Fourth Edition

Workbook in Everyday Spanish

A Comprehensive Grammar Review

Julio I. Andújar

Robert J. Dixson

PEARSON

Prentice
Hall

Upper Saddle River, New Jersey 07458

Publisher: *Phil Miller*
Senior Acquisitions Editor: *Bob Hemmer*
Assistant Director of Production: *Mary Rottino*
Editorial/Production Supervision: *Nancy Stevenson*
Executive Marketing Manager: *Eileen Bernadette Moran*
Assistant Editor: *Meriel Martínez Moctezuma*
Manufacturing Buyer: *Brian Mackey*
Full-Service Project Management: *UG / GGS Information Services, Inc.*
Cover design: Kiwi Design

This book was set in (MyriaMM_400 RG 600 NO, 11/13) by UG / GGS Information
Services, Inc. and was printed and bound at Phoenix Book Tech.

© 2004, 1997, 1991, 1958 by R. J. Dixson Associates
Published by Pearson Education, Inc.
Upper Saddle River, New Jersey 07458

Printed in the United States of America
10 9 8 7 6 5 4 3 2 1

ISBN 0-13-182514-3

Pearson Education LTD., *London*
Pearson Education Australia PTY, Limited, *Sydney*
Pearson Education Singapore, Pte. Ltd.
Pearson Education North Asia Ltd., *Hong Kong*
Pearson Education Canada, Ltd., *Toronto*
Pearson Educación de Mexico, S.A. de C.V.
Pearson Education—Japan, *Tokyo*
Pearson Education Malaysia, Pte. Ltd.
Pearson Education, *Upper Saddle River,* New Jersey

Contents

iv   Contents

Preface

Workbook in Everyday Spanish offers a tried and true approach to reviewing grammar and vocabulary. It is intended as a supplement to your main classroom text, for homework assignments and self-study through a systematic, graded presentation and practice of Spanish grammar, vocabulary and sentence structure.

As in previous editions, the fourth edition is organized into one-page *Worksheets* that present a topic and provide practice of that topic. The presentations include clear and concise English explanations of key grammatical points followed by straightforward examples that guide students through the accompanying exercises. The topics are then reinforced in self-contained *Review* sections. After most *Review* sections is a **Buscapalabras,** or word game, that keeps student interest level high.

The convenient format of *Workbook in Everyday Spanish* allows students to write directly in their books, tear out their worksheets, and submit them to their instructors for evaluation. A separate Answer Key is also available free of charge to instructors using *Workbook in Everyday Spanish* and for student purchase.

The *Fourth Edition* has been updated and enhanced by sequencing topics to correspond to the scope and sequence of most Spanish language texts. This makes the *Workbook in Everyday Spanish* ideal for use as a supplement to any Spanish language text.

Part 1

Contents

Worksheet 1.1 Definite articles and gender of nouns

Definite articles **el, la, los, las** (*the*) agree in gender and number with the noun they precede. Generally, nouns ending in **-a, -as** are feminine and take **la, las.** Nouns ending in **-o, -os** are usually masculine and take **el, los.** Several exceptions are described on p. 138. The gender of nouns ending in other vowels or in consonants must be memorized.

EXAMPLES:	**el** gato	*the cat*	**los** estudiantes	*the students*
	la gata	*the cat*	**las** vacaciones	*the vacations*
	el elefante	*the elephant*	**el** papel	*the paper*

➤ Fill in the correct definite article.

1. ___El___ libro

2. ___Las___ muchachas

3. _____ calles (f)

4. _____ cuaderno

5. _____ mujeres (f)

6. _____ hombres (m)

7. _____ profesor (m)

8. _____ cubanos

9. _____ mexicana

10. _____ señores (m)

11. _____ casa

12. _____ colores (m)

13. _____ manzanas

14. _____ papeles (m)

15. _____ ventanas

16. _____ amigos

17. _____ escuela

18. _____ médico

19. _____ primas

20. _____ hermana

21. _____ enfermera

22. _____ enfermeras

23. _____ cielo

24. _____ español (m)

25. _____ lápices (m)

26. _____ muchacho

27. _____ muchacha

28. _____ puertas

29. _____ plátanos

30. _____ padres (m)

31. _____ ciudad (f)

32. _____ noches (f)

33. _____ madre (f)

34. _____ verduras

35. _____ pan (m)

36. _____ niña

37. _____ ruidos

38. _____ profesora

39. _____ cuchillo

40. _____ cucharas

Worksheet 1.2 Indefinite articles

The indefinite article **un** (*a*) is used with a masculine noun.

EXAMPLES: **un** lápiz   *a pencil*   **un** niño   *a boy*

The indefinite article **una** (*a*) is used with a feminine noun.

EXAMPLES: **una** pluma   *a pen*   **una** camisa   *a shirt*

➤ Fill in the correct indefinite article.

1. __Un__ libro *book*
2. __Una__ pluma *feather*
3. __Un__ muchacho *boy/lad*
4. __Un__ cuchillo *cuckoo*
5. __Un__ ejercicio *exercise*
6. __Una__ pizarra *slate/blackboard*
7. __Una__ escuela *school*
8. __Un__ hermano *brother*
9. __Una__ muchacha *girl/lass*
10. __Un__ amigo *friendly/friend*
11. __Una__ amiga
12. __Una__ manzana *apple*
13. __Un__ cuaderno *notebook/exercise book*
14. __Un__ médico *medical/doctor*
15. __Una__ profesora *teacher*
16. __Un__ primo *bonus*
17. __Una__ cuchara *spoon*
18. __Un__ maestro *principal/teacher*
19. __Una__ computadora *computer*
20. __Una__ hermana *sister*

21. __Una__ puerta *door*
22. __Una__ señora
23. __Una__ familia *family*
24. __Un__ zapato *shoe*
25. __Una__ camisa *shirt*
26. __Una__ corbata *tie*
27. __Una__ ventana *window*
28. __Una__ silla *chair*
29. _____ norteamericano
30. _____ panameño
31. __Una__ sopa *soup*
32. __Una__ calle (f) *street/road*
33. __Uno__ papel (m) *piece(sheet of) paper*
34. __Una__ mujer (f) *woman*
35. __Un__ color (m) *to colour*
36. __Un__ señor (m) *male*
37. __Una__ ciudad (f) *city/town*
38. __Un__ padre (m) *father*
39. __Una__ nación *nation*
40. __Una__ madre (f) *mother*

Worksheet 1.3 Plural nouns

Nouns ending in a vowel form their plural by adding **-s** (except as noted on p. 17).

EXAMPLES:	SINGULAR:	libro	mesa	calle
	PLURAL:	libro**s**	mesa**s**	calle**s**

Nouns ending in a consonant form their plural by adding **-es** (except as noted on p. 17).

EXAMPLES:	SINGULAR:	papel	color	ciudad
	PLURAL:	papel**es**	color**es**	ciudad**es**

➤ Change to the plural.

1. libro _____

2. dólar _____

3. ventana _____

4. silla _____

5. papel _____

6. guitarra _____

7. suramericano _____

8. calle _____

9. mujer _____

10. hombre _____

11. padre _____

12. profesor _____

13. impresora _____

14. catedral _____

15. muchacha _____

16. médico _____

17. primo _____

18. venezolano _____

19. tomate _____

20. amiga _____

21. cubana _____

22. motor _____

23. cuarto _____

24. español (m) _____

25. corbata _____

26. señor _____

27. señora _____

28. familia _____

29. zapato _____

30. chaqueta _____

31. flor _____

32. cuchillo _____

33. escuela _____

34. ciudad _____

35. madre _____

36. noche _____

Worksheet 1.4 Descriptive adjectives

Adjectives usually follow the nouns they modify (**un libro** *nuevo*, **una mesa** *redonda*). Most adjectives have a masculine and a feminine form (**rojo, roja**), as well as a singular and a plural form (**rojo, rojos, roja, rojas**). All adjectives agree in number and gender with the nouns they modify.

EXAMPLES:	SINGULAR	PLURAL
MASCULINE:	el libro **rojo**	los libros **rojos**
FEMININE:	la mesa **roja**	las mesas **rojas**

➤ Supply the correct form of the adjectives in parentheses.

1. una casa _____ (bonito)
2. el libro _____ (negro)
3. los libros _____ (grueso)
4. una mesa _____ (sucio)
5. un muchacho _____ (alto)
6. una camisa_____ (amarillo)
7. un juego _____ (divertido)
8. una mujer _____ (bonito)
9. una clase _____ (nuevo)
10. un médico_____ (famoso)
11. una muchacha _____ (alto)
12. una flor _____ (blanco)
13. una lección _____ (largo)
14. dos libros _____ (caro)
15. una casa _____ (pequeña)
16. una computadora _____ (nuevo)
17. un hombre _____ (viejo)
18. dos hombres _____ (viejo)
19. una mujer _____ (rubio)

20. dos mujeres _____ (rubio)
21. dos calles _____ (ancho)
22. una profesora _____ (bueno)
23. una chica_____ (mexicano)
24. dos chicas _____ (mexicano)
25. dos ojos _____ (negro)
26. la nariz _____ (largo)
27. dos lecciones _____ (largo)
28. un sillón _____ (cómodo)
29. una silla _____ (cómodo)
30. dos sillas _____ (cómodo)
31. una manzana _____ (rojo)
32. dos camisas _____ (blanco)
33. tres plátanos _____ (maduro)
34. una noche _____ (frío)
35. un automóvil _____ (moderno)
36. dos señoras _____ (rico)
37. el médico _____ (italiano)
38. la enfermera_____ (cubano)

Worksheet 1.5 More on descriptive adjectives

Some adjectives do not have the **-o** or **-a** ending to indicate masculine or feminine gender. They have the same ending for both genders and agree in number only. These adjectives may end with a vowel (**grande, verde**) or with a consonant (**fácil, popular**). Form the plural of adjectives ending with a vowel by adding **-s** (**grandes, verdes**); form the plural of adjectives ending with a consonant by adding **-es** (**fáciles, populares**).

EXAMPLES:

el alumno **inteligente**   los alumnos **inteligentes**

la alumna **inteligente**   las alumnas **inteligentes**

el ejercicio **fácil**   los ejercicios **fáciles**

la tarea **fácil**   las tareas **fáciles**

➤ Change each of the following phrases to the plural.

1. el muchacho popular _____

2. la lección difícil _____

3. el emigrante pobre _____

4. el libro caro _____

5. el hombre italiano _____

6. el ejercicio difícil _____

7. la mujer inteligente _____

8. la flor amarilla _____

9. la comida española _____

10. la criada eficiente _____

11. el gato interesante _____

12. el niño inteligente _____

13. la muchacha baja _____

14. la mesa redonda _____

15. el reloj viejo _____

16. la ciudad grande _____

17. el pueblo grande _____

18. el libro verde _____

19. la pregunta difícil _____

20. la lección nueva _____

21. la profesora nueva _____

22. el soldado norteamericano _____

23. la pared blanca _____

24. el muchacho español _____

25. la clase fácil _____

26. el escritorio gris _____

27. la muchacha pobre _____

28. la pluma verde _____

29. el lápiz verde _____

30. el profesor nuevo _____

31. el reloj interesante _____

32. el suramericano alto _____

33. la norteamericana alta _____

34. la blusa azul _____

Worksheet 1.6 The verb *ser*

The verb **ser** is conjugated as follows:

ser (*to be*)					
yo	soy	*I am*	nosotros(as)	somos	*we are*
tú*	eres	*you are*	vosotros(as)**	sois	*you are*
usted	es	*you are*	ustedes	son	*you are*
él, ella	es	*he is, she is*	ellos, ellas	son	*they are*

➤ Supply the correct form of **ser**.

1. Nosotros _____*somos*_____ estudiantes de español.
2. El mundo _____ grande e interesante.
3. África y Asia _____ continentes enormes.
4. Europa _____ un continente también.
5. Abdul, tú _____ de África.
6. Yo _____ de Europa.
7. España _____ un país europeo.
8. Las tradiciones de España _____ bonitas.
9. Finlandia _____ un país frío.
10. Ustedes _____ de Finlandia.
11. Elena y Carlos _____ de Bogotá.
12. Bogotá _____ la capital de Colombia.
13. Los señores Garza _____ venezolanos.
14. Tú _____ de Venezuela también.
15. La señora Garza _____ una actriz famosa.
16. Yo _____ admirador de ella.
17. Nosotros _____ de varias ciudades.
18. Alicia, tú _____ de una ciudad bonita.
19. Buenos Aires _____ la capital de la Argentina.
20. Dos productos de la Argentina _____ la plata y la carne.
21. Ustedes _____ amigos de varios músicos puertorriqueños.
22. Ellos _____ populares con la gente joven.
23. Julio Iglesias _____ de España.
24. Usted _____ de Cuba.
25. Puerto Rico y Cuba _____ islas caribes.
26. La geografía _____ muy interesante, ¿verdad?

* The familiar form **tú** is mostly used with peers, family members, pets, and servants. **Usted** is used in all other cases and takes the same verb form as **él** and **ella**.

** **Vosotros** is used only in Spain; all other Spanish-speakers use **ustedes.**

Worksheet 1.7 Subject pronouns

Subject pronouns are often omitted from the sentence unless needed for clarification or emphasis. We say **somos amigos** (omitting the subject pronoun **nosotros**) because the verb form clearly indicates that the subject is first person plural. In **es interesante**, however, the subject could be **él, ella, usted, la maestra, el libro,** or anyone or anything that is second or third person singular.

➤ Supply the correct subject pronouns; include all possible choices.

1. _____ soy aficionado al cine.

2. _____ son estrellas de muchas películas.

3. _____ es un buen actor.

4. _____ es una buena actriz.

5. _____ eres admiradora de varios actores.

6. _____ son populares en los teatros.

7. _____ es vendedor de automóviles.

8. _____ eres dueño de un teatro elegante.

9. _____ somos norteamericanos.

10. _____ eres una cantante muy buena.

11. _____ soy un buen cantante.

12. _____ es una bailarina muy popular.

13. _____ es un cómico muy gracioso.

14. _____ son payasos de circo.

15. _____ son amigas de los payasos.

16. _____ somos admiradores de ella.

17. _____ son actrices y cantantes.

18. _____ somos aficionados a la televisión.

19. _____ es la esposa de un actor famoso.

20. _____ son residentes de Hollywood.

21. _____ somos turistas en Hollywood.

22. _____ es muy simpática.

23. _____ soy amigo de varios actores de teatro.

24. _____ son amables y corteses.

Worksheet 1.8 Indefinite articles with modified nouns

The indefinite article is omitted before an unmodified noun of nationality, occupation, religion, or rank that follows **ser**.

EXAMPLES: Elena **es** médico.
              Él **es** italiano.

It is always used, however, when the noun is modified.

EXAMPLES: Elena **es** un buen médico.
              Él **es** un italiano muy simpático.

➤ Supply **un** or **una** if needed.

1. Ella es _____ profesora norteamericana.

2. Pablo es _____ argentino.

3. El* señor Pérez es _____ zapatero muy bueno.

4. La señora Ruiz es _____ buena abogada.

5. Yo soy _____ cubano.

6. Ella es _____ española.

7. Jaime es _____ ingeniero.

8. Él es _____ ingeniero mecánico.

9. El señor García es _____ poeta español.

10. El señor Mendoza es _____ arquitecto.

11. Él es _____ arquitecto famoso en Chile.

12. Tú eres _____ muchacho muy cómico.

13. Ella es _____ alumna estudiosa.

14. Él es _____ médíco.

15. Isabel es _____ peluquera.

16. El doctor Soto es _____ chileno.

17. Ella es _____ muchacha muy atractiva.

18. *El diario* es _____ periódico popular.

19. Alberto es _____ capitán.

20. Él es _____ muy generoso.

21. Iliana es _____ católica.

22. Ella es _____ católica muy ferviente.

23. La maestra es _____ muchacha joven.

24. Ella es _____ puertorriqueña.

25. Somos _____ amigos de ellos.

* The definite article is used before all titles, except in direct speech.

Adjectives

➤ Supply the correct form of the adjective in parentheses.

1. La escuela es _____ (nuevo).

2. La directora es muy _____ (exigente).

3. El subdirector es un poco _____ (viejo).

4. La biblioteca es _____ (moderno).

5. Los músicos son _____ (popular).

6. El auditorio de la escuela es _____ (grande).

7. Los estudiantes son _____ (amable).

8. La profesora es_____ (grueso).

9. Los maestros son _____ (delgado).

10. María y Elena son _____ (rubio).

11. Muchos estudiantes son _____ (moreno).

12. Los salones son _____ (amplio).

13. El traje del director es _____ (azul).

14. Las cortinas de los salones son _____ (verde).

15. La lección es _____ (interesante).

16. Los ejercicios son _____ (difícil).

17. La amiga es _____ (panameño).

18. Los hijos son _____ (estudioso).

19. La maestra de gimnasia es muy _____ (simpático).

20. El timbre es _____ (eléctrico).

21. Las pizarras son _____ (verde).

22. La tiza es _____ (blanco).

23. Los deportes son _____ (saludable).

24. Las empleadas son _____ (servicial).

25. El actor principal es _____ (guapo).

26. Muchos graduados son _____ (famoso).

Name: _____ Date: _____

More on the verb *ser* and adjectives

➤ Choose the correct form.

1. Nosotros _____ (son, somos) amigos.

2. La lección de hoy _____ (es, son) difícil.

3. _____ (Los, Las) tareas de hoy también son difíciles.

4. Pepe y María son muy _____ (popular, populares).

5. La profesora es _____ (señora, una señora) alta.

6. Las puertas de la sala son _____ (grande, grandes).

7. El profesor es _____ (ingeniero, un ingeniero).

8. _____ (Nosotros, Nosotras) somos amigas.

9. El lápiz es rojo y la pluma es _____ (amarillo, amarilla).

10. Yo _____ (soy, es) alumno de español.

11. Ella _____ (soy, es) alumna de español.

12. _____ (Los, Las) padres de ella son argentinos.

13. La nueva profesora es _____ (norteamericano, norteamericana).

14. Ellas son _____ (hermanos, hermanas).

15. Nosotros _____ (son, somos) compañeros de clase.

16. _____ (Él, Ella) es la profesora de Elena.

17. Los dos muchachos son fuertes y _____ (altos, altas).

18. María es _____ (rubio, rubia) de ojos azules.

19. Caracas es una ciudad _____ (moderno, moderna).

20. Otras ciudades de Venezuela son muy_____ (antigua, antiguas).

21. Joaquín es _____ (muchacho, un muchacho) muy inteligente.

22. La familia de Enrique es muy _____ (rico, rica).

23. Los ejercicios de hoy son bastante _____(difícil, difíciles).

24. Las tareas de hoy son _____ (fácil, fáciles).

25. Joaquín es _____ (muchacho, un muchacho).

26. _____ (El señor, Señor) Ruiz es subdirector de la universidad.

27. Las escuelas de México _____ (es, son) enormes.

28. El peruano es _____ (aficionado, aficionada) a la gimnasia.

Buscapalabras

Palabras revueltas

➤ Can you circle fourteen descriptive adjectives?

B	B	L	A	N	C	O	I	A	C
X	U	O	H	V	I	E	J	O	D
D	E	N	G	U	A	P	O	U	S
S	N	U	E	V	A	L	O	R	P
R	O	J	O	A	L	I	N	D	A
P	A	Z	U	L	T	T	L	R	N
L	M	B	A	J	O	G	S	U	C
O	F	R	I	O	S	J	A	T	H
S	U	C	I	A	L	A	R	G	O

As you find the words, copy them in the spaces below:

1. _____
2. _____
3. _____
4. _____
5. _____
6. _____
7. _____
8. _____
9. _____
10. _____
11. _____
12. _____
13. _____
14. _____

Part 2

Contents

Worksheet 2.1 The present tense of regular -ar verbs

Regular -**ar** verbs (**caminar, estudiar**) are conjugated as follows:

hablar (*to speak*)			
yo	hablo	nosotros(as)	hablamos
tú	hablas	vosotros(as)	habláis
él, ella, usted	habla	ellos, ellas, ustedes	hablan

The present tense also describes daily or general actions.

EXAMPLE: El profesor siempre **habla** español en la clase.

➤ Supply the correct form of the verbs in parentheses.

1. Nosotros_____ (estudiar) mucho en la clase de español.

2. La maestra siempre _____ (hablar) español.

3. Tú _____ (mirar) las palabras en la pizarra.

4. Los estudiantes _____ (escuchar) con atención.

5. Ellos _____ (practicar) mucho la pronunciación.

6. Yo _____ (necesitar) un buen cuaderno.

7. Ella _____ (enseñar) los verbos regulares.

8. Los verbos _____ (cambiar) de una manera interesante.

9. Ella _____ (preguntar) la hora.

10. Nosotros_____ (contestar) la pregunta.

11. Un alumno _____ (ayudar) a otros alumnos.

12. Yo _____ (trabajar) mucho con los verbos regulares.

13. Los alumnos_____ (usar) cada verbo en una frase.

14. Nosotros_____ (tratar) de usar la forma correcta.

15. Tú siempre _____ (comunicar) entusiasmo en español.

16. La maestra _____ (recitar) versos en la clase.

17. Nosotros_____ (desear) cantar todos los días.

18. Hoy Catalina_____ (tocar) la guitarra.

19. Otros estudiantes _____ (comprar) discos compactos.

20. El club_____ (gastar) mucho dinero en refrescos.

21. Nosotros_____ (conversar) siempre en español.

22. Ellas _____ (tomar) limonada en cada reunión.

23. Una estudiante peruana _____ (visitar) el club.

24. Nosotros_____ (cantar) una canción para ella.

25. Los muchachos _____ (bailar) con las muchachas.

Worksheet 2.2 Subject pronouns with -*ar* verbs

With the exception of **usted/ustedes**, subject pronouns are usually omitted because the verb ending identifies the subject. The subject pronoun, however, is used for stress or emphasis and precedes the verb.

EXAMPLE: **Yo** canto, pero **ella** baila.

➤ Supply the correct subject pronoun(s); include all possible choices.

1. _____ hablamos muy poco en la biblioteca.

2. _____ busco una mesa grande.

3. _____ necesita un diccionario.

4. _____ miras el mapa de Europa.

5. _____ estudian francés.

6. _____ preparo un informe para mañana.

7. _____ compras un bolígrafo rojo.

8. _____ usamos papel blanco con líneas azules.

9. _____ hablo muchas veces con la maestra.

10. _____ ayuda a los estudiantes.

11. _____ practican deportes.

12. _____ trato de jugar tenis.

13. _____ enseña inglés muy bien.

14. _____ cantamos en voz baja.

15. _____ explico la lección a un amigo.

16. _____ escucha muy bien las explicaciones.

17. _____ pasamos dos horas en la biblioteca.

18. _____ presenta una lista de palabras nuevas.

19. _____ copia datos de un libro de consulta.

20. _____ dibujan mapas de las Antillas Mayores.

21. _____ hablan sobre los productos de Chile.

22. _____ contesto una pregunta sobre la Argentina.

23. _____ espero leer una novela interesante.

24. _____ informa sobre la poesía moderna.

25. _____ gastan mucho dinero en libros nuevos.

26. _____ deseamos leer varios libros sobre México.

Worksheet 2.3 Negation

To make a verb negative, simply place **no** to the left of the verb.

EXAMPLE: ¿**No** habla español muy bien Julia?
No, ella **no** habla español muy bien.

➤ Rewrite each sentence, making the verb negative.

1. Yo gasto mucho dinero en las tiendas. _____

2. Tú necesitas una bicicleta nueva. _____

3. Ella compra una bicicleta usada. _____

4. Usted usa un martillo en el trabajo. _____

5. ¿Es ligero ese martillo? _____

6. Nosotros pagamos demasiado aquí. _____

7. ¿Son caros los limones? _____

8. Juan trabaja en el mercado. _____

9. ¿Es moderno ese mercado? _____

10. Las manzanas pesan un kilo. _____

11. El mercado selecciona las verduras más frescas. _____

12. Los plátanos son amarillos. _____

13. ¿Son baratas las peras? _____

14. El pescado es muy caro. _____

15. El carnicero es excelente. _____

16. Él pesa las chuletas de cerdo. _____

17. El pavo pesa doce libras. _____

18. La gran venta es mañana. _____

19. Ellas buscan precios bajos. _____

20. ¿Aceptas estos dulces? _____

21. Trato de bajar de peso. _____

22. Ella desea comprar un helado. _____

23. Esta tienda es famosa. _____

24. ¿Caminamos al supermercado? _____

25. Yo compro en un mercado cerca. _____

Worksheet 2.4 More on plural nouns

The worksheet on *plural nouns* (page 4) reminded you to pluralize nouns ending in a vowel by adding **-s**, or **-es** if they end in a consonant. These additional rules must also be applied:

- Nouns ending in **-z** change **z** to **c** before adding **-es**.
- Nouns ending in **-es** or **-is,** with no accent, are the same in singular and plural.
- Nouns ending in **-n** or **-s,** with an accent on the last syllable, drop the accent in the plural.
- Other words that end in **-n** add an accent.
- Family names never change in the plural.
- These same spelling rules apply to adjectives as well as nouns.

la lu**z**	las lu**ces**
el lun**es**	los lun**es**
la lecci**ón**	las lecci**ones**
exame**n**	ex**á**men**es**
Mendoza	**los Mendoza**
capa**z**	capa**ces**

➤ Change to the singular.

1. los lápices _____
2. los franceses _____
3. los lunes_____
4. los ingleses _____
5. los jóvenes _____
6. los árboles_____
7. las mujeres _____
8. los martes _____
9. las veces_____
10. las voces _____
11. las francesas _____
12. los colores _____
13. las naciones _____

14. las narices _____
15. los actores _____
16. las actrices_____
17. las oraciones largas_____
18. los niños inteligentes _____
19. las niñas inteligentes _____
20. los cinturones rojos_____
21. las ciudades pequeñas _____
22. los cuadernos azules_____
23. las naciones grandes _____
24. las horas felices _____
25. los pescadores japoneses_____
26. los viernes y sábados _____

➤ Change to the plural.

1. el capitán del barco _____

2. la actriz capaz _____

3. el cocinero portugués _____

4. la cocinera portuguesa _____

5. el ingeniero joven _____

6. el empleado atento _____

7. la voz baja _____

8. el patrón de la fábrica _____

9. la comida costarricense _____

10. la nación europea _____

11. el papel azul _____

12. el examen fácil _____

13. la luz roja _____

14. el médico español _____

15. la señora Martinez _____

16. el coche lujoso _____

17. el limón amargo _____

18. la nación aliada _____

19. la canción popular _____

20. el lunes a las siete _____

21. el amigo alemán _____

22. la sal marina _____

23. la ciudad moderna _____

24. el reloj valioso _____

25. la primera luz _____

26. la cantidad usual _____

27. la vez anterior _____

28. el color azul _____

29. el viernes y el miércoles _____

30. la lección del jueves _____

31. el señor Pérez _____

32. la nariz larga _____

33. el punto débil _____

34. la fiera feroz _____

35. el árbol de Navidad _____

36. la lección difícil _____

37. el material inglés _____

38. la discusión final _____

39. el actor principal _____

40. el sueldo regular _____

Worksheet 2.5 Interrogative sentences

To form a question, start with an inverted question mark (¿) and place the verb before its subject.

EXAMPLE: Él corre todas las mañanas.
            ¿Corre él todas las mañanas?

➤ Change the following statements to questions.

 1. Tú mandas la ropa a la lavandería. _____

 2. Ellos usan las computadoras en la clase. _____

 3. Luisa mira mucho la televisión. _____

 4. El joven escucha la conversación. _____

 5. Pablo busca un lugar tranquilo. _____

 6. Ustedes pescan en el mar. _____

 7. Ellos hablan mucho de pesca. _____

 8. Tú cenas cerca del mar. _____

 9. Papá trabaja con ellos. _____

10. Los soldados son valientes. _____

11. El capitán saluda a los pasajeros. _____

12. El tío Carlos ayuda a los marineros. _____

13. Los novios pasean por la playa. _____

14. Catalina viaja mucho en avión. _____

15. Una amiga acompaña a Catalina. _____

16. Marta lleva mucha ropa. _____

17. Ellas hablan mucho. _____

18. Él enseña muchas horas de clases. _____

19. Ellos necesitan mucha práctica. _____

20. Los campeones ganan medallas de oro. _____

21. La natación es un deporte popular. _____

22. Tú trabajas en la tienda. _____

23. El circo viaja a muchas ciudades. _____

24. Papá compra muchos libros. _____

25. La orquesta toca el vals *Sobre las olas.* _____

Worksheet 2.6 The present tense of regular -er verbs

Regular -er verbs (**comer, aprender**) are conjugated as follows:

comer (*to eat*)			
yo	como	nosotros(as)	comemos
tú	comes	vosotros(as)	coméis
él, ella, usted	come	ellos, ellas, ustedes	comen

➤ Supply the correct form of the verb.

1. Nosotros _____ (toser) de vez en cuando.

2. Los fumadores _____ (toser) con frecuencia.

3. Los hábitos buenos _____ (proteger) la salud.

4. ¿Cómo _____ (proteger) tú la salud?

5. Andrés no _____ (beber) mucha agua.

6. Yo _____ (beber) seis vasos de agua diariamente.

7. Ella camina mucho pero _____ (correr) muy poco.

8. Ellos _____ (correr) todas las mañanas en el parque.

9. Él _____ (aprender) las reglas de seguridad.

10. Ellas _____ (aprender) los primeros auxilios.

11. Yo _____ (prometer) comer más verduras y frutas.

12. ¿ _____ (prometer) tú comer menos dulces y helados?

13. Él _____ (meter) refrescos en el refrigerador.

14. Nosotros _____ (meter) leche y jugos en el refrigerador.

15. En la escuela tú _____ (leer) mucho sobre la higiene.

16. ¿ _____ (leer) usted artículos sobre las vitaminas?

17. Nosotros _____ (comprender) la importancia de la gimnasia.

18. Yo _____ (comprender) la necesidad de tener un cuerpo sano.

19. Ellos _____ (poseer) una extensa colección de medicinas y vendas.

20. ¿ _____ (poseer) ustedes artículos peligrosos en la casa?

Worksheet 2.7 **The present tense of regular -*ir* verbs**

Regular -**ir** verbs (**vivir, escribir**) are conjugated as follows:

vivir (*to live*)			
yo	vivo	nosotros(as)	vivimos
tú	vives	vosotros(as)	vivís
él, ella, usted	vive	ellos, ellas, ustedes	viven

➤ Supply the correct form of the verb.

1. Yo _____ (asistir) a muchos conciertos.

2. Ellas _____ (asistir) a conciertos de grupos roqueros.

3. Muchos músicos profesionales _____ (vivir) en Nueva York.

4. El mariachi _____ (vivir) en Guadalajara, México.

5. Tú _____ (escribir) la letra de muchas canciones.

6. Ustedes _____ (escribir) música para la guitarra.

7. La música _____ (existir) en todas partes del mundo.

8. Los instrumentos del siglo doce no _____ (existir) hoy.

9. Nosotros _____ (discutir) la importancia de la ópera.

10. El violinista _____ (discutir) con el director.

11. Yo _____ (dividir) la orquesta en tres secciones.

12. Ella _____ (dividir) su tiempo entre Londres y París.

13. El director de la orquesta _____ (subir) la escalera.

14. Nosotros _____ (no subir) al balcón del palacio de Bellas Artes.

15. El concierto _____ (abrir) con una cantata de Mozart.

16. Ellos _____ (abrir) las puertas del teatro a las siete.

17. Los compositores a veces _____ (sufrir) mucha pobreza.

18. El perro _____ (sufrir) cuando tú tocas el violín.

19. Yo me _____ (cubrir) los oídos cuando mi hermana canta.

20. Las manos del joven pianista _____ (cubrir) las teclas del piano.

21. Los músicos _____ (recibir) el aplauso de la audiencia.

Verbs

➤ Supply the present tense of the following verbs in parentheses.

1. En mi casa, todos nosotros _____ (ayudar) a mamá con el trabajo.

2. Mi hermana _____ (sacudir) los muebles del salón.

3. Yo _____ (limpiar) el suelo y las alfombras.

4. Mi abuela _____ (insistir) en lavar los platos.

5. Yo _____ (secar) los vasos y las tazas.

6. Mamá _____ (enseñar) a mi hermana a lavar la ropa.

7. Ella _____ (coser) y mira la televisión.

8. Los niños _____ (comer) mucho.

9. Mi papá _____ (llevar) a la familia a la zapatería.

10. Nosotros _____ (comprar) varios pares de zapatos.

11. Yo _____ (arreglar) mi cuarto y el cuarto de baño.

12. Mamá _____ (meter) la ropa sucia en la lavadora.

13. Mis hermanas _____ (sacar) la ropa limpia de la secadora.

14. Mi tía _____ (planchar) los manteles y las sábanas.

15. De vez en cuando un niño _____ (romper) un juguete.

16. Papá _____ (reparar) los juguetes y los aparatos eléctricos.

17. Nosotros _____ (dividir) las tareas hogareñas entre todos.

18. Los sábados yo _____ (barrer) el patio y la sala.

19. Mañana mi hermano _____ (deber) arreglar el sótano.

20. Tú _____ (sufrir) cuando trabajas tanto.

21. Ustedes _____ (necesitar) ayudar con el trabajo.

22. ¿No _____ (comprender) ustedes que mamá necesita ayuda?

23. Los vecinos más ricos _____ (pagar) una criada.

24. En mi casa mamá no _____ (depender) de una criada.

25. Nosotros siempre _____ (cooperar) en limpiar la casa.

Subject pronouns with regular verbs

➤ Supply the subject pronoun(s).

1. _____ patinas en la pista de hielo.

2. _____ esquiamos en las montañas.

3. _____ vende boletos para la carrera de motocicletas.

4. _____ nadan en la piscina olímpica de la universidad.

5. _____ compro una canoa para remar en el lago.

6. _____ andas mucho en bicicleta en el verano.

7. _____ estudio la historia de las Olimpiadas.

8. _____ apreciamos al entrenador de los futbolistas.

9. _____ recibe muchas cartas de los aficionados.

10. _____ escribo cartas al campeón del boxeo.

11. _____ admiramos mucho al capitán del equipo.

12. _____ lees artículos sobre las corridas de toros.

13. _____ recibe los aplausos del público.

14. _____ no matan al toro en la corrida portuguesa.

15. _____ rompen a veces las banderillas.

16. _____ debemos estudiar las reglas de béisbol.

17. _____ explico a los estudiantes las jugadas de baloncesto.

18. _____ vivimos cerca del Hipódromo del Mar.

19. _____ corren rápidamente todos los caballos.

20. _____ prefieres participar en los deportes.

21. _____ no tomo café durante la temporada de fútbol.

22. _____ prohibimos el uso del tabaco y del alcohol.

23. _____ comes alimentos recomendados por el entrenador.

24. _____ compiten en muchas competencias.

25. _____ siempre tratamos de ganar.

More on verbs

➤ Change the sentences from **yo** to **tú**. Repeat the exercise for each of the other subjects: **él, ella, usted, nosotros, vosotros** (optional), **ellos**. This may be done orally and in writing by placing a strip of blank paper over the answer column.

1. Yo vivo en Santa Fe.   Tú _____

2. Yo estoy en segundo año.   Tú _____

3. Yo camino con un amigo.   Tú _____

4. Yo estudio lenguas extranjeras.   Tú _____

5. Yo hablo varios idiomas.   Tú _____

6. Yo aprendo a hablar italiano.   Tú _____

7. Yo necesito más práctica.   Tú _____

8. Yo converso con los italianos.   Tú _____

9. Yo admiro a la maestra.   Tú _____

10. Yo escucho bien su clase.   Tú _____

11. Yo debo aprender más.   Tú _____

12. Yo tengo mucha paciencia.   Tú _____

13. Yo practico la pronunciación.   Tú _____

14. Yo saludo a la maestra.   Tú _____

15. Yo paso a la pizarra.   Tú _____

16. Yo escribo una composición.   Tú _____

17. Yo cometo un error.   Tú _____

18. Yo repito una palabra.   Tú _____

19. Yo contesto una pregunta difícil.   Tú _____

20. Yo regreso a mi casa.   Tú _____

21. Yo debo hacer la tarea.   Tú _____

22. Yo uso un bolígrafo.   Tú _____

23. Yo completo los ejercicios.   Tú _____

24. Yo creo que la vida es interesante.   Tú _____

Buscapalabras bilingüe

➤ Find and circle these eight occupations in both English and Spanish: *actress, doctor, engineer, musician, principal, sailor, soldier, teacher.* Three of the words appear diagonally.

```
D   O   C   T   O   R   I   M   O   A   S   M
A   M   A   R   I   N   E   R   O   C   M   P
S   O   L   D   A   D   O   R   P   T   U   O
O   E   N   G   I   N   E   E   R   R   S   L
L   U   E   C   E   I   T   Z   I   E   I   A
D   R   O   U   N   Z   I   N   M   S   C   P
I   R   L   E   I   R   A   C   U   S   I   I
E   L   G   R   T   I   C   I   S   A   A   C
R   N   T   C   A   Z   H   P   I   I   N   N
I   M   A   E   S   T   R   A   C   L   B   I
I   R   E   H   C   A   E   T   O   O   M   R
A   O   D   I   R   E   C   T   O   R   R   P
```

English

_____

_____

_____

_____

_____

_____

_____

Spanish

_____

_____

_____

_____

_____

_____

_____

Worksheet 2.8 The possessive with *de*

In English we say (a) the boy's father or (b) the father of the boy. Spanish uses only (b) **el padre del muchacho**. The word **de** (*of*) may precede the noun (**el padre de Juan**) or the noun and its article:

EXAMPLES: el padre **del** muchacho (**de** + **el** = **del**)   el padre **de la** muchacha
el padre **de los** muchachos   el padre **de las** muchachas

➤ Supply **de** plus the article (if required): **de, del, de los, de la, de las**

1. El cuchillo es_____ carnicero.

2. La computadora es _____ secretaria.

3. Los uniformes son _____ enfermeras.

4. Los juguetes son _____ niño.

5. El diccionario es_____ maestra.

6. Los martillos _____ carpinteros son grandes.

7. Las hojas _____ árbol son verdes.

8. El vestido _____ señora es nuevo.

9. Las montañas _____ Asia son altas.

10. Los países _____ Naciones Unidas son muchos.

11. La pelota es _____ equipo de fútbol.

12. Nosotros hablamos_____ capital de Bolivia.

13. El estrella _____ película es Cantinflas.

14. Las impresoras _____ computadoras son nuevas.

15. Las noticias _____ día son buenas.

16. El precio _____ programa es demasiado alto.

17. Las preguntas _____ examen son difíciles.

18. María habla con el director _____ escuela.

19. Sancho Panza es compañero _____ Don Quijote.

20. El auto negro es_____ maestra.

21. La casa recién pintada es _____ ellos.

22. Las computadoras son _____ nosotros.

23. Las maletas grises son _____ él.

24. Las ideas mejores son _____ ustedes.

25. La entrenadora _____ tenistas chilenos es famosa.

26. El presidente _____ universidad es muy simpático.

27. La reina _____ Inglaterra es popular.

28. El abuelo_____ gemelas es generoso.

29. El inventor _____ luz eléctrica es Tomás Edison.

30. Los museos _____ ciudad son gratis.

31. El apellido _____ señor es hispano.

32. Las habitaciones _____ casa son amplias.

Worksheet 2.9 *Ser* and *estar*

Ser and **estar** both mean *to be*. **Ser** is a linking verb (see page 7). It links a noun with another noun of similar meaning (**Juan es marinero [Juan = marinero]**), or it links a noun with an adjective that describes it (**Juan es valiente [Juan = valiente]**). **Estar** indicates a temporary or acquired condition (**Juan está enfermo, Juan está en Veracruz**). In a few days, Juan will still be (**ser**) a sailor and will still be (**ser**) brave, but he may no longer be (**estar**) sick and may no longer be (**estar**) in Veracruz. Here is the present tense of **estar**:

estar *(to be)*			
yo	estoy	nosotros(as)	estamos
tú	estás	vosotros(as)	estáis
él, ella, usted	está	ellos, ellas, ustedes	están

➤ Supply the correct form of **ser** or **estar**.

1. Yo _____ enfermo.

2. Tú _____ bien.

3. Carlos _____ tenista.

4. Ellos _____ aquí.

5. El café _____ caliente.

6. El perro _____ grande.

7. Los zapatos _____ sucios.

8. Ellas _____ francesas.

9. Nosotros _____ contentos.

10. Mérida _____ en Yucatán.

11. Yo no _____ marinero.

12. Ustedes _____ de Cuba.

13. Luis _____ presente.

14. Tú _____ cansada.

15. La mesa _____ limpia.

16. Nosotros _____ norteamericanos.

17. La carne _____ fría.

18. Mi abuelo _____ viejo.

19. María _____ ausente.

20. El gato _____ negro.

21. El gato _____ enfermo.

22. Las cucharas _____ sucias.

23. Las cucharas _____ de plata.

24. La falda _____ limpia.

25. La falda _____ de seda.

26. Nosotros _____ viajeros.

27. Tú _____ muy linda.

28. Los barcos _____ en el mar.

29. Mi tía _____ de Jalisco.

30. Su casa _____ en Guadalajara.

Worksheet 2.10 More on *ser* and *estar*

➤ Supply the proper form of **ser** or **estar**, and be able to justify your choice, writing "T" for temporary, or "P" for permanent in the right margin.

                                                               T   P

1. Nosotros _____ en un buen restaurante.

2. El restaurante _____ famoso, pero caro.

3. Las selecciones del menú _____ numerosas.

4. Las servilletas y los manteles _____ limpios.

5. Todos los camareros _____ muy corteses.

6. Durante la comida uno de ellos _____ cerca de la mesa.

7. Los platos para la ensalada _____ fríos.

8. Los vasos de agua _____ grandes.

9. Un arpa* _____ en un rincón del restaurante.

10. La señorita que toca el arpa _____ joven.

11. Tres rosas amarillas _____ en cada mesa.

12. Nosotros _____ lejos de la cocina.

13. Los fumadores _____ en otra sección del restaurante.

14. Las rosas de cada mesa _____ amarillas.

15. Todos los platos _____ en una bandeja.

16. El camarero llena los vasos cuando _____ vacíos.

17. El pescado _____ bastante para dos personas.

18. El sabor del pollo _____ excelente.

19. Las papas (patatas) _____ enormes.

20. Los chícharos (guisantes) _____ en salsa blanca.

21. Yo _____ lleno y muy contento con la comida.

22. La selección de postres _____ difícil.

23. La cuenta _____ en una pequeña bandeja de plata.

24. Creemos que esta propina _____ bastante.

25. El camarero acepta el dinero y _____ contento.

* Some feminine nouns (*arpa, azúcar*) that begin with *a-* use masculine definite and indefinite articles.

Worksheet 2.11 **More on *ser* and *estar***

➤ Supply the appropriate subject pronoun(s) for the verb in each of the following sentences. Include all possibilities.

1. _____ somos miembros del club de español.

2. _____ es presidente del club.

3. _____ están aquí por primera vez.

4. _____ eres una secretaria eficiente.

5. _____ soy un tesorero de poca experiencia.

6. _____ estamos en la biblioteca.

7. _____ están sentados alrededor de una mesa grande.

8. _____ estás de pie en frente del grupo de estudiantes.

9. _____ es un miembro muy activo del club.

10. _____ son alumnos muy aplicados en todas sus clases.

11. _____ es la maestra favorita de muchos estudiantes.

12. _____ está presente en cada reunión.

13. _____ estamos aquí para planear varias actividades del club.

14. _____ estás cansado de hablar español toda la tarde.

15. _____ está nerviosa cuando habla con la maestra.

16. _____ son estudiantes de la clase superior.

17. _____ estamos en un club que consideramos importante.

18. _____ es uno de los mejores estudiantes.

19. _____ está en el tercer año de español.

20. _____ estás en el primer año.

21. _____ están en el segundo año.

22. _____ somos buenos amigos.

23. _____ son becados.

24. _____ soy miembro de un club muy activo.

25. ¿Eres _____ miembro de algún club?

Subject–verb agreement

➤ Practice with the verb forms studied so far, changing the subject of each sentence from **yo** to **él.** Be sure to change the verb to agree with the new subject. For more practice, change the subject to **tú, usted, ella, nosotros, ustedes, ellos,** and **ellas.**

1. Yo estoy en una tienda de ropa. _____

2. Yo compro una camisa nueva. _____

3. Yo miro varias corbatas. _____

4. Yo creo que son rojas. _____

5. Yo sufro de daltonismo. _____

6. Yo pido el color correcto. _____

7. Yo vivo en un clima tropical. _____

8. Yo busco ropa más ligera. _____

9. Yo quiero un traje de algodón. _____

10. Yo necesito zapatos negros. _____

11. Yo subo al primer piso. _____

12. Yo encuentro los precios muy bajos. _____

13. Yo descanso en un banco. _____

14. Yo hablo con otro cliente. _____

15. Yo soy muy listo para comprar. _____

16. Yo describo la cartera que busco. _____

17. Yo selecciono una cartera buena. _____

18. Yo entro en un ascensor. _____

19. Yo bajo a la planta principal. _____

20. Yo firmo mi nombre. _____

21. Yo cambio un cheque de viajeros. _____

22. Yo pago la cuenta. _____

23. Yo recibo el cambio. _____

24. Yo llevo las compras al coche. _____

25. Yo gasto mucho en las tiendas. _____

More on subject–verb agreement

➤ Choose the correct form and write it in the blank.

1. Los mejicanos _____ (vive, viven) en un país muy bello.

2. La capital _____ (es, eres) antigua y extensa.

3. Tú _____ (debo, debes) viajar a Guadalajara.

4. Guadalajara _____ (está, estás) en el estado de Jalisco.

5. Nosotros _____ (nadamos, nadan) allí en el lago Chapala.

6. Los mariachis _____ (cantas, cantan) en San Juan de Dios.

7. Yo _____ (escucho, escucha) la música tradicional.

8. Ellos _____ (comes, comen) en la cafetería.

9. Ella _____ (admira, admiras) la arquitectura de la Catedral.

10. Nosotros _____ (asisto, asistimos) a un drama popular.

11. El título del drama _____ (es, está) Don Juan Tenorio.

12. Los dramas del Palacio de Bellas Artes _____ (están, son) buenos.

13. El charro y la china poblana _____ (baila, bailan) en el parque.

14. Ellos _____ (reciben, recibes) el aplauso de la gente.

15. Yo _____ (aplaudo, aplaude) a los bailarines del jarabe tapatío.

16. Otros charros _____ (montamos, montan) a caballo.

17. El charro _____ (es, está) el mejor jinete de México.

18. Ustedes _____ (vemos, ven) al charro en el desfile.

19. Tú _____ (vas, voy) también a la corrida de toros.

20. El toro _____ (corre, corren) muy rápido hacia el torero.

21. Yo _____ (creemos, creo) que el torero es muy valiente.

22. Nosotros _____ (compramos, compras) en el mercado libre.

23. Ella _____ (aprende, aprendes) a regatear con los comerciantes.

24. Mi tío _____ (escoge, escogen) las legumbres y frutas en el mercado.

25. Los muchachos y las muchachas _____ (formas, forman) círculos.

26. Ellos _____ (anda, andan) a la derecha; ellas a la izquierda.

27. Esta costumbre _____ (está, es) popular entre los jóvenes.

28. México _____ (conservan, conserva) tradiciones muy bonitas.

29. Ellos _____ (descansan, descansamos) entre las dos y las cuatro.

30. Yo _____ (regresa, regreso) a México a cada oportunidad.

Part 3

Contents

Worksheet 3.1 The verb *tener*

The verb **tener** (*to have*) is conjugated in the present tense as follows:

tener (to have)			
yo	tengo	nosotros(as)	tenemos
tú	tienes	vosotros(as)	tenéis
él, ella, usted	tiene	ellos, ellas, ustedes	tienen

➤ Supply the correct form of **tener.**

1. Tú _____ un coche nuevo.

2. Tu coche _____ seis cilindros.

3. Las llantas _____ letras blancas.

4. Yo _____ un coche más grande y más viejo.

5. Nosotros _____ coches del mismo color.

6. Creo que el motor _____ un problema muy serio.

7. Algunos mecánicos _____ poco entrenamiento.

8. Yo _____ un mecánico experto y honrado.

9. Él dice que el motor _____ dos bujías malas.

10. Ustedes _____ el nombre de mi mecánico.

11. Tú _____ mucha suerte con tu coche.

12. La Ciudad de México _____ mucho tráfico.

13. Algunos chóferes _____ poca paciencia.

14. Nosotros _____ mucha experiencia.

15. Usted_____ un lote de estacionamiento.

16. El estacionamiento_____ espacio para cien automóviles.

17. Tú _____ mucha cautela cuando manejas.

18. Los peatones también _____ responsabilidades.

19. Ustedes _____ reglas para manejar y para caminar.

20. Nosotros _____ confianza en los otros chóferes.

21. Yo no_____ paciencia para manejar un taxi.

22. El taxista _____ un trabajo muy peligroso.

23. Las carreteras _____ muchos camiones grandes.

24. Cada carretera _____ su velocidad máxima.

25. ¿_____ tu licencia para manejar?

Worksheet 3.2 More on the verb *tener*

Many idioms begin with **tener.** Where English uses *to be + adjective,* Spanish may use **tener** + noun:

EXAMPLE:	ENGLISH	SPANISH	LITERAL TRANSLATION
	I am hungry.	**Tengo hambre.**	*I have hunger.*
	I am thirsty.	**Tengo sed.**	*I have thirst.*
	I am hot.	**Tengo calor.**	*I have heat.*
	I am cold.	**Tengo frío.**	*I have coldness.*
	I am afraid.	**Tengo miedo.**	*I have fear.*
	I am sleepy.	**Tengo sueño.**	*I have fear.*
	I am ashamed.	**Tengo vergüenza.**	*I have shame.*

Other idioms include **tener ganas de** (*to feel like*), **tener siete años** (*to be seven years old*), **tener razón** (*to be right*), **tener dolor de** (*to have pain in…*).

➤ Supply the correct form of **tener.**

1. A la hora de cenar yo _____ mucha hambre.

2. Tú no _____ ganas de hacer nada.

3. En el invierno, nosotros _____ frío.

4. Ellos _____ sed cuando corren mucho.

5. Cuando maneja de noche, él _____ sueño.

6. Usted _____ razón. Comer demasiado es mala costumbre.

7. Yo_____ ganas de comer más postre.

8. Tú nunca _____ dolor de estómago.

9. Mi abuelo _____ setenta y ocho años.

10. Los ancianos a veces _____ artritis.

11. Nosotros _____ calor al caminar bajo el sol.

12. Ellos_____ ganas de abrir las ventanas.

13. Elena a veces no_____ ganas de ir a trabajar.

14. Cuando falta a clase, ella _____ vergüenza.

15. Yo creo que las gemelas _____ catorce años.

16. Hoy es mi cumpleaños. _____ veinte años.

17. Nosotros _____ ganas de conocer a los toreros.

18. Los toreros no_____ miedo de los toros.

Worksheet 3.3 *Tener que*

Tener + que + infinitive is similar to *to have to + infinitive* in English:

EXAMPLES: Yo **tengo que** estudiar mucho.   *I have to study a lot.*
            Tú **tienes que** comer menos.   *You have to eat less.*

Deber and **tener que** are close in meaning, although **deber** implies a stronger obligation:

EXAMPLES: Él **tiene que** hablar.   *He has to talk.*
            Él **debe** hablar.   *He must talk.*

➤ Replace the form of **deber** with the correct form of **tener que** in the sentences below.

1. El carpintero **debe** _____ comprar un martillo nuevo.

2. Los zapateros **deben** _____ hacer zapatos bonitos y modernos.

3. La maestra **debe** _____ preparar lecciones sobre la Guerra Mundial.

4. Yo **debo** _____ practicar el piano por muchas horas.

5. Tú **debes** _____ cantar en voz más alta.

6. El taxista **debe** _____ conocer las calles de la ciudad.

7. Nosotros **debemos** _____ ayudar a los niños.

8. Los cazadores **deben** _____ usar precaución.

9. El candidato **debe** _____ recibir la mayoría de los votos.

10. Tú **debes** _____ entrenar a los peloteros.

11. Los periodistas **deben** _____ hacer muchas preguntas.

12. Ustedes **deben** _____ llamar a la policía cuando ven un crimen.

13. Nosotros **debemos** _____ avisar a los bomberos en caso de fuego.

14. Los anunciadores de radio **deben** _____ pronunciar cada sílaba
    claramente.

15. Para tener éxito en su carrera, usted **debe** _____ estudiar mucho.

16. ¿Qué **debes** _____ aprender tú para tener éxito en tu carrera o
    profesión?

Worksheet 3.4 The verb *hay* and *hay que* + infinitive

Hay, when used as a main verb in the present tense form of **haber** (literally *there to be*), is only used in the 3rd person singular meaning both *there is* and *there are*.

EXAMPLES: **Hay** un mensaje para usted.   There is a message for you.
Hay varios mensajes para usted.   There are several messages for you.
Hay mucha gente en la calle.   There are a lot of people on the street.

Hay que followed by an infinitive means strong need or obligation, similar to *have to + infinitive* in English and is the equivalent in Spanish of **deber** and **tener que.**

EXAMPLES: **Hay que** trabajar muy duro.   We have to (one has to) work very hard.
¿A qué hora **hay que** llegar?   What time must we (one) arrive?

➤ In the blanks supply either **hay** or **hay que.**

1. No _____ suficiente tiempo para terminar.

2. ¿Cuántas personas _____ en la oficina?

3. _____ decir siempre la verdad.

4. _____ cuatro computadoras en la sala, una por persona.

5. Nosotros comprendemos que _____ practicar mucho fuera de clase.

6. _____ llamar a los bomberos cuando _____ un incendio.

7. A fin de mes _____ pagar las cuentas.

8. No _____ bastante dinero para pagar todas las cuentas.

9. El jefe insiste en que _____ llegar a tiempo al trabajo.

10. _____ doce meses en el año.

11. No _____ trabajar los domingos.

12. _____ comer menos para bajar de peso.

13. _____ necesidad de aprender a usar los nuevos programas de computación.

14. Para ver el mundo _____ viajar en avión.

15. _____ muchas razones para aprender idiomas.

Worksheet 3.5 *Tener que* + infinitive

➤ In the sentences below, replace the italicized verb with the proper form of **tener que** + infinitive. If you are not certain whether a verb ends in **-ar, -er,** or **-ir,** check the verb in the vocabulary of this workbook.

1. Nosotros *protegemos* _____ la salud.

2. Tú *tomas* _____ vitaminas diariamente.

3. El señor Ruiz *camina* _____ todas las mañanas.

4. Ellas *comen* _____ menos postres.

5. Nosotros *dormimos* _____ ocho horas casi todas las noches.

6. Yo *tomo* _____ la medicina en la dosis correcta.

7. Usted *guarda* _____ cama cuando está enfermo.

8. Ella *llama* _____ al médico cuando está enferma.

9. Ustedes *aprenden* _____ a dar los primeros auxilios.

10. Tú *bebes* _____ seis vasos de agua todos los días.

11. Ellos *toman* _____ más jugos y menos refrescos.

12. Yo *evito* _____ la sal, el azúcar y el colesterol.

13. Nosotros *memorizamos* _____ el número de emergencia.

14. Juanito *va* _____ al dentista cada seis meses.

15. Tú *lees* _____ artículos sobre la nutrición y el ejercicio físico.

16. Él *practica* _____ la prevención de accidentes y enfermedades.

17. Ella *observa* _____ las reglas de seguridad en el hogar.

18. Yo *uso* _____ ropa protectora en el trabajo.

19. El carnicero *afila* _____ los cuchillos todos los días.

20. Ustedes *llevan* _____ salvavidas en sus embarcaciones.

21. ¿Qué *haces* _____ tú para cuidar tu salud?

Worksheet 3.6 More on adjectives

Descriptive adjectives (**rojo, alto, bello**) usually follow the noun they modify. Indefinite or limiting adjectives (**mucho, poco, otro, cuanto, mismo**) always precede the noun:

EXAMPLES: ropa verde   mucha ropa   azúcar blanco   mucho azúcar
           casas nuevas   otras casas   libros grandes   pocos libros

Special cases: **Cada**, regardless of the gender of the noun it modifies, remains unchanged (**cada muchacho, cada muchacha**). **Todo** always precedes both the noun and its definite article (**toda la leche, todos los días**).

➤ In the blanks, supply the correct form of the adjectives in parentheses.

1. Raquel tiene _____ (mucho) amigos.

2. Mi hermano gasta _____ (poco) dinero en restaurantes.

3. Nosotros trabajamos en la _____ (mismo) compañía.

4. ¿_____ (Cuánto) hermanos tienes tú?

5. Yo practico el piano _____ (todo) la tarde.

6. ¿Lee usted _____ (otro) periódicos también?

7. Marca _____ (cada) número otra vez con cuidado.

8. Los veinte estudiantes tienen sus _____ (propio) computadoras.

9. Casi _____ (todo) los estudiantes tienen impresoras en casa.

10. Llevo mi computadora a _____ (todo) mis clases.

11. Yo no deseo bailar con mi _____ (propio) hermana.

12. Tengo ganas de bailar con _____ (otro) chicas.

13. El director planea _____ (mucho) actividades de recreo.

14. _____ (Mucho) maestros participan en los juegos.

15. Mi _____ (segundo) reunión del día es a las diez.

16. Tengo que pasar los _____ (mismo) exámenes que ella.

17. Estamos en la _____ (último) semana del año.

18. Mi _____ (tercero) reunión es a las dos.

19. _____ (Poco) miembros del coro cantan bien.

20. Mi vecino y yo asistimos a la _____ (mismo) iglesia.

21. ¿_____ (Cuánto) muchachas participan en los deportes?

22. El _____ (primero) año en la compañía es difícil.

23. Las _____ (último) páginas del libro contienen el vocabulario.

24. Usted no sabe cuánto espero de los _____ (próximo) años.

Worksheet 3.7 Possessive adjectives

Like the adjectives in the previous exercise, possessive adjectives precede the nouns that they modify and agree with their nouns in number and gender. Only **nuestro** and **vuestro** have separate feminine forms (**nuestra, vuestra**), but all plural forms add **-s**.

ENGLISH (SINGULAR)	SPANISH (SINGULAR)	ENGLISH (PLURAL)	SPANISH (PLURAL)
my	**mi(s)**	*our*	**nuestro(s), -a(s)**
your (familiar)	**tu(s)**	*your* (familiar)	**vuestro(s), -a(s)**
your (polite), *his, her*	**su(s)**	*your* (polite), *their*	**su(s)**

➤ In the blanks, supply the possessive adjective which corresponds to the subject of the sentence.

1. Yo ahorro la mitad de _____ sueldo.

2. Yo siempre pago _____ deudas.

3. Yo uso muy poco _____ tarjetas de crédito.

4. Tú respetas a _____ vecinos.

5. Tú acompañas _____ primas.

6. Tú escuchas a _____ padre.

7. Usted trae _____ guitarra a la fiesta.

8. Usted saluda a _____ amigos.

9. Usted canta _____ canciones favoritas.

10. Él necesita _____ pluma de fuente.

11. Él tiene que usar _____ bolígrafo.

12. Él firma _____ cheques en el banco.

13. Ella abre _____ cuaderno.

14. Ella lee _____ poesías nuevas.

15. Ella memoriza _____ poema favorito.

16. Nosotros devolvemos _____ libros a la biblioteca.

17. Nosotros pagamos _____ multas.

18. Nosotros volvemos a casa en _____ camioneta.

19. Él desea vender_____ casa.

20. Ustedes piden permiso a_____ padre.

21. Ustedes ahorran _____ dinero para comprar un coche.

22. Ellas llevan _____ zapatos nuevos.

23. Ellas escogen _____ amigos con cuidado.

24. Mario llega en _____coche de último modelo.

Worksheet 3.8 More on possessive adjectives

➤ For further practice with possessive adjectives, plus a general review of plural forms, change each of the *italicized* words below to the plural. Make whatever changes are necessary in the rest of the sentence. Write the entire sentence in the space to the right.

1. Mi *libro* es nuevo. _____

2. Su *tía* es joven. _____

3. Tu *primo* es guapo. _____

4. Mi *hermana* es alta. _____

5. Nuestra *clase* es buena. _____

6. Nuestro *profesor* es simpático. _____

7. Tu *hermano* está enfermo. _____

8. Su *vecino* está enojado. _____

9. Su *jardín* es bello. _____

10. Nuestro *cuarto* es pequeño. _____

11. Mi *primo* es ingeniero. _____

12. Mi *prima* es profesora. _____

13. Su *muñeca* es bonita. _____

14. Tu *hermano* es abogado. _____

15. Su *profesor* es bueno. _____

16. Nuestra *profesora* es buena. _____

17. Mi *compañera* es inteligente. _____

18. Su *amigo* es muy fiel. _____

19. Su *reloj* es de oro. _____

20. Su *vestido* es elegante. _____

21. Su *sombrero* es moderno. _____

22. Su *joya* es costosa. _____

23. Tu *pluma* es nueva. _____

24. Mi *lección* es interesante. _____

Palabras revueltas

➤ Here are ten nine-letter words recently used in exercises. Before you can identify them, you will have to unscramble them:

T	A	C	A	M	I	O	N	E
S	O	N	C	A	U	D	E	R
E	N	T	T	I	V	I	A	S
R	A	Z	O	M	I	M	E	R
F	O	L	I	B	A	R	G	O
V	A	S	O	F	R	I	T	O
L	I	M	O	T	U	A	V	O
R	O	S	A	F	R	E	P	O
R	E	M	A	F	R	E	N	E
D	I	O	P	R	E	C	I	O

Solutions

_____ _____ _____ _____ _____ _____ _____ _____ _____ _____

_____ _____ _____ _____ _____ _____ _____ _____ _____ _____

_____ _____ _____ _____ _____ _____ _____ _____ _____ _____

_____ _____ _____ _____ _____ _____ _____ _____ _____ _____

_____ _____ _____ _____ _____ _____ _____ _____ _____ _____

_____ _____ _____ _____ _____ _____ _____ _____ _____ _____

_____ _____ _____ _____ _____ _____ _____ _____ _____ _____

_____ _____ _____ _____ _____ _____ _____ _____ _____ _____

_____ _____ _____ _____ _____ _____ _____ _____ _____ _____

Note: These same ten words will be used in the Laberinto de palabras on p. 58.

Worksheet 3.9 Irregular verbs *ir* and *ver*

Irregular verbs have one or more forms that differ from the patterns learned for conjugating regular **-ar,** **-er, -ir** verbs. Note the differences in **ir** and **ver:**

ir			
yo	voy	nosotros(as)	vamos
tú	vas	vosotros(as)	vais
él, ella, usted	va	ellos, ellas, ustedes	van

ver			
yo	veo	nosotros(as)	vemos
tú	ves	vosotros(as)	veis
él, ella, usted	ve	ellos, ellas, ustedes	ven

➤ In the blanks to the right supply the correct form of the verb in parentheses.

1. Yo _____ (ir) al teatro.

2. Yo _____ (ver) un drama.

3. Ellos _____ (ir) a Nueva York.

4. Ellos_____ (ver) una ópera italiana.

5. Usted_____ (ir) a mi casa.

6. Usted_____ (ver) la televisión.

7. Tú _____ (ir) al museo.

8. Tú _____ (ver) esculturas modernas.

9. Ellas _____ (ir) al zoológico.

10. Ellas _____ (ver) los elefantes y las girafas.

11. Nosotros _____ (ir) a España.

12. Nosotros _____ (ver) la Alhambra el primer día.

13. Ella _____ (ir) a la iglesia.

14. Ella _____ (ver) al sacerdote.

15. Ellos _____ (ir) al cine.

16. Ellos _____ (ver) muchos payasos en el circo.

17. Él_____ (ir) a Brasil.

18. Él_____ (ver) muchos lugares bellos.

19. Ustedes _____ (ir) a un restaurante caro.

20. Ustedes _____ (ver) los bailes flamencos.

21. La señora Pérez _____ (ir) a la casa de su hija.

22. La señora Pérez _____ (ver) a sus nietos.

23. ¿Cuándo _____ (ir) tú al cine?

24. ¿Qué películas _____ (ver) tú cuando vas al cine?

Worksheet 3.10 *Ir a* + **infinitive**

Ir a + infinitive is used to express intention or future action. It resembles *to be* + *going to* in English.

EXAMPLES: SPANISH   ENGLISH
     Ellos **van a** viajar en Chile.   *They are going to travel in Chile.*
     Juan **va a** estudiar francés.   *John is going to study French.*

➤ In the blank to the right, supply the correct form of **ir a** + infinitive.

1. Juanito _____ preparar su lista.

2. ¿Cuándo _____ ser tu compleaños?

3. Tus amigos _____ dar muchos regalos.

4. Yo _____ recibir muchos regalos también.

5. En las Navidades nosotros _____ dar y recibir muchos regalos.

6. Nuestros amigos en España _____ recibir y dar regalos el 6 de enero.

7. En los Estados Unidos, Papá Noel _____ trae regalos a los niños.

8. En España los Reyes Magos, Melchor, Gaspar y Baltasar _____ dejar regalos.

9. En ambos países, mucha gente _____ ir a la iglesia.

10. En las Navidades las familias _____ estar juntas.

11. Ustedes _____ preparar una gran cena.

12. Tú _____ comer cosas sabrosas.

13. Nosotros _____ a intercambiar regalos.

14. En Mexico todos_____ cantar las Posadas.

15. En España los niños _____ cantar villancicos.

16. Nosotros _____ adornar el árbol de Navidad.

17. Tú y tus vecinos _____ decorar sus casas.

18. Ellos_____ usar cientos de luces de colores.

19. Todos los familiares _____ estar juntos este año.

20. Nosotros _____ saludar a nuestros vecinos y amigos.

21. Mi tío Pepe _____ llevar su disfraz de Papá Noel.

22. Para nosotros, la Navidad _____ ser inolvidable.

23. ¿Cómo_____ celebrar tú la Navidad?

Worksheet 3.11 Demonstrative adjetives *este* and *ese*

Este (*this*) and **ese** (*that*) are demonstrative adjectives. Like other adjectives, they agree in number and gender with the nouns they modify:

EXAMPLES:

THIS	THESE	THAT	THOSE
este libro	**estos** libros	**ese** libro	**esos** libros
esta mesa	**estas** mesas	**esa** mesa	**esas** mesas

➤ Supply the correct form of **este** in the blanks.

1. _____ pluma
2. _____ libros
3. _____ ventana
4. _____ puertas
5. _____ zapatos
6. _____ silla
7. _____ cuchillo
8. _____ cuchillos
9. _____ árbol
10. _____ país
11. _____ papel
12. _____ papeles
13. _____ mesa
14. _____ ciudad
15. _____ alumnos
16. _____ corbatas
17. _____ pedazo
18. _____ color
19. _____ ruido
20. _____ niñas

➤ Supply the correct form of **ese** in the blanks.

1. _____ dinero
2. _____ noche
3. _____ página
4. _____ casas
5. _____ manzanas
6. _____ sabor
7. _____ puerta
8. _____ ruido
9. _____ lección
10. _____ computadoras
11. _____ clase
12. _____ flores
13. _____ taza
14. _____ muchachas
15. _____ autobuses
16. _____ hombre
17. _____ ejercicios
18. _____ policías
19. _____ automóviles
20. _____ montañas

Worksheet 3.12 *Este, ese, aquel*

Aquel is a third demonstrative adjective. Its feminine form is **aquella,** and its plural forms are **aquellos** and **aquellas.** While it is translated the same as **ese** (*that*), there is an important difference: **ese** refers to something near the person addressed by the speaker; **aquel** refers to something far from the speaker and the person addressed by the speaker, but possibly near a third person who is being spoken about:

EXAMPLES:	ENGLISH	SPANISH
	near me; near us	**este, esta, estos, estas**
	near you	**ese, esa, esos, esas**
	near him or her; near them	**aquel, aquella, aquellos, aquellas**

➤ Change each of the following to the plural form.

1. ese libro _____
2. esta mesa _____
3. aquel libro _____
4. esa pluma _____
5. aquella revista _____
6. esa casa _____
7. esta ciudad _____
8. aquel escritorio _____
9. ese lápiz _____
10. ese gato _____
11. esa perra _____
12. esta semana _____
13. este mes _____
14. aquel año _____
15. ese muchacho _____
16. esa rosa _____
17. ese clavel _____
18. aquella montaña _____
19. esa lección _____
20. aquel día _____
21. aquel automóvil _____

22. aquella flor _____
23. esa tienda _____
24. ese loro _____
25. aquella jaula _____
26. ese hombre _____
27. esa niña _____
28. aquella casa _____
29. esta carta _____
30. esa familia _____
31. este niño _____
32. aquel soldado _____
33. aquella compañía _____
34. esa computadora _____
35. aquel edificio _____
36. este refrigerador _____
37. esa librería _____
38. esta palabra _____
39. ese papel _____
40. esa biblioteca _____
41. esa estufa _____
42. ese árbol _____

Worksheet 3.13 Irregular verbs *hacer* and *poner*

Many irregular verbs are irregular only in the first person singular (**yo**) form. **Hacer** (*to do, to make*) and **poner** (*to put*) are good examples:

hacer			
yo	hago	nosotros(as)	hacemos
tú	haces	vosotros(as)	hacéis
el, ella, usted	hace*	ellos, ellas, ustedes	hacen

poner			
yo	pongo	nosotros(as)	ponemos
tú	pones	vosotros(as)	ponéis
el, ella, usted	pone	ellos, ellas, ustedes	ponen

*__Hace,__ the third person singular form (it) of **hacer,** is used to refer to the weather.

EXAMPLES: **Hace** mucho frío.   *It is very cold.*

➤ Supply the correct form of the verbs in parentheses.

1. Yo _____ (hacer) la comida.

2. Yo _____ (poner) la comida en la mesa.

3. Ellas _____ (hacer) la tarea.

4. Ellas _____ (poner) las manos en el teclado.

5. Hoy _____ (hacer) calor.

6. Nosotros _____ (poner) los discos en nuestras computadoras.

7. Tú _____ (hacer) tu trabajo en la fábrica.

8. Tú_____ (poner) los libros en los estantes.

9. Mi madre _____ (hacer) sus vestidos a máquina.

10. Ella _____ (poner) muchos alfileres en la tela.

11. _____ (Hacer) buen tiempo en verano.

12. Ellos _____ (poner) cubitos de hielo en cada refresco.

13. Yo_____ (hacer) mis cartas en la computadora.

14. Yo _____ (poner) los números en dos columnas.

15. Ustedes _____ (hacer) un mapa de California.

16. Ustedes _____ (poner) la ruta en el mapa.

17. La enfermera _____ (hacer) más cómodo al paciente.

18. La enfermera _____ (poner) sábanas limpias en la cama.

19. Tu coche _____ (hacer) mucho ruido.

20. Tú _____ (poner) un silenciador nuevo en tu coche.

21. Los panaderos _____ (hacer) panecillos.

22. El panadero _____ (poner) los panecillos en el horno.

23. ¿Qué _____ (hacer) usted para ganar dinero?

24. ¿Cuánto dinero _____ (poner) usted en el banco?

Worksheet 3.14 Irregular verbs *saber* and *traer*

As with many other irregular verbs, **saber** (*to know, to know how*) and **traer** (*to bring*) are irregular in the first person singular (**yo**) form:

saber			
yo	sé	nosotros(as)	sabemos
tú	sabes	vosotros(as)	sabéis
él, ella, usted	sabe	ellos, ellas, ustedes	saben

traer			
yo	traigo	nosotros(as)	traemos
tú	traes	vosotros(as)	traéis
él, ella, usted	trae	ellos, ellas, ustedes	traen

➤ Supply the correct form of the verbs in parentheses.

1. ¿ _____ (Saber) tú la receta para hacer un buen arroz con pollo?

2. Tú _____ (traer) los ingredientes de la receta.

3. Él _____ (saber) limpiar la alfombra.

4. Él _____ (traer) la aspiradora.

5. Nosotros _____ (saber) sacar fotos.

6. Nosotros _____ (traer) nuestra cámara.

7. Andrés _____ (saber) cantar canciones populares.

8. Andrés _____ (traer) su guitarra.

9. Yo _____ (saber) abrir una cuenta en el banco.

10. Yo _____ (traer) mis ahorros.

11. Ustedes _____ (saber) patinar.

12. Ustedes _____ (traer) los patines.

13. Ella _____ (saber) construir un librero.

14. Ella _____ (traer) las tablas y los clavos.

15. Usted _____ (saber) plantar los árboles.

16. Usted _____ (traer) sus palas.

17. Las señoritas _____ (saber) montar a caballo.

18. Las señoritas _____ (traer) sus propios caballos.

19. Los niños _____ (saber) hacer muñecos de papel.

20. Ellos _____ (traer) las tijeras.

21. Nosotros _____ (saber) cocinar.

22. Nosotros _____ (traer) los productos químicos.

23. ¿Qué _____ (saber) tú hacer para divertir a tus amigos?

24. ¿Qué _____ (traer) tú a la fiesta?

Worksheet 3.15 Irregular verbs *dar* and *salir*

Dar (*to give*) and **salir** (*to leave, to go out*) are also irregular in the first person singular (**yo**) form only:

dar			
yo	doy	nosotros(as)	damos
tú	das	vosotros	dais
él, ella, ustedes	da	ellos, ellas, ustedes	dan

salir			
yo	salgo	nosotros(as)	salimos
tú	sales	vosotros(as)	salís
él, ella, usted	sale	ellos, ellas ustedes	salen

➤ Supply the correct form of the verbs in parentheses.

1. El chofer _____ (salir) del automóvil.

2. El profesor de español _____ (dar) lecciones particulares.

3. Nosotros _____ (salir) del teatro.

4. Nosotros _____ (dar) nuestra opinión sobre la película.

5. Tú _____ (salir) de la iglesia.

6. Tú les _____ (dar) dinero a los pobres.

7. Yo _____ (salir) de la casa.

8. Yo le _____ (dar) una moneda al chofer del autobús.

9. El payaso _____ (salir) del circo.

10. El payaso les _____ (dar) boletos gratis a algunos niños.

11. Ustedes _____ (salir) de la selva de la India.

12. Ustedes _____ (dar) un reporte sobre los tigres.

13. Mi mamá nunca _____ (salir) de la cocina.

14. Mi mamá le _____ (dar) de comer a toda la familia.

15. Los turistas _____ (salir) del hotel.

16. Los turistas le _____ (dar) instrucciones al taxista.

17. Usted _____ (salir) del hospital después de la operación.

18. Usted les_____ (dar) las gracias al cirujano y a las enfermeras.

19. Yo _____ (salir) del taxi al llegar.

20. Yo le _____ (dar) una buena propina al taxista.

21. La actriz _____ (salir) del avión.

22. La actriz les _____ (dar) entrevistas a los periodistas.

23. ¿Estás satisfecho cuando tú _____ (salir) de un buen restaurante?

24. ¿Cuánto le_____ (dar) de propina al camarero?

Worksheet 3.16 Use of the *a personal*

When a human being is the direct object of a verb, the direct object must be preceded by the word **a**. This **a**, which is not strictly a preposition, is known as the personal **a** or **a personal**:

EXAMPLES: HUMAN BEING AS DIRECT OBJECT   NONHUMAN AS DIRECT OBJECT
          Yo veo a Juan.   Yo veo el perro de Juan.
          Tú ves al doctor.   Tú ves el coche del doctor.

➤ In the blanks, supply, as needed, the **a personal**, together with the definite or indefinite article, when used: **a, al (a + el = el), a la, a los, a las, a un, a una.** Place an X in the space if no words are required.

1. Yo veo _____ Beatriz muchas veces en el supermercado.

2. Yo veo _____ muchos alimentos en el supermercado.

3. Nosotros escribimos _____ nuestros senadores.

4. Nosotros escribimos cartas _____ los senadores.

5. El policía dirige _____ el tránsito.

6. La policía ayuda y protege_____ los ciudadanos.

7. Tú escuchas _____ tus padres.

8. Tú escuchas _____ el consejo de tus padres.

9. Ellos conocen _____ el gobernador de Utah.

10. Ellos conocen _____ el estado de Utah.

11. Carlos trae _____ María en el coche.

12. Carlos trae _____ el coche de María.

13. Mi vecino enseña _____ su loro a hablar.

14. Mi vecino enseña _____ mi hijo a cantar.

15. Yo leo _____ una bonita revista.

16. Yo veo _____ una mujer bonita en la biblioteca.

17. El chico imita _____ un chimpancé en el zoológico.

18. El chimpancé imita _____ un chico en el zoológico.

19. Nosotros contestamos _____ los alemanes en alemán.

20. Nosotros hablamos _____ alemán con los alemanes.

21. ¿Invitas tú _____ los mariachis a cantar?

22. ¿Cantan los mariachis _____ canciones rancheras?

Worksheet 3.17 Formation of adverbs

Many adverbs are formed by adding the suffix -**mente** to the feminine singular form of the adjective:

EXAMPLES:

ADJECTIVE	FEMININE SINGULAR	ADVERB
correcto	correcta	correcta**mente**
fácil	fácil	fácil**mente**
claro	clara	clara**mente**

When two or more adverbs modify the same word, -**mente** is added only to the last one:

EXAMPLE: Él habla clara y correcta**mente**.

➤ In the blanks, supply the adverbial form of the adjectives in parentheses.

1. Cristóbal Colón piensa _____ (serio) en la redondez del mundo.

2. Mucha gente escucha _____ (sospechoso) las ideas de Colón.

3. Colón no vive _____ (tranquilo) en Italia.

4. _____ (Difícil), viaja con su hijo a España.

5. La reina Isabel recibe _____ (cordial) al italiano.

6. Ella le dice que _____ (triste) no tiene el dinero necesario.

7. _____ (Generoso) ella vende sus propias joyas.

8. Colón acepta _____ (emocionado) el regalo de tres barcos.

9. Él sale _____ (respetuoso) de la corte de los reyes.

10. El almirante cree _____ (sincero) que navega hacia el Oriente.

11. Los barcos llegan _____ (inesperado) a otro continente.

12. El cree _____ (incorrecto) que los habitantes son de la India.

13. Nosotros_____ (curioso) aún los llamamos indios.

14. Hoy mencionamos _____ (respetuoso) el nombre de Colón.

15. El gran descubridor,_____ (afortunado), hace otros viajes al Nuevo Mundo.

16. En uno de esos viajes, _____ (desafortunado), resulta en una catástrofe.

17. En la Española él naufraga _____ (completo) su nave la Santa María.

18. El hermano de Colón _____ (heróico) funda un pueblo en la isla, Santo Domingo.

19. La historia de Cristóbal Colón es _____ (especial) interesante.

20. Otros descubridores contribuyen _____ (histórico) a América.

21. Ponce de León busca la Fuente de la Juventud y así explora _____ (considerable) la Florida.

22. Balboa _____ (increíble) descubre el océano Pacífico.

Name: _____ Date: _____

Irregular verbs

➤ In the blanks, supply the correct form of the verb in parentheses.

1. Tú estás en la cocina, y yo _____ (estar) en la sala.

2. Él sale a las seis, y yo _____ (salir) a las seis y media.

3. Ustedes le dan dinero a la Cruz Roja, y yo le _____ (dar) a la iglesia.

4. Ella sabe bailar bien, pero yo _____ (saber) bailar mejor.

5. Enrique hace poco ruido, pero yo _____ (hacer) mucho.

6. Ellos ponen mucha atención pero yo _____ (poner) más.

7. Tú vas a la escuela de día; yo _____ (ir) de noche.

8. Usted tiene frío, pero yo _____ (tener) calor.

9. Ellas ven películas; yo _____ (ver) los deportes.

10. Él es de Tejas, y yo _____ (ser) de Nuevo México.

11. Yo estoy en la plaza, y tú _____ (estar) en el parque.

12. Yo salgo temprano, pero ellos _____ (salir) tarde.

13. Yo doy una propina adecuada; ella _____ (dar) demasiado.

14. Yo sé la verdad; ustedes no _____ (saber) nada.

15. Yo hago naranjada, y tú _____ (hacer) limonada.

16. Yo pongo el café en la mesa; él _____ (poner) el té.

17. Yo voy a Madrid, pero ella _____ (ir) a Valencia.

18. Yo tengo sed, pero usted _____ (tener) hambre.

19. Yo veo dramas, y ustedes _____ (ver) comedias.

20. Yo soy vendedor, y él _____ (ser) gerente.

General review

➤ Choose the correct form and write it in the blank.

1. _____ (Nuestros, Nuestras) entretenimientos le deben mucho a Tomás Edison.

2. _____ (Eso, Ese) científico es el maestro de la invención.

3. _____ (La, El) luz eléctrica es su invento más importante.

4. Él también es inventor _____ (del, de el) fonógrafo.

5. _____ (Es, Eres) muy agradable tener en casa música grabada.

6. El inventor _____ (hago, hace) preguntas a su maestro.

7. El maestro _____ (es, está) enojado con el joven Tomás.

8. Tomás _____ (tiene, tiene que) abandonar sus estudios.

9. Él sólo _____ (recibe, recibo) tres meses de educación formal.

10. Su mamá es _____ (maestra, una maestra) increíble.

11. Ella le enseña mucho _____ (Tomás, a Tomás) en casa.

12. Cuando es joven hace_____ (su, sus) experimentos en Ohio.

13. Su laboratorio más famoso_____ (es, está) en Nueva Jersey.

14. El inventor es sordo, pero no _____ (completo, completamente).

15. Él también da _____ (el mundo, al mundo) la cinematografía.

16. ¿Qué_____ (hacemos, hacen) nosotros sin películas de cine?

17. Edison perfecciona _____ (los, a los) aparatos de otros inventores.

18. Hoy no tenemos_____ (que, a) gritar en el teléfono.

19. La máquina de escribir es más _____ (rápida, rápidamente).

20. Hoy_____ (nuestra, nuestras) vida es mucho mejor.

21. Yo _____ (sé, sabe) que Edison es «el Sabio del Menlo Park.»

22. Tú _____(lee, lees) mucho sobre él y ves una película de su vida.

23. Dos actores famosos _____ (tiene, tienen) el papel de Edison.

24. Mickey Rooney es Edison _____ (el, al) joven.

25. Edison el hombre _____ (es, está) Spencer Tracy.

26. Voy _____ (ir, a ir) a Nueva Jersey en el verano.

27. Deseo _____ (ver, ver a) su laboratorio en East Orange.

Worksheet 3.18 Irregular verbs *decir* and *oír*

Examine carefully the forms of **decir** and **oír,** which are more irregular than other verbs that were recently reviewed:

decir			
yo	digo	nosotros(as)	decimos
tú	dices	vosotros(as)	decís
él, ella, usted	dice	ellos, ellas, ustedes	dicen

oír			
yo	oigo	nosotros(as)	oímos
tú	oyes	vosotros(as)	oís
él, ella, usted	oye	ellos, ellas, ustedes	oyen

➤ Supply the correct form of **decir** in the blanks.

1. Ellos _____ que están muy ocupados hoy.

2. Tú _____ que vamos a tener un examen mañana.

3. Yo siempre _____ la verdad.

4. Rosa y Elena _____ que van a ir al cine esta noche.

5. Ricardo _____ que la película de hoy es muy buena.

6. ¿Por qué _____ usted que nunca va a aprender español?

7. ¡Cuidado! Juan a veces _____ mentiras.

8. ¿Qué _____ Guillermo de su nuevo trabajo?

9. Él _____ que es interesante, pero difícil.

10. ¿Por qué _____ tú que la gramática española es difícil?

11. Nosotros nunca _____ mentiras en la escuela.

12. Pedro _____ que va a estudiar para abogado.

➤ Supply the correct form of **oír** in the blanks.

1. Yo no _____ bien a la profesora desde este asiento.

2. ¿ _____ bien usted a la profesora desde ese asiento?

3. El señor Gómez no _____ bien. Es un poco sordo.

4. Tú _____ los conciertos por radio todas las tardes.

5. Yo _____ a los hijos de mi vecina desde el jardín.

6. Con tanto ruido yo no _____ nada.

7. Nosotros _____ música clásica, nada más.

8. El director _____ las ideas de los alumnos.

9. Él siempre _____ con paciencia nuestras quejas.

10. Los perros _____ a otros perros ladrar desde muy lejos.

11. Nosotros _____ muchas novelas por radio.

12. Tú _____ mucha música popular por discos compactos.

Worksheet 3.19 Irregular verbs *venir* and *querer*

The verbs **venir** and **querer** are stem-changing verbs **e → ie**. **Venir** also has a stem change in the first person singular:

venir			
yo	vengo	nosotros(as)	venimos
tú	vienes	vosotros(as)	venís
él, ella, usted	viene	ellos, ellas, ustedes	vienen

querer			
yo	quiero	nosotros(as)	queremos
tú	quieres	vosotros(as)	queréis
él, ella, usted	quiere	ellos, ellas, ustedes	quieren

➤ Supply the correct form of the verb in parentheses.

1. Lolita _____ (venir) a cenar con nosotros.

2. Lolita _____ (querer) comer a las seis.

3. Yo _____ (venir) a la oficina en autobús.

4. Yo no _____ (querer) usar mi coche para ir a trabajar.

5. Tú _____ (venir) a estudiar español.

6. Tú _____ (querer) ser presidente.

7. Nosotros _____ (venir) a la panadería del barrio.

8. Nosotros _____ (querer) comprar pan francés.

9. Ellas _____ (venir) al Palacio de Bellas Artes.

10. Ellas _____ (querer) ver el ballet folklórico de México.

11. Raúl _____ (venir) a la pista de hielo.

12. Raúl _____ (querer) patinar con sus compañeros.

13. Ustedes _____ (venir) a la Plaza Mayor de Madrid.

14. Ustedes _____ (querer) ver los edificios históricos.

15. Muchos turistas _____ (venir) a la plaza de toros.

16. Algunos turistas no _____ (querer) ver las corridas de toros.

17. Viajeros de todo el mundo _____ (venir) a Nueva York.

18. Esas muchachas _____ (querer) conocer bien la isla de Manhattan.

19. Gustavo y Esteban _____ (venir) a la biblioteca.

20. Ellos _____ (querer) ver algunos libros de consulta.

21. Yo _____ (venir) de Sevilla.

22. Yo no _____ (querer) vivir en una ciudad tan grande.

23. Tú _____ (venir) muchas veces a mi casa.

24. Tú y yo _____ (querer) oír música clásica.

Worksheet 3.20 Irregular verbs *poder* and *saber*

As helping verbs, **poder** and **saber** (*can* and *know*), normally precede the infinitive of another verb. While in English *can* and *know how* are often used interchangeably, **poder** in Spanish is strictly used with the meaning of *to be able,* as in actual physical ability to do something, or to indicate possibility, as with *may* or *might*. In English *can* is often used with the meaning of *know how to,* but in such cases in Spanish we must use **saber.**

EXAMPLES: Yo **puedo** nadar muy rápido. *I can swim very fast* (physical ability).
Yo **sé** bailar muy bien el tango. *I can dance the tango very well* (know how to).

poder			
yo	puedo	nosotros(as)	podemos
tú	puedes	vosotros(as)	podemos
él, ella, usted	puede	ellos(as)	podemos

saber			
yo	sé	nosotros(as)	sabemos
tú	sabes	vosotros(as)	sabemos
él, ella, usted	sabe	ellos(as)	saben

➤ In the following sentences, add the verbs **poder** and **saber** as needed.

1. El loro de Juan _____ (saber, poder) decir muchas palabras.

2. Yo _____ (saber, poder) pintar en acuarela.

3. Isabel _____ (saber, poder) hablar francés y alemán.

4. Es difícil _____ (saber, poder) ganar en la lotería.

5. Ricardo_____ (saber, poder) dibujar caricaturas muy chistosas.

6. Ella _____ (saber, poder) recitar lindas poesías.

7. Ese avión _____ (saber, poder) volar hasta mil kilómetros por hora.

8. Alejandro _____ (saber, poder) competir en el campeonato de boxeo.

9. María _____ (saber, poder) coser muy bien a máquina.

10. El muchacho _____ (saber, poder) manejar un automóvil bien y aún no _____ (saber, poder) pasar el examen para conducir.

11. No _____ (saber, poder) pagar todas mis cuentas este mes.

12. ¿ _____ (saber, poder) manejar un camión de carga?

13. El taxista no _____ (saber, poder) llevar a los cinco pasajeros en su vehículo porque son demasiados, y tampoco _____ (saber, poder) cómo llegar a ese lugar.

14. Mi madre _____ (saber, poder) cocinar muy bien pero ahora no _____ (saber, poder) porque no ve bien.

15. Yo _____ (saber, poder) crear el informe, pero no _____ (saber, poder) trabajar con ese nuevo programa de computadora.

Irregular verbs

➤ Change the pronoun of each sentence from **yo** to **él.** Write both the subject and the verb in the spaces to the right. For further practice, make more answer sheets for changes to other subjects: **tú, ella, usted, nosotros, ustedes, ellos.**

1. Yo tengo una vida llena de actividades. _____

2. Yo digo las frases que debo aprender en español. _____

3. Yo oigo un programa de noticias en la radio. _____

4. Yo tengo que ayudar con las tareas de la casa. _____

5. Yo hago el café para toda la familia. _____

6. Yo sé si quieren el café con o sin leche. _____

7. Yo salgo de mi casa a las ocho menos veinte. _____

8. Yo estoy en la oficina. _____

9. Yo veo las palabras nuevas en el diccionario. _____

10. Yo doy la propina al camarero. _____

11. Yo soy estudiante de español. _____

12. Yo tengo muy buenas notas en mis asignaturas. _____

13. Yo vengo a clase puntualmente. _____

14. Yo voy a estudiar derecho. _____

15. Yo digo a todos que estoy contento con la escuela. _____

16. Yo sé que los profesores trabajan muy duro. _____

17. Yo estoy dispuesto a hacer las tareas. _____

18. Yo soy miembro del equipo de béisbol. _____

19. Yo voy a participar en la competencia. _____

20. Yo tengo buena pronunciación. _____

Vocabulary check-up

➤ In the blanks, write the opposites of the following words. If you do not know the word, look for its meaning in the vocabulary at the end of the book, then try to remember its opposite.

1. fácil _____

2. pequeño _____

3. abrir _____

4. subir _____

5. entrar _____

6. hombre _____

7. madre _____

8. menos _____

9. triste _____

10. nuevo _____

11. blanco _____

12. mucho _____

13. peor _____

14. temprano _____

15. invierno _____

16. mentira _____

17. tomar _____

18. silencio _____

19. barato _____

20. calor _____

21. jugar _____

22. largo _____

23. perder _____

24. preguntar _____

25. rápido _____

26. frío _____

27. joven _____

28. vender _____

29. lejos _____

30. alto _____

31. sucio _____

32. ausente _____

33. antes _____

34. día _____

35. ir _____

36. enemigo _____

37. allí _____

38. feo _____

39. ahorrar _____

40. estos _____

41. rico _____

42. bueno _____

43. comprador _____

44. enseñar _____

45. débil _____

46. paz _____

47. actor (f.) _____

48. grueso _____

Busc apalabras

Laberinto de palabras

➤ Return to page 41. Did you unscramble all the words? Now, try to fit them into the squares below:

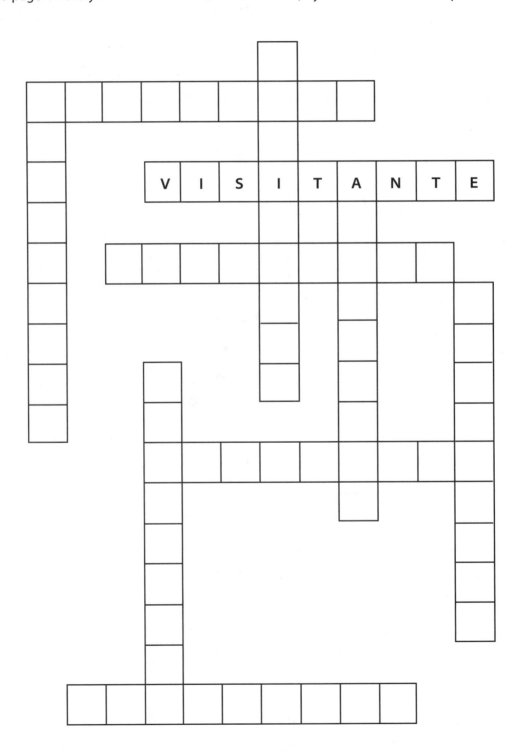

Part 4

Contents

Worksheet 4.1 Preterite tense of -ar verbs

The preterite tense (**el pretérito**) is one of the two simple past tenses. It is used to describe an action or event completed in the past. It is not used for repeated actions or actions that continue into the present or future. Regular **-ar** verbs are conjugated as follows in the preterite tense:

hablar			
yo	hablé	nosotros(as)	hablamos
tú	hablaste	vosotros(as)	hablasteis
él, ella, usted	habló	ellos, ellas, ustedes	hablaron

➤ Supply the preterite tense of the verbs in parentheses in the blanks.

1. El señor García _____ (cruzar) el océano en un barco lujoso.

2. Los pasajeros _____ (desembarcar) en Portugal.

3. Nosotros _____ (volar) en primera clase a Madrid.

4. Yo _____ (viajar) con el señor García por el sur de España.

5. Él _____ (alquilar) un automóvil en el aeropuerto.

6. Nosotros _____ (manejar) de Madrid a Sevilla.

7. José García me _____ (presentar) a su hermana Concha.

8. Ella me _____ (saludar) con una bella sonrisa.

9. Los tres _____ (cenar) en un restaurante típico de Sevilla.

10. Un trío de gitanos nos _____ (cantar) varias canciones.

11. Una bailarina _____ (presentar) un baile flamenco.

12. Los músicos _____ (tocar) muy bien la guitarra.

13. Yo sólo _____ (tomar) jugo de manzana con la comida.

14. Tú _____ (bailar) el tango.

15. Nosotros _____ (hablar) español durante toda la comida.

16. Concha _____ (conversar) con el camarero.

17. Después, tú nos _____ (llevar) a la cueva de unos gitanos.

18. Nosotros _____ (ver) familias enteras en la cueva.

19. Los gitanos también _____ (tocar) y _____ (bailar).

20. El guía _____ (mencionar) que algunos de los gitanos son ricos.

Worksheet 4.2 Preterite tense of *-er, -ir* verbs

In the preterite tense, **-er** and **-ir** verbs share the same endings:

aprender			
yo	aprendí	nosotros(as)	aprendimos
tú	aprendiste	vosotros(as)	aprendisteis
él, ella, usted	aprendió	ellos, ellas, ustedes	aprendieron

vivir			
yo	viví	nosotros(as)	vivimos
tú	viviste	vosotros(as)	vivisteis
él, ella, usted	vivió	ellos, ellas, ustedes	vivieron

➤ Supply the proper form of the verb in parentheses in the blanks.

1. Mi hermana Elena _____ (cumplir) ayer los dieciséis años.

2. Muchos de sus amigas y amigos _____ (asistir) a su fiesta de cumpleaños.

3. Ellos _____ (conocer) a Elena en el colegio.

4. Desafortunadamente, yo no _____ (hablar) mucho con ellos.

5. Todos nosotros _____ (salir) a la misma hora.

6. Elena _____ (recibir) muchos regalos.

7. Ella _____ (abrir) cada regalo con alegría.

8. Nuestros padres _____ (insistir) en invitar a los padres de las amigas, como es costumbre en los países hispanos.

9. Algunos _____ (escribir) en vez de asistir.

10. Yo sólo_____ (beber) tres vasos de agua.

11. Nosotros _____ (comer) una torta de cumpleaños muy sabrosa.

12. Los muchachos no _____ (resistir) los dulces.

13. Yo _____ (ver) muchos de mis compañeros.

14. Alberto _____ (esconder) varios dulces en el bolsillo.

15. Más tarde todos los dulces _____ (desaparecer) misteriosamente.

16. Alberto _____ (salir) temprano para la fiesta.

17. Los músicos _____ (aparecer) a las ocho en punto.

18. Yo _____ (aprender) mis canciones favoritas de niño.

19. Elena _____ (agradecer) todos sus regalos.

20. La fiesta _____ (resultar) un éxito.

Worksheet 4.3 More on the preterite tense

➤ Supply the preterite tense of the verbs in parentheses in the blanks.

1. Ayer, nosotros _____ (planear) un día de campo.

2. Nosotros _____ (caminar) a lo largo del río.

3. Mis padres y mis hermanos me _____ (acompañar).

4. Tú _____ (llevar) nuestro almuerzo en una cesta.

5. Yo _____ (escoger) un lugar cerca del río.

6. Mi mamá _____ (colocar) un mantel sobre la hierba.

7. Mis padres _____ (descansar) toda la tarde.

8. Mis hermanos y yo _____ (jugar) béisbol.

9. Después de una hora, nosotros _____ (comer) nuestro almorzar.

10. Elena _____ (ayudar) a mamá con la comida.

11. Yo _____ (tomar) un refresco de limón.

12. Papá _____ (sacar) un termo de café.

13. Yo _____ (comer) dos bocadillos (*sandwiches*) de jamón con queso.

14. Un ejército de insectos también _____ (tratar) de comer.

15. Muy pronto el sol _____ (desaparecer) completamente.

16. Yo _____ (ver) el cielo nublado.

17. Desgraciadamente, _____ (llover) mucho.

18. Nosotros _____ (recoger) rápidamente nuestra cosas.

19. Mi familia y yo _____ (correr) hacia unos árboles.

20. Un árbol muy grande _____ (ofrecer) refugio por un tiempo.

21. Después de media hora _____ (parar) de llover.

22. Nosotros _____ (regresar) a casa un poco tristes.

23. El día _____ (terminar) mal.

Worksheet 4.4 More on the preterite tense

➤ Change the following verbs from present tense to preterite tense.

1. Yo estudio _____
2. Él vive _____
3. Ellos compran _____
4. Yo escribo _____
5. Eduardo habla _____
6. Ellos viven _____
7. Elena vende _____
8. Yo espero _____
9. Tú aprendes _____
10. Usted habla _____
11. Él bebe _____
12. Yo como _____
13. Ellos comen _____
14. Tú apareces _____
15. Él sube _____
16. Yo saludo _____
17. Yo camino _____
18. Jorge recibe _____
19. Tú asistes _____
20. Yo abro _____
21. Él ahorra _____
22. Yo pregunto _____
23. Ella escribe _____
24. Ellos comen _____

25. Ellos venden _____
26. Tú vives _____
27. Yo bebo _____
28. Él admira _____
29. Ella gasta _____
30. Usted termina _____
31. Mi tío explica _____
32. Enrique sale _____
33. Tú necesitas _____
34. Él toma _____
35. Yo trato _____
36. María contesta _____
37. Ellos tratan _____
38. Luis trabaja _____
39. Tú llevas _____
40. Nosotros vemos _____
41. Nosotros tomamos _____
42. Tú caminas _____
43. Ellos planean _____
44. Yo salgo _____
45. Él responde _____
46. Yo comprendo _____
47. Tú estudias _____
48. Ella sale _____

Worksheet 4.5   Personal pronouns—prepositional forms

Personal pronouns as objects of prepositions (for *us*, with *them*) follow the patterns below:

EXAMPLES: El regalo es para **mí.**   El regalo es para **nosotros(as)**
       El regalo es para **ti.**   El regalo es para **vosotros(as).**
       El regalo es para **usted.**   El regalo es para **ustedes.**
       El regalo es para **él.**   El regalo es para **ellos.**
       El regalo es para **ella.**   El regalo es para **ellas.**

Note: Except for the first and second persons singular (**mí, ti**), the prepositional forms are identical to the subject pronouns. Note also that these same two pronouns when combined with **con** become **conmigo** and **contigo.**

➤ In the blanks, replace the words in parentheses with the appropriate prepositional pronoun.

1. Yo siempre hablo de _____ (mi hermano).

2. Hay un mensaje por correo electrónico para _____ (tú).

3. Juan estudia con _____ (Felipe y Juan).

4. Elena estudia con _____ (Carmen y María).

5. Él siempre anda con _____ (Ana y yo).

6. Ella siempre anda detrás de _____ (Pablo y tú).

7. Juan trabaja diariamente con _____ (Carlos y yo).

8. Mario trabaja diariamente con _____ (Alberto y tú).

9. Silvia sale a veces con _____ (tu primo).

10. Tu primo sale a veces con_____ (Silvia).

11. Él dice que tiene buenas noticias para _____ (tú y yo).

12. Yo tengo buenas noticias para_____ (usted y ella).

13. Tus abuelos viven muy lejos de _____ (tus padres).

14. Tu abuelo vive muy lejos de_____ (tu padre).

15. El médico conoce muy bien a _____ (las enfermeras).

16. Los médicos conocen muy bien a _____ (la enfermera).

17. Yo voy al cine con _____ (mis amigos).

18. Ella nunca va al cine sin _____ (María y yo).

19. ¿Cuándo piensas tú en _____ (yo)?

20. Quiero ir con _____ (tú).

Worksheet 4.6 More on personal pronouns—prepositional forms

REMINDER: **con + mi = conmigo**   **con + ti = contigo**
EXAMPLES: Ella va **conmigo**.   *She goes with me.*   Yo ando **contigo**   *I walk with you.*

➤ Change the following pronouns from singular to plural. Include prepositions.

1. con él _____
2. para usted _____
3. para mí _____
4. hacia mí _____
5. según tú* _____
6. conmigo _____
7. sin ti _____
8. sobre él _____
9. lejos de ti _____
10. cerca de mí _____
11. detrás de mí _____
12. en frente de ti _____
13. de él _____
14. con usted _____
15. en él _____
16. sin mí _____
17. para mí _____
18. por mí _____
19. para él _____
20. hacia ti _____

➤ Change the following pronouns from plural to singular. Include prepositions.

1. para nosotros _____
2. con ellos _____
3. para ustedes _____
4. sin nosotros _____
5. con ustedes _____
6. de nosotros _____
7. por ellas _____
8. sin nosotras _____
9. por ustedes _____
10. para ellas _____
11. con ustedes _____
12. sobre ellos _____
13. a nosotros _____
14. de ustedes _____
15. hacia ellas _____
16. a nosotros _____
17. hacia ellos _____
18. según ellas _____
19. en ustedes _____
20. entre ellos _____

*Note: After the preposition **según**, the pronouns **tú** and **yo** do not change.

Worksheet 4.7 Direct object pronouns

Direct object pronouns are placed as follows:

EXAMPLES:	ENGLISH (FOLLOW NOUN)	SPANISH (PRECEDE NOUN)	
	He sees me.	Me ve.	
	He sees you.	Te ve.	(familiar)
	He sees you.	Lo (La) ve.	(polite)
	He sees him (her).	Lo (La) ve.	
	He sees us.	Nos ve.	
	He sees you.	Os ve.	(familiar)
	He sees you.	Los (las) ve.	(polite)
	He sees them.	Los (las) ve.	

➤ Supply the direct object pronoun needed to replace the noun in parentheses and rewrite the sentences in the spaces provided.

1. Yo veo (el libro) en la mesa. _____

2. Ella necesita (esa pluma). _____

3. El profesor pone (el libro) en su cartera. _____

4. Ellos practican (los ejercicios) cuidadosamente. _____

5. Tú no necesitas más (esta computadora). _____

6. Yo veo (al señor García) en la calle con frecuencia. _____

7. Inés trae (a su amiga) a la fiesta. _____

8. El profesor busca (sus lentes) por todas partes. _____

9. Yo llamé (a usted y a María) por teléfono ayer. _____

10. Tú escribiste (la carta) por fin. _____

11. Veo (al señor López) casi todos los días. _____

12. También veo (a su esposa) con mucha frecuencia. _____

13. Yo compré (esta impresora) por cien dólares. _____

14. El médico mandó (a Carlos y a Juan) al laboratorio. _____

15. Yo abrí (las ventanas). _____

16. Él siempre envía (sus mensajes) por correo electrónico _____

17. Yo generalmente vendo (mi auto) cada tres años. _____

18. Alguien compró (el auto de mi tío). _____

19. Ella no tiene (su cartera). _____

20. Veo (a Dolores) de vez en cuando. _____

Worksheet 4.8 Indirect object pronouns

Indirect object pronouns are the same as the direct object pronouns **me, te, nos, os**, except for the third person:

	DIRECT OBJECTS	INDIRECT OBJECTS
SINGULAR:	lo, la	le
PLURAL:	los, las	les

➤ Supply the missing indirect object pronouns in the blanks.

1. Yo _____ vendo mi impresora (a ti).

2. Tú _____ pagas cien dólares (a mí).

3. Nosotros _____ hablamos (al profesor) en español.

4. El profesor no _____ habla (a nosotros) muy rápido.

5. Juan _____ escribió muchas cartas (a Angélica).

6. Angélica _____ llamó por teléfono (a sus padres).

7. Los artistas _____ cantaron (a nosotros).

8. Yo _____ pedí otra canción (a ellos).

9. Tú _____ sorprendiste (a mí) con el regalo.

10. Yo _____ regalé algo (a ella) también.

11. El maestro _____ explicó (a ti) una regla de gramática.

12. El jefe _____ explicó un plan (a los empleados).

13. Yo _____ traigo (a ti) todos mis problemas.

14. Tú _____ ayudas (a mi) a resolver mis problemas.

15. El jefe _____ ordena (a nosotros) llegar temprano.

16. Nosotros _____ prometemos (al jefe) llegar a tiempo.

17. Roberto _____ prestó (a Luisa) diez dólares.

18. Ella _____ agradeció (a Roberto) el préstamo.

19. La respuesta del estudiante _____ pareció buena (a mí).

20. Los estudiantes _____ parecen buenos (a nosotros).

21. Los veteranos _____ dicen (a mí) que van a desfilar.

22. Yo _____ mencioné (a ti) el desfile de los veteranos.

23. El banco _____ devolvió (a usted) el cheque.

24. A los bancos no _____ gustan los cheques sin fondos.

Worksheet 4.9 Redundant personal pronouns

Prepositional pronouns are used with **le, les** for emphasis or clarity because **le** and **les** can refer to you, him, her, or them. The following *redundant* prepositional phrases help to assure clarity:

EXAMPLES: SINGULAR   PLURAL
            Le doy el libro a usted *(you)*.   Les doy el libro a ustedes *(you)*.
            Le doy el libro a él *(him)*.   Les doy el libro a ellos *(them)*.
            Le doy el libro a ella *(her)*.   Les doy el libro a ellas *(them)*.

EXAMPLE: Emphasis: ¡A **mí** no **me** engaña nadie! *Nobody cheats me!*

➤ Supply the indirect object pronoun (**me, te, le, nos, os, les**) in the blanks.

1. Él _____ escribió a ella dos cartas ayer.

2. Juan siempre _____ trae a ellas muchas flores.

3. A mí no _____ importa nada su reputación.

4. A Alfredo _____ parece extraño que usted no lo llamó.

5. A ti _____ encanta bailar el tango.

6. Él siempre _____ manda a nosotros muchos regalos.

7. ¿Quién _____ enseñó a ella a escribir a máquina?

8. A mí _____ encanta aprender idiomas.

9. A mi esposa _____ encanta el clima de Puerto Rico.

10. A nosotros no _____ importan las acciones de otros.

11. ¿Qué _____ importa a ti lo que él dice?

12. A mí _____ encantan todos los deportes.

13. No _____ importa a Vicente lo que dice el profesor.

14. Él nunca _____ dice a mí lo que va a hacer.

15. A mí _____ desagradan las discusiones de política.

16. A nosotros _____ agrada mucho la profesora nueva.

17. A Vicente no _____ importa lo que dice la gente.

18. A mí _____ encantan los alumnos recién llegados del exterior.

19. Margarita _____ envió un correo electrónico a sus padres anoche.

20. A nosotros _____ pareció absurda la actitud de Raquel.

21. ¿Qué _____ parece a usted mi automóvil nuevo?

22. ¿A quién _____ prestó usted la computadora?

23. Ellos nunca _____ invitan a ti cuando van al campo.

24. A todos ellos _____ encanta nadar en la piscina.

25. ¿A usted _____ parecen fáciles los pronombres personales?

Worksheet 4.10 **The verb *gustar***

There is no verb in Spanish that corresponds exactly to *like*. To express this meaning, the verb **gustar** (*to please*) is used. In translation, the subject becomes the object, the object becomes the subject and the indirect object pronouns must be used.

EXAMPLES: | ENGLISH | SPANISH | LITERAL TRANSLATION |
|---|---|---|
| *I like the story.* | **Me gusta** el cuento. | *The story pleases me.* |
| *I like the stories.* | **Me gustan** los cuentos. | *The stories please me.* |

➤ Supply the correct form of **gustar** in the blanks, preceded by the appropriate pronoun (**me, te, le, nos, os, les**).

1. A mí _____ esquiar.

2. ¿Cuáles colores _____ a ustedes?

3. A mis padres _____ ir al cine.

4. A ellos _____ sobre todo las películas históricas.

5. El pescado frito a mí no _____ .

6. A mí _____ mucho más los mariscos.

7. A mis vecinos _____ las playas de Acapulco.

8. A mi familia _____ la playa de San Juan.

9. ¿ _____ a ustedes las casas de dos pisos?

10. A mí _____ una casa con muchas habitaciones.

11. ¿ _____ a ti el chocolate caliente estilo mexicano?

12. No, a mí _____ más el chocolate caliente sin canela.

13. A los alumnos no _____ los exámenes difíciles.

14. A otros alumnos no _____ la tarea diaria.

15. A los argentinos _____ las carreras de caballos.

16. A los españoles _____ el jai alai.

17. A mí no _____ el ruido de los helicópteros.

18. A mí tampoco _____ el ruido de los aviones.

19. A Lucía _____ comer en restaurantes.

20. A Antonio _____ más la comida preparada en casa.

21. A los niños _____ los fuegos artificiales.

22. A mí también _____ los cohetes.

23. ¿Es verdad que no _____ a usted las espinacas?

24. ¿Cuál verdura _____ más a ti?

Worksheet 4.11 More on *gustar*

A number of other verbs follow the pattern of **gustar:**

EXAMPLES: **parecer**   *to seem*   **encantar**   *to charm, delight*   **fascinar**   *to fascinate*

              importar   *to matter*   **extrañar**   *to seem strange*   **molestar**   *to bother*

The verb **disgustar** does not mean *to disgust*; it replaces the English verb *to dislike*, but literally means *to displease*.

➤ Supply the missing indirect object pronouns and the correct form of the verb in parentheses.

1. A mí _____ hablar español con el profesor. (gustar)

2. A ellos _____ fallar en el examen. (disgustar)

3. No _____ a ella el dinero que gasta en ropa. (importar)

4. A ti _____ los idiomas extranjeros. (encantar)

5. A nosotros _____ curiosa tu actitud. (parecer)

6. A mi hermana _____ las novelas policíacas. (fascinar)

7. A las mujeres no _____ decir su edad. (gustar)

8. ¿Qué _____ a ti esta corbata? (parecer)

9. ¿No _____ a tí no ver a Raquel en el baile? (extrañar)

10. A él no _____ la opinión de los demás. (importar)

11. A los senadores _____ el plan del presidente. (fascinar)

12. A mí _____ increíble la decisión del juez. (parecer)

13. A ella _____ la zona colonial de La Habana. (encantar)

14. A nosotros _____ la conducta de esa persona. (extrañar)

15. A mi señora _____ mucho ir de tiendas. (gustar)

16. ¿No _____ a ti los pingüinos? (fascinar)

17. A mí _____ mucho anoche el humo de los fumadores. (molestar).

18. No _____ a ellos la raza del candidato. (importar)

19. ¿No _____ a usted hermosa la prima de Arturo? (parecer)

20. No sabes cuánto _____ a ella la música latina. (gustar)

21. A Ramón _____ tu falta de entusiasmo. (extrañar)

22. A nosotros _____ la música brasileña. (fascinar)

23. ¿No _____ a usted ese ruido? (molestar)

24. ¿ Por qué _____ tanto a ti el resultado? (disgustar)

25. ¿A usted no _____ los mosquitos? (molestar)

Worksheet 4.12 Arithmetic

➤ For practice with cardinal numbers and arithmetical functions, compute answers to the following problems and write them in the blanks to the right.

1. Siete menos cuatro son_____ .

2. Seis menos dos son _____ .

3. Seis y (más) uno son _____ .

4. Seis y dos son _____ .

5. Cinco por (multiplicado por) dos son_____ .

6. Cinco por tres son _____ .

7. Diez menos uno son _____ .

8. Diez menos nueve es _____ .

9. Uno menos uno es _____ .

10. Siete y siete son_____ .

11. Ocho entre (dividido entre) dos son _____ .

12. Diez entre dos son_____ .

13. Siete menos seis es _____ .

14. Doce entre tres son _____ .

15. Cuatro por tres son _____ .

16. Once menos cinco son _____ .

17. Diez por tres son _____ .

18. Treinta entre diez son _____ .

19. El cincuenta por ciento (%) de diez es _____ .

20. El veinticinco por ciento de cuatro es _____ .

21. ¿Cuántos son once menos dos? _____ .

22. ¿Cuántos son doce entre tres?_____ .

23. Cinco por cuatro menos tres son _____ .

24. Diez por nueve menos cinco son _____ .

25. Quince es tres veces más que_____ .

26. Cinco dólares por cuatro son _____ dólares.

27. Un día y medio son _____ horas.

28. Una hora y media son _____ minutos.

Worksheet 4.13 Prepositions

➤ Supply the necessary prepositions in the blanks. Some common prepositions include **a, de, en, entre, para, por, sobre.**

1. Yo viajé _____ todo México el verano pasado.

2. México _____ mi es un país de mucho encanto.

3. El avión salió _____ las dos de la tarde.

4. Llegamos _____ las seis.

5. Visité el istmo _____ Tehuantepec.

6. El istmo está _____ el Pacífico y el Atlántico.

7. Es la parte más estrecha _____ México.

8. También viajé _____ la antigua ciudad de Teotihuacán.

9. Me gusta ver la luna _____ las pirámides.

10. Después de Teotihuacán viajamos _____ Oaxaca.

11. Oaxaca es la tierra _____ los zapotecas.

12. Benito Juárez nació _____ las montañas de Oaxaca.

13. Vemos estatuas de Juárez _____ todas partes.

14. La estatua _____ Morelos es la más grande de México.

15. Esta estatua está _____ la isla de Janitzio.

16. La isla es muy conocida _____ los turistas.

17. Yo ahorro mi dinero _____ hacer otro viaje a México.

18. La próxima vez voy _____ visitar Guadalajara.

19. Deseo ver _____ todo la magnífica catedral.

20. Hay un bonita parque _____ frente de la catedral.

21. Oímos las campanas _____ la tarde y a medianoche.

22. ¿Sabes _____ qué me gusta tanto?

23. Porque hay tantos lugares históricos _____ todo el país.

24. Méjico tiene algo de interés _____ todos.

25. ¡También está muy cerca _____ aquí!

General review

➤ Choose the correct form and write it in the blanks.

1. Los periódicos de hoy en español _____ (son, están) en la mesa.

2. El vocabulario del periódicos no es _____ (difícil, difíciles).

3. Me _____ (gusta, gustan) las secciones de economía y de política.

4. A ti _____ (te, tu) gusta hacer el crucigrama.

5. (Eres, Estás) _____ enojada cuando no encuentras una palabra.

6. Yo _____ (sé, sabe) la importancia de estar bien informado.

7. Gracias _____ (al, a él) periódico podemos saber muchas cosas.

8. Hay muchas noticias importantes _____ (en, sobre) la primera página.

9. No las puedo _____ (leer, leo) todas, pero sí leo la mayoría.

10. Si necesito comprar algo, _____ (yo, me) leo los anuncios.

11. Las revistas también _____ (están, son) interesantes.

12. _____ (Aquel, Aquella) revista que trajiste ayer es magnífica.

13. Me _____ (gusta, gusto) porque es toda de noticias.

14. Para oír los deportes la radio es _____ (ideal, ideales).

15. Para ver las noticias en acción la televisión _____ (es, son) buena.

16. Ayer yo _____ (veo, vi) mucha televisión.

17. _____ (Me, Yo) interesó mucho un programa sobre la salud.

18. En _____ (eso, ese) programa presentaron los peligros de fumar.

19. Hay frecuentes artículos sobre el _____ (misma, mismo) tema.

20. Un día de éstos dejamos _____ (en, de) fumar para siempre.

21. Nunca debemos de dejar _____ (en, de) aprender cosas nuevas.

22. Hoy en día podemos continuar nuestra educación sin salir _____ (de, por) casa.

23. La radio _____ (me, mi) dice lo que pasa en el mundo.

24. Las revistas _____ (me, mi) enseñan con muchas fotos.

25. La televisión _____ (te, tu) instruye, pero pone demasiados anuncios.

26. El periódico nos _____ (da, damos) los detalles.

27. Necesitamos _____ (ser, estar) bien informados.

Worksheet 4.14 Reflexive verbs

If the same person or thing is both the subject and object of a verb, the verb is said to be reflexive. It will be preceded by a reflexive pronoun:

me	*myself*	**se**	*yourself, himself, herself*	**os**	*yourselves*
te	*yourself*	**nos**	*ourselves*	**se**	*yourselves, themselves*

Lavarse, a typical reflexive verb meaning *to wash oneself,* is conjugated as follows:

lavarse			
yo	me lavo	nosotros(as)	nos lavamos
tú	te lavas	vosotros(as)	os laváis
él, ella, usted	se lava	ellos, ellas, ustedes	se lavan

Many verbs are reflexive in Spanish but not in English.

EXAMPLES: **levantarse** *to get up*   **desayunarse** *to eat breakfast*   **escaparse** *to get away*

➤ Supply the correct reflexive pronoun in the blanks.

1. Julio _____ levanta a las seis todas las mañanas.

2. Yo también _____ levanto temprano.

3. Mis padres _____ levantan antes que nosotros.

4. Todos _____ acostamos temprano también.

5. Cuando _____ pone el sol, los niños se van a la cama.

6. Nosotros _____ despertamos en la madrugada.

7. Tú _____ bañas antes que los demás.

8. Yo _____ lavo la boca después de desayunarme.

9. En mi casa, todos _____ desayunamos juntos.

10. Ellas no _____ cansan de hablar.

11. Papá _____ sienta a la cabecera de la mesa.

12. Rosa, _____ vas a enfermar si comes tantos dulces.

13. Tú tienes razón, yo _____ tengo que cuidar.

14. Rosa _____ lavó la cabeza anoche.

15. Ahora ella trata de peinar _____ de un estilo diferente.

16. Mi jefe y yo _____ preparamos para ir de viaje en avión.

17. Nosotros no _____ aburrimos en el largo vuelo.

18. ¿Por qué _____ quedaste después de las cinco?

19. ¿Cómo_____ llama su cantante favorito?

Worksheet 4.15 More on reflexive verbs

➤ Supply the present tense of the verbs in parentheses in the blanks.

1. Ellos _____ (levantarse) a las seis todas las mañanas.

2. ¿Es verdad que usted _____ (llamarse) Enrique?

3. No, usted _____ (equivocarse); me llamo Roberto.

4. Ella _____ (cansarse) cuando trabaja demasiado.

5. ¿A qué hora _____ (desayunarse) tú?

6. Yo siempre _____ (desayunarse) antes de las siete.

7. Yo siempre _____ (aburrirse) mucho en las fiestas de los Ruiz.

8. Ella _____ (quedarse) en casa todos los viernes.

9. El profesor _____ (enojarse) mucho si llegamos tarde a clase.

10. La profesora _____ (quedarse) después de su última clase.

11. Mis padres siempre _____ (levantarse) temprano.

12. Tú siempre _____ (peinarse) con mucho cuidado.

13. Juan dice que él _____ (aburrirse) en las reuniones.

14. ¿Cómo_____ (llamarse) los compañeros de Arturo?

15. Yo siempre _____ (ponerse) los lentes para leer.

16. Nosotros _____ (ponerse) a trabajar a las nueve.

17. Las muchachas hoy día _____ (pintarse) mucho la cara.

18. Yo _____ (enfermarse) si como demasiado.

19. Si Marina _____ (equivocarse) se pone nerviosa.

20. Los jefes siempre _____ (marcharse) después que nosotros.

21. El nuevo contador _____ (llamarse) Roberto Esparza.

22. Yo _____ (bañarse) casi siempre con agua fría.

23. Tú siempre _____ (ponerse) nervioso antes de volar en avión.

24. Los domingos no tenemos que _____ (levantarse) temprano.

25. ¿ _____ (preocuparse) tú mucho por la contaminación del

    ambiente?

Worksheet 4.16 More on reflexive verbs

Definite articles are used with parts of the body and articles of clothing in reflexive constructions.
Compare Spanish and English.

EXAMPLES:	ENGLISH	SPANISH	LITERAL TRANSLATION
	I wash my hands.	**Me lavo las manos.**	*I wash myself the hands.*
	You put on your coat.	**Te pones el abrigo.**	*You put yourself the coat.*

➤ Supply the definite article in the blanks.

1. Tú te pones _____ guantes (m).

2. Yo me pongo _____ bufanda.

3. Ella se quita _____ abrigo.

4. Él se quita _____ chaqueta.

5. Ellos se lavan _____ manos (f).

6. Nosotros nos lavamos _____ cara.

7. Elena se pintó _____ labios.

8. Juana se quitó _____ maquillaje (m).

9. La criada se pone _____ delantal (m).

10. Los pilotos se ponen _____ uniformes (m).

11. ¿Cuándo se cepilla usted _____ dientes (m)?

12. ¿Cuándo se lava usted _____ cara?

13. La niña se ensució _____ vestido.

14. El niño se lastimó _____ rodillas.

15. Mi papá se lastimó _____ pie.

16. Yo me corté _____ dedo con el cuchillo.

17. ¿Te secas tú _____ pelo con secador eléctrico?

18. ¿Cómo te mordiste _____ lengua?

19. ¿Por qué se pone el chofer _____ lentes oscuros?

20. ¿Por qué se quita el charro _____ sombrero?

21. ¿Cómo te rompiste _____ impermeable (m)?

22. ¿Cuándo se va a cortar ella _____ uñas?

23. Me cepillé _____ traje antes de salir.

24. Abuelito se pone _____ dentadura postiza al levantarse.

Worksheet 4.17 Reflexive verbs—infinitive form

When a reflexive verb is assisted by one or more preceding verbs, the pronoun may precede the first verb or may be attached to the infinitive. Note also that the reflexive pronoun must have the same person and number as the subject:

EXAMPLES: REFLEXIVE CONSTRUCTIONS

Yo quiero lavar**me** el pelo.
Tú vas a quitar**te** el abrigo.
Ella piensa pintar**se** los labios.
Nosotros debemos peinar**nos** bien.
Ustedes quieren cansar**se** más.

ALTERNATE CONSTRUCTION

Yo **me** quiero lavar el pelo.
Tú **te** vas a quitar el abrigo.
Ella **se** piensa pintar los labios.
Nosotros **nos** debemos peinar bien.
Ustedes **se** quieren casar.

➤ Copy the infinitives into the blanks, then attach the correct reflexive pronouns.

1. Yo quiero _____ (levantar) temprano mañana.

2. Nosotros vamos a _____ (acostar) a las diez.

3. Ellos deben _____ (retirar) también.

4. Tú no puedes _____ (despertar) tarde.

5. Todavía puedo _____ (peinar).

6. Todos podemos _____ (equivocar) a veces.

7. Yo necesito _____ (poner) una chaqueta.

8. Él debe _____ (bañar) por la mañana.

9. No quiero _____ (lastimar) en el trabajo.

10. Ella tiene ganas de _____ (desayunar).

11. Ella trata de _____ (secar) el pelo al sol.

12. Nosotros empezamos a _____ (poner) la ropa.

13. Gloria sabe _____ (arreglar) la vida.

14. Carlos, no debes_____ (quitar) los zapatos en el cine.

15. El coronel piensa _____ (quedar) en el ejército.

16. Yo quiero _____ (ganar) la vida como policía.

17. Los jóvenes quieren _____ (pasear) por los jardines.

18. Ustedes no deben _____ (preocupar) por eso.

19. Yo empecé a _____ (enojar) con uno de ellos.

20. Debemos _____ (bajar) del autobús en la esquina.

Worksheet 4.18 Alternate reflexive construction

➤ Rewrite the sentences on p. 77, using the alternate reflexive construction.

1. _____
2. _____
3. _____
4. _____
5. _____
6. _____
7. _____
8. _____
9. _____
10. _____
11. _____
12. _____
13. _____
14. _____
15. _____
16. _____
17. _____
18. _____
19. _____
20. _____

Reflexive verbs

➤ Change the following sentences from **yo** to **él.** In the blanks to the right, write **Él** plus the corresponding form of the italicized verb.

1. Yo *me llamo* Roberto. _____

2. Yo *me lavo* las manos muchas veces al día. _____

3. Yo *me baño* todos los días. _____

4. Yo *me levanto* temprano excepto los sábados. _____

5. Yo no *me canso* fácilmente. _____

6. Yo *me pongo* la chaqueta cuando hace frío. _____

7. Yo *me cepillo* los dientes tres veces al día. _____

8. Yo *me peino* con mucho cuidado. _____

9. Yo *me desayuno* antes que mi padre. _____

10. Yo *me enojo* cuando los niños se pelean. _____

11. Yo *me pongo* ropa de lana en el invierno. _____

12. Yo *me canso* de vez en cuando. _____

13. Yo *me enfermo* raras veces. _____

14. Yo *me seco* la cara con la toalla. _____

15. Yo *me arreglo* las uñas cada semana. _____

16. Yo *me limpio* los zapatos cuando se ensucian. _____

17. Yo no *me apuro* demasiado. _____

18. Yo *me asusto* cuando la gente maneja muy rápido. _____

19. Yo *me pongo* nervioso en los exámenes. _____

20. Yo *me afeito* con una máquina eléctrica. _____

21. Yo *me caso* después de graduarme de la universidad. _____

22. Yo no *me preocupo* sin necesidad. _____

23. Yo nunca *me aburro* en el trabajo. _____

24. Yo *me quedo* en casa cuando estoy resfriado. _____

25. A propósito, *me llamo* Cisneros. _____

Note: Repeat orally each of the above sentences, substituting the other subject pronouns **tú, usted,**
ella, nosotros, ustedes, ellos, ellas.

More on reflexive verbs

➤ Change the following reflexive verbs from present tense to preterite tense.

1. Yo me canso. _____

2. Ella se casa. _____

3. Tú te enojas. _____

4. Ella se baña. _____

5. Yo me preocupo. _____

6. Yo me asusto. _____

7. Ella se arregla. _____

8. Yo me arreglo. _____

9. Tú te cansas. _____

10. Él se quita las botas. _____

    _____

11. Yo me desayuno. _____

12. Usted se asusta. _____

13. Tú te aburres. _____

14. Nosotros nos aburrimos. _____

    _____

15. Yo me apuro. _____

16. Usted se apura. _____

17. Ella se preocupa. _____

18. Yo me enfermo. _____

19. Ellas se bañan. _____

20. Juan se queda. _____

21. Tú te retiras. _____

22. Nosotros nos levantamos. _____

    _____

23. Yo me quedo. _____

24. Usted se peina. _____

25. Tú te afeitas. _____

26. Yo me afeito. _____

27. Ella se cuida. _____

28. Él se retira. _____

29. Él se apura. _____

30. Yo me aburro. _____

31. Él se enoja. _____

32. Isabel se asusta. _____

33. Pedro se casa. _____

34. Yo me peino. _____

35. Ella se mira. _____

36. Ellos se levantan. _____

    _____

37. Él se desayuna. _____

38. Elena se quita el reloj. _____

    _____

39. Ellas se pintan. _____

40. Yo me baño. _____

41. Él se asusta. _____

42. Usted se aburre. _____

43. Ustedes se levantan. _____

    _____

44. Tú te enfermas. _____

 **Buscapalabras**

Buscapalabras geográfico

➤ The following word search puzzle contains the names of thirteen South American and Central American countries. As you find them, place their names in the blank spaces:

V	A	R	G	E	N	T	I	N	A	P	
E	C	U	A	D	O	R	R	I	C	A	N
N	B	O	L	I	V	I	A	C	O	N	
E	P	G	U	A	T	E	M	A	L	A	
Z	E	C	H	I	L	E	A	R	P	M	
U	R	U	G	U	A	Y	S	A	A	U	
E	U	R	O	P	A	R	U	G	N	E	
L	L	I	P	A	R	A	G	U	A	Y	
A	C	O	L	O	M	B	I	A	M	E	
D	A	S	H	O	N	D	U	R	A	S	

1. _____   8. _____

2. _____   9. _____

3. _____   10. _____

4. _____   11. _____

5. _____   12. _____

6. _____   13. _____

7. _____

Part 5

Contents

Worksheet 5.1 Use of infinitives

The only verb form that can follow a preposition is the infinitive. Some verbs require a particular preposition before the infinitive:

EXAMPLES:

acabar de esquiar	*to have just skied*
aprender a esquiar	*to learn to ski*
dejar de esquiar	*to stop skiing*
empezar a esquiar	*to begin to ski, to start skiing*
enseñar a esquiar	*to teach to ski*
estar por esquiar	*to be about to ski*
ir a esquiar	*to be going to ski*
pensar en esquiar	*to think about skiing*
quedar en esquiar	*to agree to ski*
soñar con esquiar	*to dream about skiing*
tratar de esquiar	*to try to ski*

➤ Supply the correct form of the verb in parentheses. Include the correct preposition if required.

1. Yo aprendí _____(usar) las computadoras.

2. Yo trato_____(educar) bien a mis hijos.

3. Yo quiero _____(ayudar) a mi amigo.

4. Yo trato_____(conocer) a todos mis compañeros.

5. Yo voy_____(tomar) el examen para manejar.

6. Hoy dejo_____(fumar).

7. Yo sé _____(explicar) la regla.

8. Yo empiezo _____(escribir) la regla en la pizarra.

9. Yo empiezo _____(entender) la radio en español.

10. Yo sé _____(pronunciar) bastante bien las palabras.

11. Yo sueño_____(esquiar) este invierno.

12. Yo necesito_____(tener) mucha paciencia.

13. Yo acabo_____(hacer) varias preguntas.

14. Yo trato_____(escuchar) todo lo que él dice.

15. Me encanta _____(aprender) español.

Worksheet 5.2 Preterite tense of *ser* and *ir*

Ser and **ir** share the same forms in the preterite tense.

EXAMPLE: **Yo fui**   *I was* or *I went*

Both verbs are conjugated as follows:

		ir		
yo	fui	nosotros(as)	fuimos
tú	fuiste	vosotros(as)	fuisteis
él, ella, usted	fue	ellos, ellas, ustedes	fueron

➤ Supply the correct preterite form of the verb in parentheses.

1. Él _____ (ser) la persona que nos acompañó.

2. Él _____ (ir) al cine con nosotros.

3. Yo no _____ (ser) la persona con quien hablaron ayer.

4. Yo no _____ (ir) a trabajar ayer.

5. ¿Cuándo _____ (ser) tú presidente del club?

6. ¿ _____ (Ir) tú a la reunión anoche?

7. Ellos _____ (ser) los culpables del accidente.

8. Ellos _____ (ir) a su casa.

9. ¿Por qué _____ (ser) importante la batalla de Lepanto?

10. Cervantes _____ (ir) a pelear en esa batalla.

11. Yo _____ (ir) al baile con Cristina.

12. Yo _____ (ser) su compañero y nadie más bailó con ella.

13. _____ (Ser) en enero cuando te enfermaste.

14. Tú _____ (ir) al hospital el 15 de enero.

15. ¿ _____ (ir) ustedes a ver la producción de Carmen?

16. En la obra, nosotros _____ (ser) toreros.

17. Anteayer tú _____ (ser) muy amable conmigo.

18. Ayer yo _____ (ir) a ayudarte.

19. Tú _____ (ser) capaz de entrar sin pagar.

20. ¿Por qué _____ (ir) tú al circo sin dinero?

21. Roberto _____ (ser) Papá Noel en la fiesta.

22. Los niños _____ (ir) a recibir juguetes.

23. Ella _____ (ser) la muchacha que ganó ayer.

24. Nosotros _____ (ir) a su casa para felicitarla.

Worksheet 5.3 Preterite tense of *dar* and *ver*

Ver is a regular verb. Although **dar** is an **-ar** verb, it usually takes **le, les** and sometimes it takes the same endings as **ver.** (Accent marks are very seldom required of one-syllable verbs.)

dar			
yo	di	nosotros(as)	dimos
tú	diste	vosotros(as)	disteis
él, ella, usted	dio	ellos, ellas, ustedes	dieron

ver			
yo	vi	nosotros(as)	vimos
tú	viste	vosotros(as)	visteis
él, ella, usted	vio	ellos, ellas, ustedes	vieron

➤ Supply the preterite tense of the verb in parentheses.

1. Tú _____ (ver) mucha nobleza y generosidad.

2. Tú le _____ (dar) un cheque a la Cruz Roja.

3. Yo _____ (ver) la infracción que cometiste.

4. Yo le _____ (dar) la pelota al otro equipo.

5. Ayer ella _____ (ver) un gato hambriento.

6. Ella le _____ (dar) de comer.

7. Nosotros _____ (ver) los juegos olímpicos por televisíon.

8. Ellos le _____ (dar) una medalla.

9. Yo _____ (ver) a varios amigos allí.

10. No sabes cuánta risa me _____ (dar).

11. Nosotros _____ (ver) el robo de un coche.

12. Nosotros le _____ (dar) la información a la policía.

13. Yo _____ (ver) a una amiga en la playa.

14. Yo le _____ (dar) limonada de mi termo.

15. El maestro _____ (ver) los errores en mi trabajo.

16. Él me _____ (dar) otra página de ejercicios.

17. Yo _____ (ver) el anuncio en el periódico.

18. Ella me _____ (dar) algunas galletas.

19. Tú _____ (ver) el peligro a tiempo.

20. Tú me _____ (dar) un grito de aviso.

21. Nosotros no _____ (ver) el coche.

22. El claxon nos _____ (dar) mucho susto.

23. Yo _____ (ver) a muchas amigas en tu casa ayer.

24. Sí, ellas me _____ (dar) una despedida de soltera.

Worksheet 5.4 Preterite tense of *leer* and *caer*

When the addition of a verb ending results in an **i** between vowels, change the **i** to **y**.

leer			
yo	leí	nosotros(as)	leímos
tú	leíste	vosotros(as)	leísteis
él, ella, usted	leyó	ellos, ellas, ustedes	leyeron

caer			
yo	caí	nosotros(as)	caímos
tú	caíste	vosotros(as)	caísteis
él, ella, usted	cayó	ellos, ellas, ustedes	cayeron

Note: **Caer** is often used with reflexive pronouns (**caerse**).

➤ In the blanks, supply the preterite tense of **leer.**

1. Yo _____ la noticia del accidente en el periódico.

2. María _____ la carta de su hermano con mucho interés.

3. ¿ _____ usted la carta que ella recibió la semana pasada?

4. La profesora _____ en voz alta el poema que yo escribí.

5. Tomás _____ muchos libros durante sus vacaciones.

6. Tú _____ esas dos novelas muy rápido.

7. Todo el mundo _____ la noticia del asesinato.

8. ¿ _____ ustedes el discurso del senador en el periódico?

9. Sí, Enrique y yo lo _____ juntos anoche.

10. Antonio y su hermano _____ los libros que les regalé.

11. Tú _____ en silencio las noticias internacionales.

12. Todo el mundo _____ las noticias del terremoto.

➤ In the blanks, supply the preterite tense of **caer.**

1. La madre de Alberto se _____ en la calle ayer.

2. Tú te _____ una vez en el mismo lugar.

3. Mi compañero se resbaló y se _____ en la nieve.

4. La noticia _____ sobre el país como una bomba.

5. La anciana se _____ en el portal de la casa.

6. La niña se _____ en la piscina y se lastimó.

7. Los dos niños se _____ de la cama durante la noche.

8. Las hojas de los árboles se _____ temprano este año.

9. Tú fácilmente _____ en la trampa.

10. Todos mis libros _____ al suelo durante el terremoto.

11. El avión _____ en el lago.

12. La lluvia _____ a cántaros.

Worksheet 5.5 Preterite tense of *oír* and *traer*

Oír has the same vowel change to **y** as **leer** and **creer**. **Traer** is irregular:

oír			
yo	oí	nosotros(as)	oímos
tú	oíste	vosotros(as)	oísteis
él, ella, usted	oyó	ellos, ellas, ustedes	oyeron

traer			
yo	traje	nosotros(as)	trajimos
tú	trajiste	vosotros(as)	trajisteis
él, ella, usted	trajo	ellos, ellas, ustedes	trajeron

➤ In the blanks, supply the preterite tense of **oír.**

1. Yo no _____ el discurso del presidente ayer.

2. Por lo visto, ellos no _____ a Nicolás tocar a la puerta.

3. Tú no _____ el despertador esta mañana.

4. Yo _____ los gritos del niño.

5. Ella _____ las disculpas de José pacientemente.

6. El profesor te _____ sin mucho interés.

7. Nosotros _____ los mismos cuentos varias veces.

8. María dio un salto cuando _____ su nombre.

9. Ellos no nos _____ entrar.

10. Anoche yo _____ las noticias de las once.

11. Anoche nosotras _____ el mismo programa por radio.

12. ¿Por qué no _____ tú mis razones?

➤ In the blanks, supply the preterite tense of **traer.**

1. Mis padres me _____ muchas cosas de México.

2. ¿Qué _____ usted de Nueva York para sus hermanas?

3. Hoy no _____ mi computadora.

4. Raquel _____ a dos amigos a la fiesta anoche.

5. El cartero no te _____ hoy ni una sola carta.

6. Su abuelo le _____ un tren eléctrico de Nueva York.

7. Cecilia _____ los últimos modelos de vestidos de París.

8. Tú me _____ una blusa preciosa.

9. Juan y Pedro _____ muchos recuerdos de la India.

10. Yo _____ varios regalos para mis hijas.

11. ¿ _____ tú muchas cosas bonitas del Canadá?

12. Él no _____ su tarea hoy y el profesor se enojó.

Irregular preterite verbs

➤ In the blanks, supply the correct preterite form of the verb in parentheses.

1. Ella _____ (caerse) en la escalera.

2. La pobre _____ (ir) al hospital en la ambulancia.

3. En la tormenta _____ (caerse) muchas ramas del olmo.

4. Los truenos y relámpagos _____ (ser) horribles.

5. Nosotros _____ (ver) tu fotografía en el periódico.

6. Yo _____ (leer) el artículo sobre la boda de ustedes.

7. Tus amigos les _____ (traer) regalos muy bonitos.

8. Yo _____ (oír) mi canción favorita por la radio.

9. Esta vez el cantante _____ (ser) Enrique Iglesias.

10. Tú y yo lo _____ (ver) hace tres años en Miami.

11. El año pasado mi esposa y yo _____ (ir) a Arizona de vacaciones.

12. Mi tía nos _____ (dar) comidas muy sabrosas en el rancho.

13. Nosotros _____ (traer) naranjas y toronjas en el coche.

14. Yo no _____ (caerse) del caballo ni una sola vez.

15. La verdad es que él _____ (caerse) dos veces.

16. ¿A dónde _____ (ir) tú la semana pasada?

17. Yo no te _____ (ver) por ninguna parte.

18. No puedo nadar. Yo no _____ (traer) mi traje de baño.

19. Mi padre _____ (caerse) en la fábrica donde trabaja.

20. El accidente no _____ (ser) serio.

21. Yo _____ (creer) en tu explicación del arte moderno.

22. Los libros me _____ (dar) otras teorías.

23. En la biblioteca ustedes _____ (leer) teorías muy distintas.

24. Tú me _____ (traer) un ejemplar de *Lazarillo de Tormes*.

25. Yo _____ (creer) que Cervantes escribió esa obra.

26. Ahora sé que el autor _____ (ser) anónimo.

More on irregular preterite verbs

➤ Change the following subjects and verbs to the preterite tense.

1. Yo traigo _____
2. Él lee _____
3. Tú ves _____
4. Yo creo _____
5. Ellos traen _____
6. Él da_____
7. Ellas van _____
8. Ella es _____
9. Nosotros somos _____
10. Tú traes _____
11. Yo voy _____
12. Él oye_____
13. Yo me caigo _____
14. Tú lees _____
15. Él cree _____
16. Usted trae _____
17. Yo soy _____
18. Usted va _____
19. Ellos dan _____
20. Nosotros vemos _____
21. Ellos oyen _____
22. Tú te caes _____

23. Nosotros leemos _____
24. Ellos creen_____
25. Ella trae _____
26. Ustedes son_____
27. Tú vas _____
28. Ustedes dan _____
29. Juan ve _____
30. Tú oyes _____
31. José se cae _____
32. El niño lee _____
33. Usted cree_____
34. Nosotros traemos _____
35. Tú eres_____
36. María va_____
37. Los niños dan _____
38. Todo el mundo va_____
39. Nadie oye _____
40. Todos se caen _____
41. ¿Quién lee? _____
42. Nadie cree_____
43. Todos van _____
44 . Nadie va _____

Vocabulary check-up—number and gender

➤ Supply the other three forms of each noun.

MASCULINE SINGULAR	MASCULINE PLURAL	FEMININE SINGULAR	FEMININE PLURAL
1. hermano			
2. chico			
3. niño			
4. primo			
5. cuñado			
6. hijo			
7. profesor			
8. alumno			
9. dueño			
10. artista			
11. director			
12. novio			
13. cubano			
14. alemán			
15. español			
16. maestro			
17. muchacho			
18. abuelo			
19. turista			
20. actor			
21. tío			
22. inglés			
23. venezolano			
24. estudiante			
25. víctima			

General review

➤ Choose the correct form and write it in the blank.

1. Me _____ (gusta, gustan) las cuatro estaciones del año.

2. Las flores de la primavera _____ (es, son) muy bonitas.

3. La rosa es mi flor _____ (favorita, favoritas).

4. Ayer yo _____ (fui, fue) de paseo al jardín botánico.

5. Esta noche _____ (voy a, voy al) concierto en el parque.

6. Ella quiere patinar, pero yo no _____ (sé, sabe) patinar.

7. _____ (Nadie, A nadie) le gusta el mal tiempo.

8. En el verano pasado yo pasé _____ (varios, varias) días en el lago.

9. Los deportes acuáticos son _____ (mi, mis) favoritos.

10. Nosotros pescamos _____ (mucho, muchos) en el río.

11. Ahora _____ (estamos, somos) en el otoño.

12. En octubre las hojas de los árboles empezaron a _____ (caer, caerse).

13. Ésta es también la temporada _____ (del, de el) fútbol.

14. El equipo de mi universidad siempre trata _____ (de, a) ganar.

15. Los estudiantes _____ (regresas, regresan) a la universidad.

16. A ellas _____ (le, les) gusta mucho el otoño.

17. Para _____ (me, mí) es bonito también el invierno.

18. Mi familia va _____ (con mí, conmigo) a las montañas.

19. Allí_____ (podemos, podemos a) esquiar.

20. _____ (Este, Aquel) hombre allá lejos esquía bien.

21. ¿A ti qué te_____ (gustas, gusta) hacer en el invierno?

22. ¿Cuál estación _____ (es, eres) tu favorita?

23. ¿Te gusta más _____ (ir, ir a) la playa o a las montañas?

24. ¿Piensas mucho _____ (en, de) las vacaciones de verano?

Worksheet 5.6 Order of object pronouns

Indirect object pronouns always precede direct object pronouns.

EXAMPLES: Juan me dio **el libro.**   Juan **me lo** dio.
Ella nos regaló **las revistas.**   Ella **nos las** regaló.

➤ Rewrite each of the following sentences, replacing the italicized nouns with the correct form
of the direct object pronoun.

1. Él me mandó *los libros.* _____

2. Ella me mandó *las revistas.* _____

3. Él nos explicó *la lección.* _____

4. Ellas te explicaron *el cuento.* _____

5. Tú me prometiste *el dinero.* _____

6. Nosotros te prometimos *los fondos.* _____

7. El cartero me trajo *la carta* esta mañana. _____

8. La camarera nos trajo *las ensaladas.* _____

9. El señor López me dio *las flores.* _____

10. Los señores Ibarra nos dieron *los dulces.* _____

11. Tú me enseñas *la gramática francesa.* _____

12. Yo te enseño *el vocabulario español.* _____

13. Ellos me entregaron *los planos.* _____

14. Ella nos entregó *el cheque de viajeros.* _____

15. Mis padres me compraron *la bicicleta.* _____

16. Tu mamá te compró *el vestido nuevo* para la fiesta. _____

17. El panadero me vendió *los pasteles.* _____

18. La anciana nos vendió *las tortillas.* _____

19. Benito siempre me lleva *la ropa* a la tintorería. _____

20. Yo siempre te saco *la basura* a la calle. _____

21. Ellos nos llevaron *las maletas* al aeropuerto. _____

22. Susana me envió *la fotografía de su familia.* _____

23. ¿Quién me dejó *esta nota?* _____

24. Te dejé *el mensaje* junto al teléfono. _____

25. El maestro nos escribió *la fecha* en la pizarra. _____

26. Tus abuelos te escribieron *las cartas* desde Madrid. _____

Worksheet 5.7   Indirect object pronoun *se*

Both direct and indirect object pronouns begin with (*l*) in the third person. To avoid repetition of this sound, Spanish changes the indirect object pronoun (**le, les**) to **se**. The possible combinations are: **se lo, se la, se los, se las.** To clarify the indirect object pronoun **se**, the redundant pronouns [see page 68] are often used.

EXAMPLES: Juan **le dio el regalo a Carlos.**   Juan **se lo** dio **a él.**
Pablo **les dio los regalos a las chicas.**   Pablo **se los** dio **a ellas.**

➤ In the blanks, supply the verb and its indirect and direct object pronouns. The indirect object pronoun must correspond to the words in parentheses and will precede the direct object pronoun.

1. Juan las mandó (a mí). _____

2. José las mandó (a ella). _____

3. Su amigo lo trajo de Uruguay (a ella). _____

4. Tú las trajiste esta mañana (a ellos). _____

5. El profesor los explicó bien (a mí). _____

6. Ella lo dio (a Miguel). _____

7. María las prestó (a mí). _____

8. Margarita las prestó (a ellos). _____

9. Yo lo mandé la semana pasada (a ellas). _____

10. El profesor los lee en español (a nosotros). _____

11. Yo siempre lo presto (a usted). _____

12. Ellos la explicaron muy claramente (a él). _____

13. Tú la explicaste muy claramente (a mí). _____

14. Esteban la explicó muy claramente (a ella). _____

15. Yo las mandé ayer (a usted). _____

16. Yo lo di el mes pasado (a ustedes). _____

17. Él la trajo ayer (a ella). _____

18. Nosotras los prestamos el año pasado (a ellos). _____

19. El lo contó todo ayer (a mí). _____

20. Tú lo llevaste el mes pasado (a él). _____

21. Nadie lo regaló (a mí). Yo lo compré. _____

22. ¿Quién lo mandó (a usted)? _____

Worksheet 5.8 Personal pronouns with infinitives

When two verbs are used together, you will recall that the second one must be an infinitive. Object pronouns may be placed in front of the first verb (**lo quiere vender**) but are more commonly attached to the infinitive (**quiere venderlo**).

➤ In the blanks, supply the correct object pronoun, adding it to the infinitive in place of the words in italics.

1. Mi padre quiere mirar *los televisores.* _____

2. Yo quiero ver *el refrigerador.* _____

3. Él va a escoger *la alfombra.* _____

4. Tú vas a pedir *las sillas.* _____

5. Nosotros pensamos vender *el piano.* _____

6. Ustedes piensan comprar *las lámparas.* _____

7. Yo sé seleccionar *las cortinas.* _____

8. Tú sabes colgar *los retratos.* _____

9. Yo necesito probar *el sofá.* _____

10. Ella necesita comprar *la estufa.* _____

11. Ellos desean examinar *la mesa.* _____

12. Usted desea ver *el sofá-cama.* _____

13. Yo tengo que reemplazar *el cristal.* _____

14. Tú tienes que lavar *el mantel sucio.* _____

15. Nosotros debemos cambiar *el cartucho de la impresadora.* _____

16. Ellas planean modernizar *la cocina.* _____

17. Nosotros tratamos de agrandar *el garaje.* _____

18. Mi primo trata de construir *la casa ideal.* _____

19. Ella espera encontrar *antigüedades.* _____

20. Yo espero reparar *la radio estereofónica.* _____

21. Tú debes pintar todas *las paredes.* _____

22. Ustedes deben mezclar *las pinturas.* _____

23. Él tiene miedo de romper *los platos.* _____

24. Nosotros tenemos miedo de perder *las llaves.* _____

Worksheet 5.9 More on personal pronouns with infinitives

Both the indirect and direct object pronouns may be attached to an infinitive to form a single word. Remember that the indirect object must precede the direct object and that the vowel in the infinitive ending will have a written accent mark.

EXAMPLES: Juan quiere **darme el libro**.   Juan quiere **dármelo**.
            Yo trato de **venderte las sillas**.   Yo trato de **vendértelas**.

Note: **Se** replaces **le, les** when two personal pronouns are used: **Yo quiero dárselo a ellos.**

➤ In the blanks, rewrite the verb, adding the correct indirect object pronoun to the infinitive, in place of the words in parentheses.

1. Él no desea *mandarlo (a mí)*. _____

2. Andrés no quiere *darlo (a ella)*. _____

3. Tú no vas a *llevarlos (a ellos)*. _____

4. Enrique puede *traerlo (a mí)*. _____

5. Después de *darlo (a él)*, usted puede volver a su casa. _____

6. Papá dice que está cansado de *explicarlo (a nosotros)*. _____

7. ¿Puede usted *hacerlo (a mí)* ahora mismo? _____

8. ¿Por qué no quiere usted *darlo (a ella)*? _____

9. Tú vas a *leerla (a nosotros)* esta noche. _____

10. Voy a tratar de *hacerlo (a usted)* pronto. _____

11. ¿Cuándo van a *mandarlo (a ustedes)*? _____

12. Yo no puedo *traerlo (a usted)* mañana. _____

13. Tú tienes que *enviarlo (a ella)* hoy. _____

14. Él no puede *traerlo (a ustedes)* antes del mediodía. _____

15. Yo estoy cansado de *decirlo (a él)*. _____

16. Nosotros no podemos *prestarlo (a ellos)*. _____

17. Él no está interesado en *prestarlo (a ellos)*. _____

18. ¿Por qué no quiere usted *darlo (a ella)*? _____

19. Tengo que *comprarlo* hoy *(para él)*. _____

20. ¿Por qué no quiere *contarlo* usted *(a mí)*? _____

21. ¿Por qué no quieres tú *decirlo (a ellos)*? _____

22. ¿Cuándo va usted a *darlo (a mí)*? _____

23. A mí no me gusta *venderlo (a ellos)*. _____

24. Ellos no quieren *prestarlo (a nosotros)*. _____

Worksheet 5.10 Preterite tense of *hacer* and *decir*

The verbs **hacer** and **decir** are both irregular in the preterite tense. The stem vowel of both verbs changes to **i.**

hacer			
yo	hice	nosotros(as)	hicimos
tú	hiciste	vosotros(as)	hicisteis
él, ella, usted	hizo	ellos, ellas, ustedes	hicieron

decir			
yo	dije	nosotros(as)	dijimos
tú	dijiste	vosotros(as)	dijisteis
él, ella, usted	dijo	ellos, ellas, ustedes	dijeron

➤ In the blanks, supply the preterite tense of the verb in parentheses.

1. Ayer yo _____ (hacer) la ensalada para la cena.

2. Mamá _____ (decir) que a ella le gusta.

3. Ellos _____ (hacer) demasiado ruido con sus guitarras eléctricas.

4. La vecina le _____ (decir) algo a la policía.

5. Tú _____ (hacer) planes detallados para viajar por Europa.

6. Nosotros _____ (decir) que tú planeaste todo muy bien.

7. María _____ (hacer) el vestido para la fiesta ella misma.

8. Sus amigas _____ (decir) que lo hizo muy bonito.

9. ¿Quiénes _____ (hacer) estas sabrosas galletas?

10. Nosotros les _____ (decir) que las hicimos nosotros.

11. Yo _____ (hacer) todo lo posible para hablar con ellos.

12. Ellos no _____ (decir) casi nada.

13. El niño no le _____ (hacer) caso a la criada.

14. La criada _____ (decir) que el niño se portó mal.

15. Ayer _____ (hacer) mucho calor.

16. Tú _____ (decir) que yo me quejé demasiado del calor.

17. El domingo yo no _____ (hacer) absolutamente nada.

18. Yo les _____ (decir) que descansé todo el día.

19. Tú _____ (hacer) bien en llamarlos enseguida por teléfono.

20. Ellos _____ (decir) que llamaste a tiempo.

21. Él _____ (hacer) sacrificios para educar a sus hijos.

22. El hijo mayor _____ (decir) que su padre se sacrificó mucho.

23. ¿Qué _____ (hacer) con tus ahorros?

24. Yo le _____ (decir) lo que gastamos en el viaje al Japón.

Worksheet 5.11 Preterite tense of *querer* and *venir*

Like **hacer** and **decir,** the verbs **querer** and **venir** also change the stem vowel to **i** in the preterite:

querer			
yo	quise	nosotros(as)	quisimos
tú	quisiste	vosotros(as)	quisisteis
él, ella, usted	quiso	ellos, ellas, ustedes	quisieron

venir			
yo	vine	nosotros(as)	vinimos
tú	viniste	vosotros(as)	vinisteis
él, ella, usted	vino	ellos, ellas, ustedes	vinieron

➤ In the blanks, supply the preterite tense of the verb in parentheses.

1. Alfredo no _____ (venir) a tiempo anoche.

2. Él dijo que _____ (querer) llegar tarde.

3. Los otros _____ (venir) en el mismo autobús.

4. Yo _____ (querer) viajar en mi propio coche.

5. Anoche tú _____ (venir) tú a la fiesta con varios amigos.

6. Mi hermana _____ (querer) conocer a cada uno.

7. ¿Por qué no _____ (venir) a la clase ayer?

8. Yo _____ (querer) ver el campeonato de tenis en televisión.

9. Ellos _____ (venir) temprano para ver mejor el desfile.

10. Nosotros también _____ (querer) venir temprano.

11. Mi tía _____ (venir) a casa para mostrar su camioneta nueva.

12. Nosotros_____ (querer) comprarnos una semejante.

13. El perro_____ (venir) cuando lo llamé.

14. Yo _____ (querer) darle de comer.

15. Nosotros no _____ (venir) hasta las once y media.

16. Mis papás_____ (querer) ir de compras antes de volver.

17. Los niños _____ (venir) al parque con sus padres.

18. Anita_____ (querer) jugar con sus amigas.

19. ¿Tú _____ (venir) en el tren desde Nueva York?

20. Sí, yo no _____ (querer) volar como hice el año pasado.

21. Yo _____ (venir) a casa anoche muy tarde.

22. ¿Por qué no _____ (querer) tú esperarme allí?

Worksheet 5.12 Preterite tense of *poner* and *saber*

Poner and **saber** change their stem vowels to **u** in the preterite tense.

poner			
yo	puse	nosotros(as)	pusimos
tú	pusiste	vosotros(as)	pusisteis
él, ella, usted	puso	ellos, ellas, ustedes	pusieron

saber			
yo	supe	nosotros(as)	supimos
tú	supiste	vosotros(as)	supisteis
él, ella, usted	supo	ellos, ellas, ustedes	supieron

Saber means *to know* (*how*), but in the preterite it can mean *to find out*.

➤ In the blanks at the right, supply the preterite tense of the verb in parentheses.

1. Él _____ (poner) las flores en la mesa.

2. Yo no _____ (saber) agradecérselas.

3. El niño _____ (ponerse) la camisa al revés.

4. Carlitos no _____ (saber) ponérsela correctamente.

5. ¿Dónde _____ (poner) tú las llaves del coche?

6. ¿No _____ (saber) tú dónde las dejaste?

7. José _____ (ponerse) de mal humor porque no lo invitaste.

8. Nosotros no _____ (saber) su dirección.

9. La criada _____ (poner) la ropa afuera a secar.

10. Ella no _____ (saber) hasta después que tenemos una secadora eléctrica.

11. Mi hija _____ (ponerse) zapatos blancos para salir.

12. Afortunadamente, yo _____ (saber) limpiárselos ayer.

13. ¿Por qué _____ (poner) usted tantos sellos en esa carta?

14. Yo no le _____ (poner) el franqueo correcto.

15. El año pasado tú no _____ (poner) ni un centavo en el banco.

16. ¿Cómo _____ (saber) tú eso?

17. Los niños se _____ (poner) los cinturones de seguridad.

18. Gracias a su papá, ellos _____ (saber) hacerlo.

19. El médico _____ (poner) a su paciente en el hospital.

20. ¡Qué lástima! Nosotros no _____ (saber) nada del accidente.

21. El niño _____ (ponerse) el dedo pulgar en la boca.

22. Su mamá no _____ (saber) cómo curarle de ese hábito.

Worksheet 5.13 Preterite tense of *tener* and *poder*

Tener and **poder** also change their stem vowels to **u.**

tener			
yo	tuve	nosotros(as)	tuvimos
tu	tuviste	vosotros(as)	tuvisteis
él, ella, usted	tuvo	ellos, ellas, ustedes	tuvieron

poder			
yo	pude	nosotros(as)	pudimos
tú	pudiste	vosotros(as)	pudisteis
él, ella, usted	pudo	ellos, ellas, ustedes	pudieron

➤ In the blanks, supply the preterite tense of the verb in parentheses.

1. Yo _____ (tener) que dejar mucha comida en mi plato.

2. Yo sólo _____ (poder) comer un poco.

3. Mi tío _____ (tener) que vender su automóvil.

4. Afortunadamente, mi hermano _____ (poder) comprárselo.

5. Ellos _____ (tener) la intención de visitarlos anoche.

6. Desgraciadamente, ellos no _____ (poder) hacerlo.

7. Tú _____ (tener) que comprar llantas nuevas.

8. Tú _____ (poder) pagarlas con tu tarjeta de crédito.

9. Mi sobrina _____ (tener) un accidente serio.

10. Por dos días ella no _____ (poder) andar sin muletas.

11. Nosotros no _____ (tener) tiempo para terminar el trabajo.

12. Tomás y yo no _____ (poder) encontrar la casa.

13. Yo no sé por qué tú _____ (tener) que gritar a tu abuela.

14. Pues ella dice que no _____ (poder) oírme.

15. El chofer _____ (tener) que comprar gasolina.

16. Él _____ (poder) comprarla en la próxima esquina.

17. Nosotros _____ (tener) mucha suerte en la selva.

18. Nosotros _____ (poder) fotografiar muchos animales salvajes.

19. ¿ _____ (Tener) ustedes que trabajar el sábado?

20. _____ (Poder) ganar mucho más dinero, pero no quisimos.

21. Ayer yo _____ (tener) la oportunidad de conocer a Liliana.

22. La verdad es que no _____ (poder) pensar en nada qué decirle.

Worksheet 5.14 Preterite tense of *estar* and *andar*

Estar and **andar** do not change the vowel in their stems, but they share the same irregular endings:

estar			
yo	estuve	nosotros(as)	estuvimos
tú	estuviste	vosotros(as)	estuvisteis
él, ella, usted	estuvo	ellos, ellas, ustedes	estuvieron

andar			
yo	anduve	nosotros(as)	anduvimos
tú	anduviste	vosotros(as)	anduvisteis
él, ella, usted	anduvo	ellos, ellas, ustedes	anduvieron

Note: **andar** means *to walk* and also *to go around (with)*.

➤ In the blanks, supply the preterite tense of **estar.**

1. Yo _____ un mes en el hospital el año pasado.
2. ¿Dónde_____ tú anoche?
3. Nosotros _____ en casa toda la noche.
4. Juan _____ en la oficina hasta las cinco.
5. Elena _____ muy enferma la semana pasada.
6. ¿Dónde_____ usted hace dos días?
7. ¿Dónde _____ sus amigos Manuel y Enrique anoche?
8. Creo que ellos _____ en casa de Dolores.
9. ¿Cuándo _____ usted enfermo?
10. Las muchachas _____ de compras todo el día.
11. Tú _____ enojado conmigo casi dos meses.
12. Yo _____ muy ocupado todo el día ayer.

➤ In the blanks, supply the preterite tense of **andar.**

1. Nosotros _____ descalzos en la playa ayer.
2. El niño _____ en bicicleta toda la tarde.
3. Las niñas _____ por el parque toda la tarde hoy.
4. ¿Quién _____ en mi jardín?
5. Tú estás cansada porque _____ mucho esta tarde.
6. Yo _____ en las tiendas más de tres horas ayer.
7. Nosotros _____ por todas partes en busca del perro.
8. ¿Por dónde _____ usted ayer?
9. Ellos _____ con mucho cuidado para no despertarme.
10. Tú _____ en cuatro patas para hacer reír al niño.
11. El señor Morales _____ por toda Europa cuando joven.
12. Ella se enojó porque nosotros no _____ con ella.

Irregular verbs

➤ Supply the preterite tense of the verbs in parentheses.

1. Mi madre _____ (estar) enferma todo el día ayer.

2. Yo _____ (tener) que cuidar a mis hermanitos.

3. Nosotros le _____ (traer) su medicina y sus comidas.

4. En la noche ella _____ (ponerse) mucho mejor.

5. Yo _____ (ver) a tu tía Teresa en la calle.

6. La pobre mujer _____ (caerse) en la calle y casi la golpeó un coche.

7. Gracias a Dios, el chofer _____ (poder) frenar a tiempo.

8. Ella _____ (decir) que va a tener más cuidado en adelante.

9. Nosotros no _____ (poder) encontrar a nuestro perro.

10. Lo buscamos por todas partes pero no lo _____ (encontrar).

11. Anoche por fin lo _____ (oír) en el patio.

12. Nosotros nunca _____ (saber) por qué no volvió antes.

13. ¿Por qué no _____ (querer) ir al cine con nosotros?

14. Ya vi esa película que ustedes _____ (ir) a ver.

15. Además, _____ (poner) demasiada violencia en muchas escenas.

16. Mi familia y yo _____ (andar) por toda Disneylandia.

17. Yo no _____ (saber) hacer el ejercicio.

18. Yo traté de hacerlo pero no _____ (poder).

19. ¿Lo _____ (hacer) tú?

20. ¡Claro que sí! Para mí _____ (ser) fácil.

21. Fernando _____ (traer) un invitado al club.

22. Ellas _____ (venir) por primera vez.

23. Muchos jóvenes _____ (querer) bailar con ellas.

24. Ellas no _____ (poder) bailar con todos.

More on irregular verbs

➤ Change the subjects of the following sentences to third person singular **él** or **ella**, and write the new sentences in the spaces to the right.

1. Fui al cine anoche con Juan. _____

2. Traje a Elena a la fiesta anoche. _____

3. Vi a Enrique en la calle ayer. _____

4. Me caí en la calle ayer. _____

5. Leí esa novela el año pasado. _____

6. Estuve en casa de María el miércoles. _____

7. Hice muchas cosas ayer. _____

8. Dije la verdad. _____

9. No quise ir al cine con ellas anoche. _____

10. Vine a clase hoy en autobús. _____

11. Puse los libros en el escritorio. _____

12. No supe nada de su llegada hasta ayer. _____

13. No tuve tiempo para llamarle a usted. _____

14. No pude asistir a clase ayer. _____

15. Estuve toda la tarde ayer en casa de Arturo. _____

16. No oí lo que dijo el profesor. _____

17. Le di a José la carta de usted. _____

18. No creí el cuento de Joaquín. _____

19. Puse las maletas en el automóvil. _____

20. Hice todo lo posible por llegar a tiempo. _____

21. Vi dos buenas películas anoche. _____

22. Fui al médico ayer. _____

23. Tuve que hacer mucha tarea ayer. _____

24. Traje una pelota a la playa. _____

For further practice, repeat the preceding sentences orally, changing the subject to **tú, usted, nosotros, ellos, ustedes.**

More on irregular verbs

➤ Change the following from present to preterite tense.

1. Yo hago _____

2. Él tiene _____

3. Yo estoy _____

4. Él anda _____

5. Tú puedes ir _____

6. Yo traigo _____

7. Usted lee _____

8. Yo leo _____

9. Tú sabes _____

10. Ella se cae _____

11. Nosotros vamos _____

12. Yo quiero _____

13. Tú vienes _____

14. Yo lo digo _____

15. Él hace _____

16. Nadie lee _____

17. Ellas van _____

18. Yo oigo _____

19. Tú traes _____

20. Él pone _____

21. Yo doy _____

22. Tú eres _____

23. Yo voy _____

24. Tú tienes _____

25. Juan está _____

26. Yo ando _____

27. Nosotros vamos _____

28. Nadie está _____

29. Todos saben _____

30. Yo pongo _____

31. Tú se lo das _____

32. Ellos vienen _____

33. Él dice _____

34. Tú quieres _____

35. José quiere _____

36. Nosotros somos _____

37. María sabe _____

38. Ellos tienen _____

39. Nadie sabe _____

40. Ustedes tienen _____

41. Él puede ir _____

42. Pablo se pone _____

43. Tú haces _____

44 . Nadie va _____

General review

➤ Choose the correct form and write it in the blank.

1. Juan y Enrique van _____ (junto, juntos) al juego de béisbol.

2. El nuevo alumno _____ (llama, se llama) Jorge.

3. Los alumnos de esta clase _____ (son, están) muy aplicados.

4. Ellos son también muy _____ (inteligente, inteligentes).

5. El profesor López nos enseña _____ (leer, a leer) en español.

6. Anoche saludé _____ (el profesor, al profesor) en la calle.

7. El domingo yo _____ (fui, fue) al cine con Elena.

8. Ella _____ (trajiste, trajo) a su hermanito.

9. Juanito siempre tiene _____ (mucho, mucha) hambre.

10. Yo _____ (les, los) compré dulces y refrescos.

11. Además, el chico _____ (hice, hizo) mucho ruido.

12. No pienso _____ (escribirles, escribirlos) una carta.

13. ¿_____ (Estuviste, Estuvisteis) tú enferma?

14. ¿Te llevaron _____ (a ti, a tú) al hospital?

15. Te ves muy bien _____ (ayer, hoy).

16. ¿_____ (Gustó, Te gustaron) las comidas?

17. Mi tío me _____ (dije, dijo) que le gustaron.

18. Pero cree que no dan _____ (suficiente, suficientes) comida.

19. Estos señores _____ (son, están) del Brasil.

20. Tú tratas _____ (de, a) hablarles en español.

21. Ellos no _____ (pudieron, pusieron) entender lo que dijiste.

22. ¿Nunca _____ (supiste, supo) lo que dijeron?

23. Su lengua _____ (esta, es) semejante pero es otra.

24. A los brasileños les _____ (gusta, gustan) mucho la música.

Part 6

Contents

Worksheet 6.1 Prepositions

➤ In the blanks, supply the necessary prepositions.

1. Yo voy _____ estudiar para abogado.

2. Espero asistir _____ una universidad famosa.

3. Yo solicito admisión _____ varias universidades.

4. Hablo con algunas _____ teléfono.

5. Yo enseñé _____ esquiar a mi tío.

6. Mi tío conoce_____ muchos abogados.

7. Él es un juez famoso _____ la capital.

8. Yo le digo que sueño _____ ser abogado.

9. Nunca dejo _____ estudiar muy duro para serlo.

10. El abogado debe hablar claramente y _____ voz alta.

11. ¿Le gusta _____ él leer mucho?

12. Él aprende _____ interpretar las leyes.

13. Creo que está a punto _____ llover.

14. Mis estantes ya están llenos _____ libros.

15. Sueño_____ leerlos todos.

16. No dejo _____ leer todos los días.

17. Yo leo las frases en Latín _____ dificultad.

18. Es importante aprender _____ entenderlas bien.

19. Quiero ayudar _____ la gente a resolver sus problemas.

20. Las leyes nos garantizan justicia _____ todos.

21. Juan nunca piensa _____ ayudar a los demás.

22. El abogado representa _____ los acusados.

23. También representa _____ los culpables.

24. Es imporante proteger los derechos _____ todos.

25. No se puede vivir _____ trabajar.

Worksheet 6.2 Odd word out

➤ Which word does not fit with the others? If necessary, consult the master vocabulary for any unfamiliar word.

EXAMPLE: Juan   Ernesto   Pablo   Felipe   (María)

1. cinco	sus	siete	ocho	nueve
2. gasto	perro	tigre	elefante	vaca
3. guitarra	acordeón	martillo	piano	violín
4. taxista	futbolista	violinista	entrevista	artista
5. doctor	enfermera	cirujano	contador	médico
6. amable	feo	simpático	cariñoso	bueno
7. caricatura	coche	automóvil	contador	médico
8. carpintero	carnicero	panadero	helicóptero	bombero
9. cama	mesa	silla	estufa	derecha
10. hombre	mujer	propina	muchacho	chica
11. japonés	interés	español	portugués	francés
12. pie	cabeza	oreja	piedra	ojo
13. hablar	lugar	pescar	empezar	dar
14. ciudad	continente	universidad	estado	país
15. sé	sabes	sabemos	saber	sabor
16. escuela	maestra	cuaderno	tarea	deuda
17. de	se	en	con	sin
18. cheque	muñeca	dinero	dólar	moneda
19. casa	museo	biblioteca	hospital	obra
20. título	nieto	padre	hermano	tío
21. suelo	pared	puerta	viento	ventana
22. tú	yo	nos	él	ustedes
23. uniforme	jaula	sombrero	guantes	traje
24. jai alai	tenis	fútbol	baloncesto	aparato
25. fui	fuiste	fuego	fueron	fuimos
26. gris	rojo	blanco	azul	joya
27. limonada	naranja	manzana	plátano	pera
28. postre	carne	fruta	piscina	legumbre
29. siglo	sílaba	día	mes	año
30. río	lago	océano	mar	llanta

Worksheet 6.3 Stem-changing -*ar* verbs

Certain verbs are identified as stem-changing (radical-changing) in the present tense. In some of these forms, a stressed **o** changes to **ue** and a stressed **e** changes to **ie.**

contar (ue)			
yo	cuento	nosotros(as)	contamos
tú	cuentas	vosotros(as)	contáis
él, ella, usted	cuenta	ellos, ellas, ustedes	cuentan

pensar (ie)			
yo	pienso	nosotros(as)	pensamos
tú	piensas	vosotros(as)	pensáis
él, ella, usted	piensa	ellos, ellas, ustedes	piensan

➤ In the blanks, supply the present tense of the verb in parentheses. **Contar** means *to count* or *to tell*; **contar con** means *to count on*. **Pensar** means *to think* or *to plan*; **pensar en** means *to think about*.

1. Mi padre nos _____ (contar) muchas historias de España.

2. Nosotros_____ (pensar) mucho en viajar a España.

3. Yo siempre _____ (contar) con mis amigos.

4. Yo _____ (pensar) que los buenos amigos son muy importantes.

5. Tú _____ (contar) los uniformes para el equipo de fútbol.

6. Tú _____ (pensar) que falta el uniforme de alguien.

7. Si no puedo dormir, _____ (contar) ovejas.

8. Ella _____ (pensar) que todo va bien.

9. Nosotros no _____ (contar) con la cooperación de Ana.

10. Ustedes _____ (pensar) que ella no es sincera.

11. El sargento _____ (contar) con la disciplina de los soldados de su unidad.

12. Él_____ (pensar) que todos están presentes.

13. ¿Por qué _____ (contar) tú el dinero tantas veces?

14. ¿ _____ (Pensar) tú que te engañó?

15. Mi abuelo _____ (contar) anécdotas de su juventud.

16. Él_____ (pensar) que los coyotes roban las gallinas.

17. Él nos _____ (contar) las aventuras de Pancho Villa.

18. Ustedes _____ (pensar) viajar a México este verano.

19. El niño _____ (contar) las estrellas del cielo.

20. Nosotros_____ (pensar) que es imposible.

21. El muchacho _____ (contar) el dinero que ganó.

22. Yo no _____ (pensar) comprar más discos.

Worksheet 6.4 More on stem-changing -*ar* verbs

The following -**ar** verbs are also stem-changing:

acostar(se)	**(ue)**	**mostrar**	**(ue)**
almorzar	**(ue)**	**recordar**	**(ue)**
encontrar	**(ue)**	**soñar**	**(ue)**

➤ Supply the present tense of the verb in parentheses.

1. Los niños _____ (soñar) con ser astronautas.

2. Ellos _____ (encontrar) muchos artículos en las revistas.

3. Tú _____ (acostarse) a la misma hora todas las noches.

4. Toda la familia _____ (almorzar) a la misma hora.

5. No _____ (recordar) lo que dijo mi tío.

6. Él nos _____ (mostrar) muchos trucos que nos hacen reír.

7. Los niños _____ (soñar) con animales feroces.

8. Nunca _____ (recordar) mis sueños.

9. Yo _____ (acostarse) tarde algunas veces.

10. Nosotros no _____ (almorzar) fuera casi nunca.

11. Juan me _____ (mostrar) su auto nuevo.

12. Yo no _____ (encontrar) ni uno que me gusta.

13. Ella nunca _____ (almorzar) sola.

14. Tú siempre _____ (encontrar) a una amiga con quien comer.

15. Él dice que nunca _____ (soñar).

16. Yo le _____ (mostrar) un artículo sobre los sueños.

17. ¿A qué hora _____ (acostarse) tú?

18. Él viene a las diez si _____ (recordar) hacerlo.

19. Nosotros no _____ (encontrar) nada que comer en la nevera.

20. ¿Por qué no _____ (almorzar) ustedes en ese restaurante?

21. ¿Con qué _____ (soñar) tú con más frecuencia?

22. Yo nunca _____ (recordar) mis sueños.

23. Ella nos _____ (mostrar) su traje nuevo.

24. Lo estrena _____ (almorzar) con su novio.

Worksheet 6.5 More on stem-changing -*ar* verbs

The following -**ar** verbs are also stem-changing:

calentar	(ie)	empezar	(ie)
cerrar	(ie)	negar(se)	(ie)
comenzar	(ie)	nevar	(ie)
despertar(se)	(ie)	sentar(se)	(ie)

➤ Supply the present tense of the verb in parentheses.

1. Este horno _____ (calentar) mucho la cocina.

2. Si tú _____ (empezar) a cocinar, más vale abrir la ventana.

3. En el invierno yo _____ (sentarse) cerca de la ventana.

4. Me gusta ver el jardín cuando _____ (nevar).

5. Yó siempre _____ (despertarse) a la misma hora.

6. Es verdad. Yo no lo _____ (negar).

7. Mis primos _____ (comenzar) hoy a pintar la casa.

8. ¿Por qué ellos no _____ (cerrar) las ventanas antes de pintar?

9. Ustedes _____ (calentar) la casa en invierno.

10. ¿Por qué no _____ (sentarse) tú junto a mí?

11. Él dice que ella se enfada mucho. Ella lo _____ (negar).

12. Él _____ (empezar) a criticarla demasiado.

13. Yo me preocupo cuando _____ (nevar) mucho y tengo que manejar.

14. Son las diez y ya _____ (empezar) a nevar mucho.

15. ¿A qué hora _____ (cerrarse) las tiendas los viernes?

16. La mayoría _____ (comenzar) a cerrarse a las seis en punto.

17. En el verano, nosotros _____ (despertarse) más temprano.

18. Nosotros _____ (negarse) a levantarnos temprano.

19. Yo _____ (calentar) el café un poco más.

20. Cuando hace frío y _____ (nevar) afuera, prefiero el café más caliente.

21. Si hace frío, ella _____ (despertarse) durante la noche.

22. Ella se levanta y _____ (cerrar) la ventana.

23. Los González _____ (sentarse) en la primera fila del teatro.

24. El concierto _____ (comenzar) a las ocho.

Worksheet 6.6 Stem-changing -*er* verbs

Some -**er** verbs also have **o → ue** or **i → ie** stem changes:

volver (ue)			
yo	vuelvo	nosotros(as)	volvemos
tu	vuelves	vosotros(as)	volvéis
él, ella, usted	vuelves	ellos, ellas, ustedes	vuelven

perder (ie)			
yo	pierdo	nosotros(as)	perdemos
tu	pierdes	vosotros(as)	perdéis
él, ella, usted	pierde	ellos, ellas, ustedes	pierden

Other verbs in this category include **defender(se) (ie), devolver (ue), entender (ie), llover (ue), mover (ue), poder (ue), querer (ie).**

➤ Supply the present tense of the verb in parentheses.

1. Yo nunca _____ (perder) los libros de la biblioteca.

2. Yo no _____ (querer) pagar las multas.

3. El tráfico _____ (moverse) muy despacio ahora.

4. Siempre es así cuando _____ (llover).

5. ¿Por qué no me _____ (devolver) mis discos?

6. Porque yo _____ (querer) escucharlos una vez más.

7. El acusado _____ (defender) sus derechos.

8. El abogado _____ (volver) a ayudarlo por segunda vez.

9. Ernesto _____ (perder) los lentes cada vez que viaja.

10. Yo no _____ (entender) como puede comer tanto.

11. Raquel _____ (volver) de Guatemala pasado mañana.

12. Nosotros _____ (poder) recibirla en el aeropuerto.

13. Te _____ (devolver) la computadora que me prestaste.

14. Yo no _____ (querer) tanta responsabilidad.

15. Ricardo me _____ (volver) a pedir dinero.

16. Él nunca te _____ (devolver) el dinero que le prestas.

17. Este tren _____ (moverse) más rápido fuera de la ciudad.

18. ¡Ojalá! Nosotros no _____ (querer) perder más tiempo.

19. El soldado _____ (defenderse) contra el enemigo.

20. En realidad él no _____ (querer) hacerle daño a nadie.

21. Es primera vez que nuestro equipo de fútbol _____ (perder).

22. Si _____ (llover) no hay partido hoy.

Preterite tense

All of the following verbs are stem-changing in the present but regular in the preterite. Note, however, that verbs ending in **-zar** change the **z** to **c** in the first person singular, preterite tense.

EXAMPLES: comen**zar**   empe**zar**   almor**zar**

comen**cé**   empe**cé**   almor**cé**

➤ Change each of the following to the preterite tense.

1. Él entiende. _____

2. Yo almuerzo. _____

3. Ella encuentra. _____

4. Tú muestras. _____

5. Yo me acuerdo. _____

6. Ellos pierden. _____

7. El día empieza. _____

8. Juan cuenta. _____

9. Nadie piensa. _____

10. Tú vuelves. _____

11. Ella pierde. _____

12. Devolvemos. _____

13. Él se sienta. _____

14. Nos sentamos. _____

15. Tú cierras. _____

16. Se despierta. _____

17. Todos cuentan. _____

18. Yo comienzo. _____

19. Se sientan. _____

20. No entiendo. _____

21. Te acuestas. _____

22. Leonora cuenta. _____

23. Ellos vuelven. _____

24. Tú entiendes. _____

25. Yo comienzo. _____

26. María piensa. _____

27. Yo pierdo. _____

28. Empezamos. _____

29. Mi tío muestra. _____

30. Él empieza. _____

31. Lola cierra. _____

32. Pablo defiende. _____

33. Yo me acuesto. _____

34. No te acuerdas. _____

35. Yo encuentro. _____

36. Elena mueve. _____

37. Nadie vuelve. _____

38. Se acuestan. _____

39. Te despiertas. _____

40. Tú entiendes. _____

41. Llueve mucho. _____

42. Tú almuerzas. _____

Worksheet 6.7 Stem-changing *-ir* verbs

Note the stem change in the present of each of the following **-ir** verbs:

consentir (ie)	**mentir (ie)**	**divertir(se) (ie)**	**sentir(se) (ie)**
convertir(se) (ie)	**preferir (ie)**	**dormir(se) (ue)**	**morir (se) (ue)**

consentir			
yo	consiento	nosotros(as)	consentimos
tú	consientes	vosotros(as)	consentís
él, ella, usted	consiente	ellos, ellas, ustedes	consienten

➤ Supply the present tense of the verb in parentheses.

1. De todas las chicas de mi clase, yo _____ (preferir) a Lola.

2. Yo casi_____ (morirse) de miedo al hablar con sus padres.

3. Yo _____ (sentirse) por fin el más afortunado del mundo.

4. Sus padres _____ (consentir) en dejarme salir con ella.

5. Yo _____ (dormir) muy contento cuando pienso en mi primera cita.

6. El sábado yo_____ (sentirse) muy nervioso.

7. Yo no _____ (mentir) cuando digo que estoy distraído.

8. Nosotros_____ (divertirse) mucho en la playa.

9. Miguelito es un niño travieso y_____ (mentir) mucho.

10. A los diez años él _____ (convertirse) en un buen muchacho.

11. Él siempre _____ (consentir) en hacer lo que dice su mamá.

12. A las nueve en punto él va a la cama y_____ (dormir).

13. Él _____ (divertirse) con sus amigos.

14. Si _____ (morirse) de hambre, él no se queja.

15. Más que nada _____ (preferir) ayudar a sus padres.

16. Sus padres _____ (sentirse) muy orgullosos de él.

17. El padre de Isabel _____ (consentir) en comprarle un coche.

18. Ella _____ (sentirse) muy contenta con su nuevo coche.

19. El gato de Isabel se llama Tobi. Tobi _____ (dormir) con Isabel.

20. Un día Tobi _____ (morirse), y su papá le compra otro gatito, Chucho.

21. Ella dice que no echa de menos a Tobi, pero _____ (mentir).

22. Un gato no _____ (convertirse) en otro gato.

23. Al principio ella _____ (preferir) recordar a su primer gato.

24. Poco a poco ella _____ (divertirse) mucho con Chucho.

Worksheet 6.8 More on stem-changing -ir verbs

We have practiced with many **e → ie** and **o → ue** stem changes. A third stem change in the present, **e → i**, occurs in the following **-ir** verbs:

EXAMPLE **conseguir competir despedir(se) medir pedir repetir seguir servir vestir(se)**

pedir			
yo	pido	nosotros(as)	pedimos
tu	pides	vosotros(as)	pedís
él, ella, usted	pide	ellos, ellas, ustedes	piden

➤ Supply the present tense of the verb in parentheses.

1. Juan y Carlos _____ (competir) en la clase de trigonometría.

2. Juan _____ (medir) los ángulos de varios triángulos.

3. Carlos _____ (pedir) más problemas para hacer en casa.

4. Los dos _____ (conseguir) libros avanzados le matemáticas.

5. Juan y Carlos _____ (seguir) los ejemplos exactamente.

6. Ellos _____ (repetir) las reglas para aprenderlas bien.

7. Nosotros_____ (vestirse) con ropa elegante.

8. Mamá _____ (servir) un desayuno muy nutritivo.

9. Nosotros_____ (despedirse) de ella y nos fuimos.

10. Nosotros_____ (seguir) el sendero que sube a las montañas.

11. Nuestros mapas nos _____ (servir) para no perdernos.

12. Nosotros no _____ (competir) en llegar a la cima.

13. ¿ _____ (Medir) tú los ingredientes cuando cocinas?

14. Sí, yo siempre_____ (seguir) la receta.

15. ¿Tienes un menú favorito que _____ (repetir) mucho?

16. No, yo _____ (servir) algo nuevo cada noche.

17. ¿Qué_____ (pedir) usted en los restaurantes elegantes?

18. No voy. No quiero _____ (ponerse) corbata.

19. Ana _____ (vestirse) muy elegante para su despedida de soltera.

20. En la fiesta ella _____ (conseguir) muchos regalos útiles.

21. Sus amigas _____ (servir) pastel y helado.

22. Ella _____ (repetir) las gracias a todas sus amigas.

23. La fiesta _____ (seguir) hasta muy tarde.

24. Cuando ellas _____ (despedir) ya es casi medianoche.

Stem-changing *-ir* verbs

The verbs in the following sentences change in the present from
o → ue, e → ie or from **e → i. Reír** (*to laugh*) and **sonreír** (*to smile*)
change from **e** to **í.**

➤ Supply the present tense of the verbs in parentheses.

1. Carlos siempre _____ (dormirse) en el tren.

2. Yo _____ (sentirse) muy contento con mi adelanto en español.

3. La profesora _____ (divertir) mucho a los estudiantes.

4. Nosotros_____ (reírse) muchas veces en su clase.

5. Si cometemos un error, ella _____ (sonreírse) y nos corrige.

6. Primero que nada, la maestra siempre nos _____ (pedir) la tarea.

7. Si no tengo mi tarea, no le _____ (mentir) a la maestra.

8. De todas mis clases, yo _____ (preferir) ésta.

9. Buenos días, Rosa. ¿Cómo _____ (sentirse)?

10. Estoy mejor, pero no _____ (dormir) bien en este hospital.

11. ¿Te _____ (servir) ellos buena comida?

12. Yo _____ (pedir) lo que quiero, y la enfermera me lo trae.

13. ¿Cómo _____ (seguir) la garganta? ¿Te duele todavía?

14. No, sólo me duele cuando _____ (reírse).

15. Entonces yo no te _____ (repetir) el chiste que oí anoche.

16. Ay, ¿quién _____ (divertirse) en el hospital?

17. Mis hermanos _____ (competir) en la natación.

18. Yo _____ (sentir) mucho orgullo cuando ganan trofeos.

19. Ellos _____ (vestirse) en traje de baño.

20. Ellos _____ (repetir) los mismos saltos hora tras hora.

21. Por mi parte, yo no _____ (servir) para competir.

22. Yo _____ (morirme) de tanto entrenamiento.

23. Yo _____ (preferir) emplear el tiempo en otras cosas.

24. Pero no _____ (mentir) al decir que les envidio su talento.

Worksheet 6.9 Preterite tense stem-changing -*ir* verbs

Those -**ir** verbs with stem changes in the present tense will also have a stem change in the third person preterite tense, both singular and plural. These changes will be from **e → i** or from **o → u**.

sentir (e→i)			
yo	sentí	nosotros(as)	sentimos
tú	sentiste	vosotros(as)	sentisteis
él, ella, usted	sintió	ellos, ellas, ustedes	sintieron

dormir (o→u)			
yo	dormí	nosotros(as)	dormimos
tú	dormiste	vosotros(as)	dormisteis
él, ella, usted	durmió	ellos, ellas, ustedes	durmieron

➤ In the blanks, supply the preterite tense of **sentir**.

1. Yo no _____ (sentirse) bien ayer.

2. Tú no _____ (sentirse) bien ayer tampoco.

3. Yo _____ (sentirse) obligado a pagar por el libro que perdí.

4. La abuela _____ (sentir) mucho la ausencia de sus nietos.

5. Nosotros_____ (sentir) no poder continuar el curso.

6. Tú _____ (sentir) mucho frío anoche.

7. ¿Por qué no _____ (sentirse) bien usted ayer?

8. Yo _____ (sentir) mucho no estar en casa cuando Julio llamó.

9. Tomás_____ (sentirse) muy triste cuando murió su perro.

10. Nosotros_____ (sentir) no verlos cuando fuimos a Panamá.

➤ In the blanks, supply the preterite tense of **dormir**.

1. El niño _____ (dormir) muy mal anoche.

2. Raquel _____ (dormirse) inmediatamente al acostarse.

3. Yo también_____ (dormirse) en seguida.

4. Tú _____ (dormirse) en el tren.

5. El perro_____ (dormir) ayer en mi silla favorita.

6. Las niñas_____ (dormir) una siesta en la playa.

7. Tú _____ (dormirse) anoche durante el programa de televisión.

8. Juan _____ (dormir) en casa de Luis.

9. Yo _____ (dormir) bien cuando pasé la noche en el desierto.

10. Nosotros _____ (dormir) la siesta ayer domingo.

Worksheet 6.10 More on preterite tense of stem-changing -*ir* verbs

In addition to **sentir e → i** and **dormir o → u** (see previous worksheet), several other verbs are stem-changing in the preterite tense:

despedirse (i)	**divertirse (i)**	**mentir (i)**	**morir (u)**	**pedir (i)**
preferir (i)	**reírse (i)**	**reñir (i)**	**repetirse (i)**	**sentir (u)**
seguir (i)	**servir (i)**	**vestirse (i)**		

➤ Supply the preterite tense of the verbs in parentheses.

1. El Domingo de Pascua, mi tío _____ (vestirse) de conejo.

2. Los niños _____ (divertirse) mucho.

3. Mi hermanita le _____ (pedir) huevos de Pascua.

4. Mis padres _____ (reírse) al ver la inocencia de los niños.

5. Después, mi madre nos _____ (servir) chocolate caliente.

6. Mis primos en México _____ (preferir) el Día de los Muertos.

7. Ellos _____ (vestirse) de piratas, payasos y fantasmas.

8. Algunos _____ (repetir) que les gusta espantar a la gente.

9. El vecino dijo que casi _____ (morirse) de espanto.

10. La verdad es que _____ (mentir) para divertir a ___

11. En el Día de los Inocentes todos _____ (m___

12. Todos _____ (divertirse) con la___

13. Gracias al buen humor, nosotros no _____ (re___

14. Las mentiras y las bromas _____ (se___

15. Los peregrinos _____ (despedirse) de Inglaterra.

16. Ellos _____ (seguir) rumbo a América y la liber___.

17. Fue difícil, pero ellos _____ (preferir) quedarse en el Nuevo Mundo.

18. Muchos _____ (morir) durante el primer año.

19. Los indios les _____ (servir) de buenos amigos y los ayudaron.

20. Ayer, el 4 de julio, nosotros _____ (sentir) mucho orgullo.

21. Yo _____ (preferir) recordar a los héroes de la Revolución.

22. Muchos _____ (morir) en la lucha por la independencia.

23. También fue un día cuando todos _____ (divertirse).

24. Los fuegos artificiales _____ (servir) bien para celebrar la fecha.

Preterite tense of stem-changing -ir verbs

➤ Change each of the following from the present to the preterite tense.

1. Yo prefiero _____
2. Él se divierte _____
3. Él se muere _____
4. Tú pides _____
5. Él repite _____
6. Ella sirve _____
7. Yo me río _____
8. Tú te vistes _____
9. Yo me despido _____
10. Ella se siente _____
11. Yo me duermo _____
12. Ellos repiten _____
13. Eso no sirve_____
14. Ellos se ríen_____
15. Yo me visto _____
16. Nadie se divierte _____
17. Tú mientes _____
18. Ella prefiere _____
19. Él pide _____
20. Esto sirve_____
21. Todos se ríen_____
22. Tú te despides _____

23. Yo repito _____
24. Tú te duermes _____
25. Nadie prefiere_____
26. Tomás lo siente_____
27. Algunos se visten _____
28. Todos duermen _____
29. Nosotros pedimos _____
30. Ellos riñen _____
31. El profesor se ríe_____
32. Nadie se despide _____
33. Tú me lo repites _____
34. Los niños piden _____
35. ¿Quién se muere?_____
36. Nadie se viste _____
37. Eduardo se despide _____
38. Ella nunca pide_____
39. Él nunca miente _____
40. Tú prefieres_____
41. Ellos siempre piden _____
42. Tú te ríes _____
43. Ella se viste _____
44. ¿Cuál sirve? _____

Name: _____ Date: _____

General review

➤ Choose the correct form and write it in the blanks.

1. Ellos trataron _____ (de, a) llamarnos al mediodía.

2. Anoche _____ (me acuesto, me acosté) a medianoche.

3. ¿Qué hora es? _____ (Es, Son) las cinco y media.

4. Yo _____ (sé, se) que van a cenar a las siete y cuarto.

5. A mí no me gusta _____ (levantar, levantarme) antes de las ocho.

6. _____ (Este, Esto) periódico es del veinte de marzo.

7. Arturo se sienta _____ (delante, delante de) mí.

8. Anoche _____ (acosté, me acosté) después de las diez.

9. Yo me encontré con _____ (el, al) profesor a las dos menos cuarto.

10. Vamos a _____ (despedir, despedirnos) de los García el lunes.

11. Tú me _____ (pidio, pediste) un favor ayer por la mañana.

12. Jaime _____ (enfermó, se enfermó) a principios de abril.

13. Él_____ (puso, se puso) bien a fines de abril.

14. Los novios _____ (se casaron, casaron) el catorce de junio.

15. Ella es la _____ (única, único) persona que vino a la reunión.

16. A la una Isabel empezó _____ (leer, a leer).

17. Yo tengo_____ (a, que) ver al maestro antes de las ocho.

18. Ramón _____ (estuve, estuvo) aquí a mediados de octubre.

19. Juan dijo que no vio a _____ (alguien, nadie) anteayer.

20. Pasado mañana voy _____ (a ver, ver) a mis tíos.

21. A mis padres no_____ (le, les) gusta viajar en agosto.

22. Yo me _____ (puse, puso) a estudiar a principios de mayo.

23. El primero de diciembre, él _____ (viajo, viajó) a Tejas.

24. Hoy por la mañana mi hijito _____ (vistió, se vistió) solo.

Worksheet 6.11 More on prepositions

➤ In the blanks, supply the necessary prepositions required to complete the meaning of each sentence.

1. Me encontré en la calle ayer _____ el hermano de Luis.

2. Vamos a empezar el nuevo curso _____ principios de mayo.

3. Tú vienes aquí de vez _____ cuando para ayudarnos a nosotros.

4. Yo le doy _____ comer a mi perro dos veces al día.

5. Más que nada a mí me gusta mucho montar _____ caballo.

6. El joven ingeniero se enamoró _____ ella enseguida.

7. Como _____ costumbre, tú llegaste tarde a la clase hoy.

8. Ellos viven cerca _____ nosotros desde hace cuatro años.

9. Felipe se sienta _____ frente de mí en la iglesia.

10. Voy a salir hoy, a pesar _____ lo que dijo el médico ayer.

11. Ellos no pudieron encontrar a Diego _____ ninguna parte.

12. Tú te llevas bien _____ todo el mundo.

13. Ellos van a tardar mucho _____ hablar español bien.

14. Ayer traté varias veces _____ llamarlo a usted.

15. Ricardo se parece mucho _____ su hermano mayor.

16. Ellos hablaron conmigo _____ teléfono tres veces ayer.

17. Este lápiz que compré en la papelería no sirve _____ nada.

18. Él va a salir _____ Nueva York el miércoles.

19. Tú vas a volver del centro _____ seguida.

20. Tengo que tomar esta medicina tres veces _____ día.

21. Este vestido que compré para la fiesta es _____ algodón.

22. Su sombrero nuevo es _____ un color oscuro.

23. El niño se echó _____ llorar enseguida.

24. Tú vienes a mi casa _____ mucha frecuencia.

Worksheet 6.12 Imperfect tense of -*ar* verbs

Spanish has two simple past tenses. The preterite tense is used for single, completed actions. The imperfect tense is used for repeated actions or those begun in the past and continuing into the present or future.

EXAMPLES:	PRETERITE	EXPLANATION
	Mi primo viajó.	*He travelled once and is not still travelling.*
	IMPERFECT	EXPLANATION
	Mi primo viajaba.	*He used to travel at various times.*
	Mi primo viajaba.	*He was travelling and still is.*
	Mi primo viajaba cuando se enfermó.	*He was travelling when he got sick.*

Regular **-ar** verbs are conjugated in the imperfect tense as follows:

hablar (to speak)			
yo	hablaba	nosotros(as)	hablábamos
tú	hablabas	vosotros(as)	hablabais
él, ella, usted	hablaba	ellos, ellas, ustedes	hablaban

➤ Supply the imperfect tense of the verbs in parentheses.

1. En mi niñez yo _____ (hablar) italiano.

2. Mi padre _____ (viajar) frecuentemente a la Argentina.

3. Él _____ (comprar) cosas muy bonitas allí.

4. Un día nos dijo que _____ (desear) vivir en Buenos Aires.

5. Todos los días él _____ (estudiar) español.

6. Yo aprendí que la palabra "burro" no _____ (significar) mantequilla.

7. Mis hermanitos _____ (pelearse) mucho.

8. Mis padres _____ (tratar) de separarlos.

9. Poco a poco ellos _____ (portarse) mejor.

10. Pablo le _____ (ayudar) a Raúl con las matemáticas.

11. Raúl le _____ (enseñar) a Pablo a jugar fútbol.

12. En años recientes uno siempre _____ (acompañar) al otro.

13. El profesor nos _____ (explicar) la historia de México muy bien.

14. Nosotros _____ (imaginarse) fácilmente la época azteca.

15. En nuestra imaginación _____ (escuchar) a Moctezuma.

16. El emperador _____ (hablar) con los conquistadores.

17. Los españoles _____ (conquistar) a los indios.

18. Desgraciadamente, todos _____ (luchar) en una horrible guerra.

Worksheet 6.13 Imperfect tense of -er and -ir verbs

In the imperfect tense, **-er** and **-ir** verbs share the same endings.

comer			
yo	comía	nosotros(as)	comíamos
tú	comías	vosotros(as)	comíais
él, ella, usted	comía	ellos, ellas, ustedes	comían

vivir			
yo	vivía	nosotros(as)	víviamos
tú	vivías	vosotros(as)	vivíais
él, ella, usted	vivía	ellos, ellas, ustedes	vivían

➤ Supply the imperfect tense of the verbs in parentheses.

1. Hace muchos años mis abuelos _____ (vivir) con nosotros.

2. Yo recuerdo que ellos _____ (salir) de vez en cuando.

3. Ellos _____ (asistir) mucho a eventos culturales.

4. Mi abuelo nos _____ (divertir) con cuentos de su juventud.

5. Diariamente mi abuelita nos _____ (leer) espisodios de la Biblia.

6. Nosotros _____ (querer) mucho a nuestros abuelitos.

7. En la escuela mi hermana siempre_____ (recibir) buenas notas.

8. Ella _____ (aprender) muy fácilmente todo lo que estudiaba.

9. A veces yo _____ (tener) celos de ella.

10. Adelita _____ (recibir) muchos honores en la comunidad.

11. Todos _____ (decir) que ella tenía mucha inteligencia.

12. Es verdad. Ella _____ (poseer) muchos talentos.

13. Cuando yo viajaba, yo _____ (perder) muchas cosas.

14. Yo _____ (tener) miedo de perder los boletos de vuelta.

15. Mi memoria en aquel entonces no _____ (valer) para nada.

16. Nosotros _____ (coger) muchos resfriados en Nueva York.

17. La familia _____ (sufrir) mucho a causa del frío.

18. Además la nieve _____ (cubrir) las calles completamente.

19. Nosotros _____ (tener) que manejar con mucho cuidado.

20. En el invierno _____ (poner) llantas especiales.

21. Durante aquel año todos _____ (hacer) algo para ganar dinero.

22. Mi hermano y yo _____ (vender) periódicos y revistas.

23. Mis hermanas _____ (coser) ropa para los vecinos.

24. Mis primos _____ (trabajar) en una tienda.

Worksheet 6.14 Imperfect tense of *ser, ir, ver*

Three important verbs are irregular in the imperfect tense:

ir			
yo	iba	nosotros(as)	íbamos
tú	ibas	vosotros(as)	ibais
él, ella, usted	iba	ellos, ellas, ustedes	iban

ser			
yo	era	nosotros(as)	éramos
tú	eras	vosotros(as)	erais
él, ella, usted	era	ellos, ellas, ustedes	eran

ver			
yo	veía	nosotros(as)	veíamos
tú	veías	vosotros(as)	veíais
él, ella, usted	veía	ellos, ellas, ustedes	veían

➤ Supply the imperfect tense of the verbs in parentheses.

1. Antes de jubilarme, yo _____ (ser) vendedor de libros.

2. Yo _____ (ir) a las ciudades más grandes de cinco estados.

3. Yo _____ (ver) a los gerentes de más de cien librerías.

4. Mi prima _____ (ser) aficionada a los conjuntos de rock and roll.

5. Elena _____ (ir) a muchos conciertos en Los Ángeles.

6. Ella _____ (ver) a todos los conjuntos más célebres.

7. Benito Juárez _____ (ser) presidente por esos tiempos.

8. Él _____ (ir) a muchas partes para conocer mejor al pueblo.

9. Él _____ (ver) como vivían en cada ciudad.

10. Nosotros _____ (ser) muy buenos amigos entonces.

11. _____ (Ir) juntos a todas partes.

12. Siempre _____ (ver) las mismas películas.

13. Según mi padre, mis abuelos _____ (ser) rusos.

14. Antes de emigrar a los Estados Unidos, ellos ya _____ (hablar) inglés en casa.

15. Mi padre nunca _____ (oír) hablar nada de ruso.

16. Nosotros _____ (ir) anualmente al jardín zoológico.

17. Nos fascinó un grupo de pingüinos. _____ (Ser) muy graciosos.

18. Los _____ (ver) por horas entrar y salir del agua.

19. Nuestro entrenador de fútbol _____ (ser) muy exigente.

20. Algunos de nosotros _____ (ir) a los juegos con un poco de miedo.

21. A pesar de esto, nosotros lo _____ (ver) como a un padre.

22. La reunión _____ (ser) a las cuatro.

23. Allí _____ (ir) también mi antigua novia.

24. Hacía mucho tiempo que no la _____ (ver).

Imperfect tense

Because they represent continuing actions, the verbs in the following exercise are among the most commonly used in the imperfect tense. In this tense they are all regular verbs.

➤ Supply the imperfect tense of the verbs in parentheses.

1. Ellos no _____ (saber) que yo tenía un automóvil nuevo.

2. Yo _____ (creer) que Carlos estaba en casa.

3. Entonces nosotros no _____ (pensar) en casarnos.

4. Tú _____ (tener) la idea de que ella hablaba español bien.

5. Yo no _____ (entender) por qué ella se portaba así.

6. Ellos _____ (sentir) mucho no poder ir con nosotros.

7. Yo no _____ (saber) que él escribía novelas.

8. Nosotros no _____ (poder) ver la película desde allí.

9. Tú _____ (creer) que yo viví en México varios años.

10. Él _____ (pensar) llegar antes que nosotros.

11. ¿_____ (Saber) tú que Juan estaba en el hospital?

12. María _____ (creer) que sus compañeros estaban en el parque.

13. Yo no _____ (pensar) estudiar mis lecciones esta noche.

14. Ellos no _____ (poder) encontrar un apartamento barato.

15. Rafael _____ (saber) que Alberto tenía malas notas.

16. Tú _____ (creer) que Raquel estaba enferma desde ayer.

17. Yo _____ (esperar) ir con ustedes a las playas de Acapulco.

18. Nosotros _____ (pensar) ir a Nueva York, pero vamos a Santa Fe.

19. Yo _____ (sentirse) muy mal hasta que fui al médico.

20. Ellos le _____ (deber) dinero al tesorero del club.

21. Luis _____ (sentirse) muy apenado por su equivocación.

22. Él le _____ (deber) al Banco de Zamora más de mil dólares.

Worksheet 6.15 *Iba a* + infinitive

Page 42 reviewed **ir a** + infinitive (*am, is, are going to*). The equivalent expression in the past tense (*was, were going to*) makes use of the imperfect tense of **ir** (page 123).

EXAMPLES: **Yo iba a estudiar,** pero dejé mi libro en la escuela.
I was going to study, but I left my book in school.

Íbamos a manejar, pero mi hermano tenía el coche.
We were going to drive, but my brother had the car.

➤ In the blanks, supply the imperfect tense of **ir a** + infinitive.

1. Yo _____
   (llamar) a Juan anoche, pero no tenía su número
   de teléfono.

2. Ellos _____
   (entregar) los paquetes ayer, pero no tuvieron
   tiempo.

3. Nosotros _____
   (acostarse) temprano anoche, pero unos amigos
   llegaron de visita.

4. Elena y yo _____
   (pasear) al parque, pero hacía demasiado frío.

5. Yo _____
   (acostarse) temprano anoche, pero tenía mucho
   trabajo.

6. Nosotros _____
   (levantarse) temprano, pero teníamos
   demasiado sueño.

7. Tú _____ (jugar) a las
   cartas anoche, pero Dora no se sentía bien.

8. Mi hermano _____
   (ir) a los Estados Unidos a estudiar, pero cambió
   de idea.

9. Yo _____
   (estudiar) francés el año pasado pero cambié
   a español.

10. Tú _____
    (escribir) varias cartas anoche, pero estabas muy
    cansado.

11. Yo _____
    (ir) a la iglesia, pero me levanté muy tarde.

12. Ellos _____
    (estudiar) medicina, pero les faltaba el dinero.

13. Nosotros _____
    (ir) a la playa, pero llovió.

14. Ellos _____
    (casarse) en junio, pero decidieron esperar hasta
    diciembre.

15. ¿Por qué _____
    (vender) ustedes el coche que compraron el año
    pasado?

16. Él dijo que _____
    (pensar) en al asunto antes de decidir.

17. Yo le _____
    (prestar) dinero a Pedro, pero descubrí que no
    tenía suficiente.

18. Diana _____
    (cortarse) el pelo, pero su madre no la dejó.

Imperfect tense

➤ Change **yo** to **tú** in each of the following sentences, and copy the subject and verb in the spaces to the right. For additional practice (orally or by writing on separate sheets of paper), change the subject next to **él** or **ella, usted, nosotros, ustedes,** and **ellos** or **ellas.**

1. *Yo estudiaba* español con el señor García. _____

2. *Yo iba* a la escuela en autobús. _____

3. *Yo veía* al maestro en el parque con frecuencia. _____

4. *Yo era* un alumno muy aplicado. _____

5. *Yo contestaba* siempre cortésmente al profesor. _____

6. *Yo miraba* televisión todas las noches. _____

7. Yo siempre *hablaba* con ellos en español. _____

8. *Yo almorzaba* en casa todos los días. _____

9. *Yo comía* en casa de Juan con mucha frecuencia. _____

10. *Yo leía* muchas novelas durante el verano. _____

11. *Yo tenía* que devolverlas a la biblioteca. _____

12. *Yo seguía* mi horario diariamente. _____

13. *Yo me levantaba* muy temprano todas las mañanas. _____

14. Yo siempre *salía* de casa a la misma hora. _____

15. *Yo me acostaba* temprano de lunes a viernes. _____

16. Yo siempre *dormía* muy bien. _____

17. Yo siempre *me despertaba* a la misma hora. _____

18. *Yo me vestía* rápidamente para no llegar tarde. _____

19. *Yo prefería* comer en casa cada vez que podía. _____

20. *Yo jugaba* al tenis cuando vivía en Miami. _____

21. *Yo le prestaba* dinero a todo el mundo. _____

22. *Yo me reía* mucho de los chistes de Andrés. _____

More on the imperfect tense

➤ Change the verbs in the following sentences from present tense to imperfect tense. Read each new sentence and be sure that you understand its altered meaning.

1. Nosotros *viajamos* muchas veces a Europa. _____

2. Tú *andas* por los bulevares de París. _____

3. Ellos *ven* las óperas en La Scala. _____

4. Yo *asisto* a las corridas de toros de Madrid. _____

_____

5. Ella *pinta* paisajes en los Pirineos. _____

6. Ustedes *tratan* de hablar portugués. _____

7. Nosotros *compramos* relojes en Suiza. _____

8. Él *admira* las ruinas en Roma. _____

9. Mi cuñado *sube* a la Torre Eiffel. _____

10. Yo *veo* el Arco de Triunfo todos los días. _____

11. Tú *vas* a los museos de Madrid. _____

12. Ricardo *es* aficionado a la pelota. _____

13. La tía Luisa *busca* conchas en la playa. _____

14. Todos *comemos* mariscos en Galicia. _____

15. A mí me *encantan* las catedrales. _____

16. A ti te *gustan* los teatros elegantes. _____

17. Muchos hoteles *son* grandes palacios. _____

18. Los autobuses de Londres *tienen* dos pisos. _____

_____

19. Los griegos *bailan* día y noche. _____

20. A todos les *gusta* patinar en el hielo en Holanda. _____

_____

21. Cuando *estoy* en Europa estoy feliz. _____

22. ¿*Viajas* tú a Sudamérica con frecuencia? _____

More on the imperfect tense

➤ Change the verbs in the following sentences from preterite tense to imperfect tense. Read each new sentence and be sure that you understand its altered meaning.

1. Yo *manejé* el coche de mi papá. _____

2. Yo lo *hice* sin permiso de él. _____

3. El *pensó* que yo era demasiado joven. _____

4. Por un mes él no me *dejó* montar en bicicleta. _____

   _____

5. En la noche yo no *pude* salir de mi cuarto. _____

6. ¡Qué sorpresa! Al mes siguiente me *prestó* su coche. _____

   _____

7. *Valió* la pena pedir permiso, ¿verdad? _____

8. Mi tío me *dio* dinero para comprar dulces. _____

9. Yo *escogí* dulces de chocolate. _____

10. Yo *comí* demasiado helado también. _____

11. Además yo *fui* al mercado a comprar galletas. _____

12. Mamá me *dijo* que yo iba a engordar. _____

13. Ella *fue* muy inteligente. _____

14. Yo t*uve* que bajar de peso. _____

15. Nosotros *esquiamos* en Colorado. _____

16. Yo *me caí* a cada rato. _____

17. Mi prima *tuvo* más suerte. _____

18. Ella *aprendió* muy rápidamente. _____

19. Pronto *conoció* a todos los entrenadores. _____

   _____

20. Si hacía mucho frío, ella no *dejó* de esquiar. _____

21. No *te pudiste* imaginar la envidia que me daba. _____

   _____

Vocabulary check-up

➤ Complete the following to show who sells things in different shops.

1. El _____ vende leche en la _____.

2. El _____ vende dulces en la _____.

3. El _____ vende carne en la _____.

4. El _____ vende libros en la _____.

5. El _____ vende zapatos en la _____.

6. El _____ vende pan en la_____.

7. El _____ vende joyas en la_____.

8. El _____ vende flores en la _____.

9. El _____ vende papel en la _____.

10. El _____ vende muebles en la_____.

➤ Complete the following sentences to show who works in a particular location.

1. El _____ *(waiter)* trabaja en el _____.

2. El _____ *(barber)* trabaja en la_____.

3. La _____ *(doctor)* trabaja en el _____.

4. El _____ *(cook)* trabaja en la _____.

5. El _____ *(gardener)* trabaja en el_____.

6. El _____ *(tailor)* trabaja en la_____.

7. La _____ *(teacher)* trabaja en la _____.

8. El _____ *(programmer)* trabaja con las _____.

9. La_____ *(actress)* trabaja en el_____.

10. El _____ *(secretary)* trabaja en la _____.

Busapalabras

Palabras revueltas

➤ This word search puzzle contains all the words in the second part of each sentence in the previous worksheet. Some words will be found horizontally, and some words will be found vertically.

```
R  J  A  R  D  I  N  F  L  O  R  E  R  I  A  PI
E  S  C  C  A  R  N  I  C  E  R  I  A  P  S  A
S  J  O  Y  E  R  I  A  E  T  H  G  C  E  A  N
T  D  F  I  C  I  N  A  S  E  O  E  O  L  S  A
A  U  I  S  O  T  R  A  C  A  S  S  C  U  T  D
U  L  C  O  C  I  N  E  U  T  P  I  I  Q  R  E
R  C  I  P  A  P  E  L  E  R  I  A  N  U  E  R
A  E  N  A  D  E  R  I  L  O  T  I  A  E  R  I
N  R  A  N  E  R  A  Z  A  P  A  T  E  R  I  A
T  I  T  A  R  O  M  U  E  B  L  E  R  I  A  Y
E  A  C  O  M  P  U  T  A  D  O  R  A  A  L  I
L  E  C  H  E  R  I  A  L  I  B  R  E  R  I  A
```

Horizontal

_____

_____

_____

_____

_____

_____

_____

_____

_____

Vertical

_____

_____

_____

_____

_____

_____

_____

_____

Worksheet 6.16 Future tense

The same endings are used for all **-ar, -er,** and **-ir** verbs that are regular in the future tense. Notice that these endings are added to the entire infinitive:

	yo	tú	él/ella/ud.	nosotros	vosotros	ellos/ellas
hablar:	hablaré	hablarás	hablará	hablaremos	hablaréis	hablarán
comer:	comeré	comerás	comerá	comeremos	comeréis	comerán
vivir:	viviré	vivirás	vivirá	viviremos	viviréis	vivirán

EXAMPLES: Yo te paga**ré** mañana   *I shall pay you tomorrow.*
            ¿Cena**rás** con Ana?   *Will you have dinner with Ana?*

➤ Supply the future tense of the verbs in parentheses.

1. Mañana yo _____ (estar) en San Francisco.

2. Yo _____ (trabajar) allí en un banco.

3. Yo _____ (conocer) a muchas personas.

4. En el banco yo _____ (ayudar) a mucha gente con sus ahorros.

5. También yo les_____ (prestar) dinero.

6. El martes nosotros _____ (divertirse) mucho.

7. Mi padre, mi hermanito, y yo _____ (ir) al río.

8. Nosotros _____ (llegar) allí antes de las siete de la mañana.

9. Los tres_____ (pescar) en el río todo el día.

10. Con suerte, nosotros _____ (regresar) con muchos pescados.

11. Esta noche Isabel me _____ (acompañar) al cine.

12. Papá me_____ (dejar) usar el coche por primera vez.

13. A ella le _____ (gustar) la película porque es una comedia musical.

14. Isabel _____ (pasar) el verano en México con sus padres.

15. Ella _____ (hablar) español muy bien a su regreso.

16. Un día de éstos, mis padres _____ (comprar) una casa grande.

17. El sábado, ellos _____ (ver) más casas que se venden.

18. Sólo _____ (visitar) casas de dos plantas.

19. Ellos _____ (necesitar) cuatro dormitorios.

20. Mis dos hermanas no _____ (dormir) en la misma habitación.

21. Tú _____ (aprender) mucho en la clase de geometría.

22. Muy pronto tú _____ (resolver) los problemas más complicados.

23. Si vas a ser ingeniero, _____ (usar) la geometría diariamente.

24. Con ese curso te _____ (preparar) para el cálculo.

Worksheet 6.17 More on future tense

➤ Supply the preterite and the future tense of each of the following present tense verbs. Include the subjects in each answer.

PRESENT TENSE	PRETERITE TENSE	FUTURE TENSE
1. Yo trabajo		
2. Él estudia		
3. Ellos compran		
4. Yo escribo		
5. Ella trae		
6. Yo me levanto		
7. Tú te acuestas		
8. Nosotros vamos		
9. Juan lee		
10. Usted come		
11. Él vuelve		
12. Ellos hablan		
13. María está		
14. Yo almuerzo		
15. Tú necesitas		
16. Él prepara		
17. Ella baila		
18. Yo veo		
19. Él vive		
20. Tú prefieres		
21. Él pide		
22. Ellos reciben		
23. Ella se viste		
24. Nadie oye		

Worksheet 6.18 Future tense of *caber, haber, poder, querer, saber*

All verbs have regular endings in the future tense, but a few common verbs have irregular stems. The following verbs simply drop the **e** from the stem:

caber		haber*		poder		querer		saber	
cabré	cabremos	habré	habremos	podré	podremos	querré	querremos	sabré	sabremos
cabrás	(cabréis)	habrás	(habréis)	podrás	(podréis)	querrás	(querréis)	sabrás	(sabréis)
cabrá	cabrán	habrá	habrán	podrá	podrán	querrá	querrán	sabrá	sabrán

➤ Supply the future tense of the verbs in parentheses.

1. Mañana _____ (haber) mucho trabajo que hacer en casa.

2. Yo no _____ (poder) ir a la playa con ustedes.

3. Tú _____ (querer) conocer a mi tío Manuel.

4. Él_____ (saber) ayudarte con la construcción de tu casa.

5. No_____ (caber) todos en el cochecito de ustedes.

6. ¿ _____ (Poder) usar nosotros la camioneta de tus papás?

7. La policía _____ (saber) proteger a los candidatos políticos.

8. _____ (Haber) suficientes policías para acompañar a cada uno.

9. Tantos abrigos no _____ (caber) en este ropero.

10. _____ (Haber) lugar para más abrigos en el ropero de arriba.

11. ¿ _____ (Saber) tú entenderte con los franco-canadienses?

12. Sí, nosotros_____ (poder) entendernos fácilmente.

13. Dos docenas de rosas no _____ (caber) en este florero.

14. _____ (Haber) un florero más grande en la cocina.

15. Mis compañeros _____ (querer) escuchar discos en la fiesta.

16. ¿ _____ (Saber) tú escoger las canciones que les gustan más?

17. ¿Cuándo_____ (poder) yo probar las famosas galletas de tu mamá?

18. Ella _____ (querer) servirte algunas en tu visita mañana.

19. ¿Quién _____ (saber) la dirección del consulado boliviano?

20. Seguramente _____ (haber) un directorio de consulados en el hotel.

*__Haber__, as an independent or principal verb, has the following forms in the present, preterite, imperfect, and future tenses: **hay, hubo, había, habrá**. As a principal verb, **haber** is the equivalent of the English *there is* or *there are* (see Worksheet 3.4, page 36). Thus, **Hay muchos alumnos ausentes hoy.** means *There are many students absent today*. **Habrá muchos alumnos ausentes mañana.** means **There will be many students absent tomorrow.**

Worksheet 6.19 Future tense of *poner, salir, tener, venir*

All the verbs in the previous worksheet dropped the vowel of the infinitive ending. **Poner, salir, tener,** and **venir** replace that dropped vowel with a **d**:

	yo	tú	él, ella, usted	nosotros(as)	vosotros(as)	ellos, ellas, ustedes
poner	pondré	pondrás	pondrá	pondremos	pondréis	pondrán
salir	saldré	saldrás	saldrá	saldremos	saldréis	saldrán
tener	tendré	tendrás	tendrá	tendremos	tendréis	tendrán
valer	valdré	valdrás	valdrá	valdremos	valdréis	valdrán
venir	vendré	vendrás	vendrá	vendremos	vendréis	vendrán

➤ Supply the future tense of the verbs in parentheses.

1. _____ (Poner) el dinero que me diste en el banco.

2. Pronto _____ (tener) bastante para comprarme un coche.

3. Daniel_____ (tener) su guitarra en la fiesta esta noche.

4. ¡Qué bueno! ¿A qué hora _____ (venir)?

5. Nosotros_____ (salir) juntos por primera vez.

6. Todos _____ (ponerse) ropa muy elegante.

7. Ellos no están de acuerdo. ¿Cuál _____ (tener) razón?

8. Alfredo _____ (venir) más tarde. Él sabrá decidir.

9. Si vas a graduarte, _____ (tener) que ver menos televisión.

10. Después de este programa, yo _____ (ponerse) a estudiar.

11. Si no me pongo la chaqueta,_____ (tener) frío en el estadio.

12. ¡Buena idea! Nosotros _____ (salir) juntos.

13. ¿ _____ (Venir) tus padres a California este año?

14. ¡Sí! Ellos ya _____ (tener) sus boletos para fines de mayo.

15. ¿Dónde_____ (poner) ella el piano que piensa comprar?

16. Creo que ella _____ (tener) que ponerlo en la sala.

17. ¿ _____ (Salir) ustedes tarde del estadio?

18. Sí, pero nosotros _____ (venir) directamente a casa después.

19. El profesor Vidal_____ (componer) una canción.

20. El programa _____ (contener) muchas canciones originales.

21. El gobierno_____ (imponer) impuestos sobre tu aumento de sueldo.

22. Sí, pero todavía _____ (valer) la pena ganar más dinero.

Worksheet 6.20 Future tense of *hacer* and *decir*

Two other verbs are irregular in the future tense. **Hacer** and **decir** both drop the letters **c** and **e** before adding the future tense endings.

hacer			
yo	haré	nosotros(as)	haremos
tú	harás	vosotros(as)	haréis
él, ella, usted	hará	ellos, ellas, ustedes	harán

decir			
yo	diré	nosotros(as)	diremos
tú	dirás	vosotros(as)	diréis
él, ella, usted	dirá	ellos, ellas, ustedes	dirán

➤ Supply the future tense of the verbs in parentheses.

1. Yo te _____ (decir) los nombres de los candidatos.

2. Entonces yo _____ (hacer) una lista para los miembros.

3. Yo averiguaré el nombre del joven y se lo _____ (decir).

4. ¿Cuándo _____ (hacer) usted eso?

5. Si le preguntas a Juan, no te _____ (decir) la verdad.

6. Entonces, ¿qué _____ (hacer) nosotros para saberla?

7. Ese dependiente nos _____ (decir) el precio.

8. ¿Qué _____ (hacer) ustedes si no tienen bastante dinero?

9. Nosotros te _____ (decir) el fin del cuento.

10. Tú me _____ (hacer) dichoso si termina felizmente.

11. ¿Me _____ (decir) usted cuándo está lista la cena?

12. Sí, además yo _____ (hacer) mi receta favorita.

13. El juez muy pronto nos _____ (decir) su decisión.

14. Creo que él la _____ (hacer) con poca dificultad.

15. Si escuchas bien, te _____ (decir) el alfabeto griego.

16. ¿Me _____ (hacer) tú también una lista de las letras?

17. ¿Qué _____ (decir) tus padres acerca de esto?

18. No sé, pero ellos me _____ (hacer) decirles la verdad.

19. El profesor nos _____ (decir) nuestras notas el lunes.

20. ¿Por qué les _____ (hacer) esperar hasta entonces?

21. ¿Me _____ (decir) tú lo que yo necesito hacer?

22. Tú _____ (hacer) la ensalada; yo prepararé la carne.

Future tense

➤ For further practice with the future tense, change the subject of the following sentences from **yo** to **él**, and write the subject and verb in the spaces to the right. You may also practice changing the **yo** to **tú, nosotros,** and **ellos.**

1. *Yo volveré* el primero de septiembre. _____

2. *Yo hablaré.* _____

3. *Yo me quedaré* allí dos meses. _____

4. *Yo iré* a Europa en avión a principios de Marzo. _____

5. *Yo traeré* muchos regalos para mis hijos. _____

6. *Yo escribiré* esa carta antes del sábado. _____

7. *Yo saldré* alrededor del dos de agosto. _____

8. *Yo tendré* mucho que hacer pasado mañana. _____

9. *Yo sabré* muy pronto la fecha exacta de la fiesta. _____

10. *Yo haré* todo lo posible para visitar a mis amigos. _____

11. *Yo vendré* aquí a las seis y cuarto. _____

12. *Yo comeré* en un restaurante nuevo esta noche. _____

13. *Yo dejaré* los libros en la mesa. _____

14. *Yo leeré* cinco novelas durante el verano. _____

15. *Yo podré* hacerlo a ratos. _____

16. *Yo diré* solamente la verdad en cuanto al robo. _____

17. *Yo estaré* de vuelta al mediodía. _____

18. *Yo me levantaré* temprano mañana. _____

19. *Yo seré* el mejor alumno de la clase. _____

20. *Yo estudiaré* más de ahora en adelante. _____

21. *Yo empezaré* a estudiar francés el año próximo. _____

22. *Yo pondré* las ciruelas en una canasta. _____

23. *Me las comeré* más tarde. _____

24. *Yo obtendré** los datos necesarios. _____

*Contener, detener, obtener, retener, and sostener are all conjugated the same as **tener.**
The meaning of these verbs becomes clear if **-tener** is translated as *-tain.*

General review

To review regular and irregular verbs in the preterite, imperfect, and future tenses, complete the following columns. Include the subject pronoun with each entry.

PRESENT	PRETERITE	IMPERFECT	FUTURE
1. Yo pongo			
2. Él dice			
3. Ella está			
4. Yo hago			
5. Ellas comen			
6. Tú quieres			
7. Él sabe			
8. Yo vengo			
9. Ella tiene			
10. Usted sale			
11. Tú puedes			
12. Él pone			
13. Yo me acuesto			
14. Tú vas			
15. Ellos salen			
16. Nosotros somos			
17. Yo tengo			
18. Él almuerza			
19. Yo veo			
20. Él pierde			
21. Ella hace			
22. Yo vuelvo			
23. Tú estás			
24. Usted sabe			

Worksheet 6.21 More on articles

Many nouns do not end in **-o.** Furthermore, some nouns ending in **-o** are feminine; some nouns ending in **-a** are masculine. Still others use **él** in the feminine singular. Here are the rules:

1. Some words are exceptions: **la mano, el día, la foto.**
2. Nouns with the suffix **-dad, -tad, -tud, -ción** or **-ez** will be feminine (**la libertad, la realidad, la creación, la niñez**).
3. Nouns beginning with a stressed (**a**) sound, regardless of gender, will use **el** (**el arpa, el hacha, but las arpas, las hachas**).
4. Most Greek derivatives ending in **-ma, -pa, -ta** will be masculine (**el tema, el mapa, el poeta**).
5. Some nouns will change meaning according to gender (**el cometa,** *comet;* **la cometa,** *kite;* **el frente,** *the front part;* **la frente,** *the forehead;* **el policía,** *the police officer;* **la policía,** *police force;* **el papa,** *pope;* **la papa,** *potato;* **la radio,** *radio;* **el radio,** *radium, radius*).

➤ Supply the definite article for each of the following nouns.

1. _____ hambre
2. _____ amistad
3. _____ rapidez
4. _____ hadas
5. _____ loción
6. _____ drama
7. _____ realidad
8. _____ manos
9. _____ prontitud
10. _____ agua
11. _____ condición
12. _____ álgebra
13. _____ amo
14. _____ lealtad
15. _____ hada
16. _____ almeja

17. _____ mapa
18. _____ día
19. _____ actor
20. _____ actriz
21. _____ arte
22. _____ aguas
23. _____ poema
24. _____ ángel
25. _____ timidez
26. _____ acta
27. _____ lentitud
28. _____ posición
29. _____ pared
30. _____ clima
31. _____ verdad
32. _____ armas

Worksheet 6.22 Shortened adjectives (*apócope*)

The following adjectives drop their final -o when preceding the noun they modify: **bueno, malo, uno, alguno (algún), ninguno (ningún), primero, tercero.**

The final -a is not dropped in the following adjectives: **buen chico, buena chica; ningún muchacho, ninguna muchacha; el tercer niño, la tercera niña.**

The adjectives **grande** and **ciento** drop the final syllable before the nouns they modify, regardless of gender:

EXAMPLES: el **gran** hombre, la **gran** mujer; **cien** toros, **cien** vacas

Some adjectives change meaning when moved from the right to the left of the modified noun:

EXAMPLES: | **mujer grande** | *large woman* | **camisa nueva** | *new shirt* |
|---|---|---|---|
| **gran mujer** | *great woman* | **nueva camisa** | *fresh shirt* |
| **soldado pobre** | *penniless soldier* | **único libro** | *only book* |
| **pobre soldado** | *unfortunate soldier* | **libro único** | *unique, unmatched book* |

➤ Supply the proper form of the adjectives in parentheses.

1. (grande) presidente_____

2. (grande) _____ presidente

3. (bueno)_____ día

4. (bueno) _____ días

5. (primero) _____ capítulo

6. (malo) alumno _____

7. (malo) _____ muchacho

8. (nuevo) _____ cortinas

9. (limpio) agua _____

10. (ninguno) _____ nación

11. (alguno) _____ programa

12. (único) actriz _____

13. (ciento) _____ palomas

14. (alguno) _____ manera

15. (ninguno) _____ mapa

16. (grande) _____ señora

17. (tercero) _____ año

18. (tercero)_____ arte

19. (nuevo) iglesia _____

20. (alguno)_____ hombre

21. (uno) _____ chico

22. (uno) _____ chica

23. (grande)_____ reina

24. (primero) _____ rey

Worksheet 6.23 More on shortened adjectives

➤ Move the italicized adjective from the left side to the right side of the modified noun. Be able to explain any change in meaning. In the blanks, write the noun followed by the correct form of the adjective.

1. Mañana será el *primer* día de octubre. _____

2. Aquel vecino siempre fue un *mal* alumno. _____

3. El científico nació en un *gran* país. _____

4. Yo quiero ayudar a esa *pobre* mujer. _____

5. Pronto empezaremos a estudiar el *tercer* libro. _____

6. Por mi parte, no tengo un *gran* apetito. _____

7. El año pasado fue un *buen* año para nosotros. _____

8. La madre del señor Chávez es una *gran* señora. _____

9. Él no tiene un *gran* interés en aprender francés. _____

10. Él tenía la apariencia de una *mala* persona. _____

11. Planeamos una fiesta para el *tercer* día del mes. _____

12. Mañana vamos a estudiar la *tercera* lección. _____

13. Anoche ayudé a un *pobre* hombre en la calle. _____

14. Yo te aseguro que María es una *buena* muchacha. _____

15. Su hermano Guillermo también es un *buen* muchacho. _____

16. El lunes fue el *primer* día de clases. _____

17. Juan no pone un *gran* interés en sus estudios. _____

18. San Francisco tiene un *buen* clima. _____

19. Los Pérez viven en el *tercer* piso del hotel. _____

20. Yo no tengo *ningún* deseo de ir a Europa. _____

21. Mentir es una *mala* costumbre. _____

22. Hoy tuvimos un *buen* día en la escuela. _____

General review

➤ Choose the correct form and write it in the blanks.

1. Hoy es el _____ (primer, primero, primera) día del mes.

2. A mí me gusta mucho _____ (el, la) clima de San Francisco.

3. A ellos _____ (le, les, los) gusta mucho viajar por México.

4. Me dicen que tú eres una _____ (buen, buena) muchacha.

5. Tu hermano es un _____ (buen, bueno) chico también.

6. _____ (Esta, Este) pluma que me prestaste no sirve.

7. _____ (Hay, Había, Habrá) muchos alumnos ausentes mañana.

8. A ti no te gusta la playa _____ (también, tampoco).

9. No vi a _____ (alguien, nadie) en el jardín.

10. Él no tiene _____ (ningún, ninguno) amigo en la escuela.

11. Yo _____ (levantaba, me levantaba) siempre a la misma hora.

12. _____ (Hay, Habrá) mucha actividad en la escuela mañana.

13. Ayer me _____ (encontré, encontraba) con ella en la calle.

14. Colón _____ (llegó, llegaba) a América en 1492.

15. Yo _____ (dormí, me dormí) enseguida anoche.

16. El niño no sabe _____ (vestir, vestirse) sin ayuda.

17. Voy a _____ (acostumbrar, acostumbrarme) a gastar menos.

18. Nosotros empezamos _____ (de, a) estudiar juntos.

19. Yo _____ (fue, fui) anoche al cine con Roberto y Félix.

20. Venezuela es un _____ (gran, grande) país.

21. Estamos un poco cansados _____ (ir, de ir) al mismo sitio.

22. Hay _____ (una, un) mapa grande en la pared del salón.

23. Tú no oyes bien _____ (el profesor, al profesor).

24. Juan no _____ (quise, quiso) ir con nosotros a la feria.

Vocabulary check-up

➤ Choose the correct form or answer and write it in the blank.

1. Si yo hago algo enseguida, lo hago (con dificultad, con poco interés, inmediatamente, despacio).

    _____

2. Lo opuesto de mojado es (grande, seco, ancho, pesado). _____

3. Si digo que Juan se puso bravo, eso quiere decir que Juan (se cayó, se acostó, se enojó, sonrió).

    _____

4. ¿Cuál de estas cosas se encuentra en un restaurante? (caballo, piscina, postre, nubes) _____

5. ¿Cuál de estos verbos está en el presente? (hago, puse, pudo, era) _____

6. Si usted tiene mucho calor, ¿qué hace con su chaqueta?(quitármela, ponérmela, colgarla, limpiarla)

    _____

7. Lo opuesto de ancho es (chico, grande, alto, estrecho). _____

8 ¿Quién le sirve en un restaurante? (piloto, chofer, camarero, médico). _____

9. Un sinónimo de muchacho es (joven, señor, camarero, profesor). _____

10. ¿En que estación del año hace más calor en los Estados Unidos? (primavera, verano, otoño, invierno)

    _____

11. ¿En qué estación del año hace más frío en los Estados Unidos? (primavera, verano, otoño, invierno)

    _____

12. ¿Cuál de estas palabras es masculina? (escuela, pluma, mapa, mesa) _____

13. ¿Cuál de estas palabras es femenina? (brazo, mano, ojo, cuello) _____

14. Si veo a alguien de vez en cuando, lo veo (con frecuencia, nunca, temprano por la mañana, a veces).

    _____

15. Si tengo sueño por la mañana es que necesito (comer, tomar algo, dormir más, levantarme). _____

16. Tal vez es (siempre, quizás, seguramente, nunca). _____

17. Poco a poco quiere decir (rápidamente, al poco rato, temprano, gradualmente). _____

18. ¿Cuál de estos idiomas se habla en el Brasil? (español, francés, italiano, portugués) _____

19. El tercer mes del año es (mayo, marzo, febrero, enero)._____

20. Si hoy es miércoles, que día fue ayer? (lunes, martes, sábado, domingo)_____

21. ¿Cuál de estos países se encuentra al norte de los Estados Unidos? (Venezuela, Cuba, México, Canadá)

    _____

22. ¿Si hoy es martes, que día será pasado mañana? (domingo, lunes, miércoles, jueves)

    _____

Part 7

Contents

Worksheet 7.1 Comparison of adjectives (comparative degree)

English has two ways to form the comparative of adjectives: *pleasanter* (*than*) and *more pleasant* (*than*). Spanish has only one: **más agradable (que).**

EXAMPLES: Juan es **más alto** que su hermano.   *John is taller than his brother.*
Esta calle es **más ancha** que la otra.   *This street is wider than the other.*

Spanish has four forms that are irregular:

bueno	→	**mejor**	*better*	**grande**	→ **mayor**	*bigger, older*
malo	→	**peor**	*worse*	**pequeño**	→ **menor**	*smaller, younger*

➤ In the blanks, supply the comparative degree of the adjective in parentheses, including **más** or **menos** (**que**) when required. Make necessary agreements in number and gender.

1. Estas pirámides son _____ (alto) las pirámides egipcias.

2. Los cocineros franceses son _____ (moderno) los argentinos.

3. Este apartamento es _____ (caro) ciertas casas.

4. Estos ejercicios son _____ (fácil) los de ayer.

5. Nuestro clima es _____ (frío) el de Panamá.

6. Las peras son _____ (dulce) las manzanas.

7. El pudín sabe _____ (bueno) el pastel.

8. La fecha es _____ (importante) la hora.

9. El gato parece _____ (grande) el perro.

10. Sus rosas son _____ (bonito) mis claveles.

11. Tú eres _____ (alta) mis otras amigas.

12. El tigre es _____ (feroz) el león.

13. Los libros son _____ (caros) los de este año.

14. La civilización tolteca es _____ (antiguo) la azteca.

15. Los mosquitos son _____ (pequeños) las moscas.

16. El vestido negro es _____ (popular) el rojo.

17. El coche anda _____ (rápido) el autobús.

18. Según la enfermera, tú te sientes _____ (bueno) nunca.

19. Como alumno, Felipe es _____ (aplicado) yo.

20. La margarina es _____ (saludable) la mantequilla.

21. Caracas es una ciudad _____ (importante) Maracaibo.

22. Las campanas de la iglesia son _____ (grande) la de la escuela.

Worksheet 7.2 Comparison of adjectives (superlative degree)

The superlative form of adjectives generally requires the combination of (1) definite article + (2) noun + (3) **más** + (4) adjective + (5) **de**. The noun can sometimes be omitted. With **mejor, peor, mayor,** and **menor** the word **más** is eliminated:

EXAMPLE: Juan es **el alumno más aplicado de** la clase.   *John is the most studious boy in the class.*
                           (1)   (2)   (3)   (4)   (5)   (1) (3)   (4) (2) (5)

POSITIVE	COMPARATIVE (+ QUE)	SUPERLATIVE (+ DE)
ancha	**más ancha**	**la más ancha**
altos	**más altos**	**los más altos**
buena (mala)	**mejor (peor)**	**la mejor (peor)**
grande (pequeño)	**mayor (menor)**	**la mayor (menor)**

➤ In the blanks at the right, supply the superlative degree of the adjective in parentheses. Make necessary agreements in number and gender, and use **mejor** and **mayor** wherever possible.

(Note these symbols: — add one word; — — add two words;   *definite article already precedes noun)

1. Este jardín es — — (hermoso) de la ciudad.   _____

2. Esta estación es — — (frío) del año.   _____

3. Estos ejercicios son — — (útil) de todo el libro.   _____

4. Como alumno, Juan es — — (malo) de la clase.   _____

5. La fiesta de esta noche va a ser — — (bueno) del año.   _____

6. Tokío es la ciudad* — (poblado) del mundo.   _____

7. Tú eres el alumno* — (diligente) de la clase.   _____

8. Este libro es — — (práctico) de todos.   _____

9. Esta reunión — — (importante) de todo el año.   _____

10. Estas flores son — — (bello) de la estación.   _____

11. Buenos Aires es la ciudad* — (bonito) de la Argentina.   _____

12. El chocolate es el sabor* — (preferido) por los niños.   _____

13. Tú eres la muchacha* — (inteligente) de la clase.   _____

14. Julio es — — (bueno) profesor de la universidad.   _____

15. Esta lección es — — (largo) del libro de español.   _____

16. Estos edificios son — — (moderno) de Caracas.   _____

17. Sudamérica tiene los animales*— (extraño) del mundo.   _____

18. En Colombia se cosecha el café* — (sabroso) que hay.   _____

19. En Egipto se cultiva — — (bueno) algodón del mundo.   _____

20. El Everest es la montaña — — (alto) del mundo.   _____

Worksheet 7.3 More on comparison of adjectives (superlative degree)

➤ For further practice with the superlative degree of adjectives, change the italicized words to the plural.

EXAMPLE: **el traje más nuevo** to **los trajes más nuevos**

1. Compraron *la mejor casa* de la ciudad. _____

2. Estuvimos allí *el peor día* del mes. _____

3. Hicimos *el ejercicio más difícil* del libro. _____

4. Viste *la mejor película* del año. _____

5. Estudiamos en *el aula más grande* de la escuela. _____

6. Alquilaron *el apartamento más lujoso* del edificio. _____

_____

7. Viven en *la casa más hermosa* de la ciudad. _____

8. Estuve en Lima durante *el día más frío* del invierno. _____

9. Tú compraste *el sombrero más bonito* de la tienda. _____

_____

10. Viajamos en *el barco más rápido* de la compañía. _____

11. Visitamos *el museo más importante* de la ciudad. _____

_____

12. Pasé allí *la peor semana* de mi vida. _____

13. Recuerdo bien *el día más feliz* de mi infancia. _____

14. Pagué en ese hotel *el precio más alto* que recuerdo. _____

_____

15. Viven en *el barrio más elegante* de la ciudad. _____

16. Visitamos *el estado más rico* del país. _____

17. Descubriste *el mejor restaurante* de la ciudad. _____

18. Estuvimos en *la ciudad más antigua* de Europa. _____

19. Cruzamos *el río más ancho* de África. _____

20. Escalamos *la montaña más alta* de México.

21. En Guatemala hice *la mejor compra* del viaje. _____

22. Él escribió *la mejor novela* de ese período. _____

Worksheet 7.4 More on comparison of adjectives

The expression **que** (*than*) usually follows the comparative degree; however, **que** is replaced by **de** when it precedes an expression of quantity, kind, class, or place.

EXAMPLE: **más que yo, menos que ayer,** *but* **más de diez, menos de una docena.**

➤ In the blanks, supply **de (del)** or **que,** whichever is correct.

1. Guadalajara es la ciudad más grande _____ Jalisco.

2. Mi cuarto tiene más ventanas _____ la sala.

3. Tú eres mucho más estudioso _____ tus primos.

4. Él habla español mejor _____ su hermano.

5. Tú tienes más _____ diez amigos en la escuela.

6. El señor es más generoso _____ los otros vecinos.

7. Tuvimos que esperar más _____ veinte minutos.

8. Ella vino más temprano _____ los otros maestros.

9. Hicieron más _____ tres viajes a Europa en un año.

10. Ésta es la época más cálida _____ año.

11. Tú estás más pálida hoy _____ nunca.

12. Hoy me siento un poco peor _____ ayer.

13. Estos ejercicios son los más fáciles _____ todo el libro.

14. Ella comió más _____ diez galletas esta tarde.

15. Tuve que esperar más _____ una hora para ver al dentista.

16. París es probablemente más interesante _____ las otras capitales europeas.

17. María y Elena son las mejores alumnas _____ nuestra clase.

18. Estos ejercicios son más fáciles _____ los que acabamos de hacer.

19. Las frutas este año son mejores _____ las del año pasado.

20. Estas rosas son las más bellas _____ jardín.

21. Es el periódico más popular _____ Nicaragua.

22. Ellos son los peloteros más conocidos _____ equipo brasileño.

Worksheet 7.5 Comparison of adverbs

Adverbs are compared the same as adjectives (see page 144):

EXAMPLE: ADJECTIVE: Carlos es **más sincero** que Alberto.
           ADVERB: Carlos habla **más** sinceramente que Alberto.

Bien and **mal** are irregular:

ADJECTIVE		ADVERB		COMPARATIVE DEGREE
bueno (*good*)	or	**bien** (*well*)	=	**mejor** (*better*)
malo (*bad*)	or	**mal** (*badly*)	=	**peor** (*worse*)

➤ In the blanks, supply the comparative form of the adverbs in parentheses.

1. Él habla español _____ (rápidamente) _____ los otros alumnos.

2. Ella puede hacer este trabajo _____ (fácilmente) _____ yo.

3. Juan habla español _____ (mal) _____ los otros miembros de su familia.

4. Le escuchamos_____ (atentamente) _____ sus propios

    amigos.

5. Hoy vinieron a la clase _____ (temprano) _____ ayer.

6. Elena baila mucho _____ (bien) _____ su hermana.

7. Tú estudias ahora_____ (diligentemente)_____ el año

    pasado.

8. Ellos entienden inglés _____ (bien) _____ español.

9. El viejo habla ahora _____ (lentamente)_____ nunca.

10. Parece que él trabaja _____ (cuidadosamente) _____ los

    otros trabajadores.

11. Yo puedo hacer estos ejercicios _____ (rápidamente) _____ antes.

12. Teresa aceptó el fracaso _____ (valientemente) _____ su hermana.

13. Los Pérez nos recibieron _____ (alegremente) de lo_____

    esperábamos.

14. Pablo habla _____ (claramente)_____ los otros estudiantes.

15. Isabel entiende inglés _____ (bien) _____ los demás.

16. Ella habla inglés en la escuela _____ (frecuentemente) _____ en

    casa.

17. Su hermano sabe matemáticas _____ (bien) _____ su hermano.

18. Mi profesor explica la lección _____ (claramente) _____ el de Carmen.

Worksheet 7.6 Comparison of equality (adjectives and adverbs)

In the expressions *as + adjective + as* and *as + adverb + as*, the first *as* will be **tan** and the second *as* will be **como.**

EXAMPLE: *The cat is as big as the dog.*   El gato es **tan grande como** el perro.
My car goes as fast as your truck.   Mi coche anda **tan rápidamente como** tu camión.
Chicago is not as far as Miami.   Chicago no está **tan lejos como** Miami.

➤ In the blanks, supply **tan** and **como** plus the indicated adjective or adverb. Make whatever changes are necessary in gender, number, or form.

1. Aquellas muchachas no son _____ (bonito) _____ éstas.

2. Tú eres casi _____ (alto) _____ tu padre.

3. Esta calle es _____ (ancho) _____ el Paseo de la Reforma.

4. Ellos no son _____ (joven) _____ nosotros.

5. Hoy no estoy _____ (cansado) _____ ayer.

6. Tú hablas español _____ (bueno, bien) _____ los otros alumnos.

7. Él no puede hacer ese trabajo_____ (fácil) _____ ella.

8. Elena no juega tenis _____ (buen, bien) _____ su hermana.

9. Los alumnos son _____ (estudioso)_____ los del año pasado.

10. Ninguna otra revista es _____ (popular) _____ ésta.

11. La hermana mayor no es _____ (inteligente) _____ la menor.

12. Nosotros no somos _____ (rico)_____ los Ramírez.

13. Los estudiantes no leen_____ (rápido) _____ el profesor.

14. Nueva York no es _____ (interesante) _____ Washington.

15. Esta iglesia no es _____ (viejo)_____ la catedral.

16. Las peras no son _____ (sabroso)_____ las manzanas.

17. Los gatos no son _____ (fiel)_____ los perros.

18. Las mujeres no son _____ (alto) _____ los hombres.

19. Esta mesa es_____ (largo) _____ ancha.

20. Este hotel es_____ (bonito) _____ el Palacio Nacional.

21. Ella no es _____ (listo) _____ ustedes creen.

22. Este sillón no es _____ (cómodo) _____ me parecía.

Worksheet 7.7 Comparison of equality (nouns)

In the expressions *as much* (noun) *as* and *as many* (noun) *as*, the first *as* will be **tanto(s)** and the second *as* will be **como**:

EXAMPLES: *My car has as many cylinders as your truck.*
Mi coche tiene **tantos** cilindros **como** tu camión.

The cookies do not contain as much sugar as the candies.
Las galletas no contienen **tanto** azúcar **como** los dulces.

➤ In the blanks, supply **tanto como** plus the necessary noun. Make **tanto** agree in number and gender with the noun that it modifies.

1. Vamos a estar en la biblioteca _____ tiempo _____ mi primo.

2. Mi primo no lee _____ libros _____ yo.

3. Yo tengo_____ amigos_____ mi hermana.

4. Ella no conoce a_____ estudiantes _____ antes.

5. La maestra nos da _____ exámenes _____ la del año pasado.

6. No tenemos que escribir_____ composiciones _____ antes.

7. La clase de español no tiene _____ estudiantes _____ la clase de inglés.

8. Nuestras clases no tienen _____ muchachas _____ muchachos.

9. Esta casa no tiene _____ valor_____ la de ustedes.

10. Mi nueva casa no tiene _____ cuartos_____ la suya.

11. Hoy no hace_____ calor_____ ayer.

12. Este mes no tiene _____ días lluviosos_____ en abril.

13. Estos niños hacen _____ ruido _____ todos los niños.

14. Yo creo que sus juegos causan _____ ruido _____ los de nosotros.

15. No tengo _____ ahorros _____ los vecinos.

16. Tú gastas _____ dinero _____ toda mi familia.

17. Roberto no come_____ dulces _____ su esposa.

18. María come _____ legumbres _____ su marido.

19. Rosa no conoce a_____ pilotos _____ su padre.

20. Ese piloto no tiene_____ horas de vuelo _____ el padre de Rosa.

21. La señora Rivera tiene _____ recetas _____ mi madre.

22. Ella prepara _____ comidas_____ mamá.

Comparison of equality/inequality (adjectives, adverbs, nouns)

➤ Choose the correct form and write it in the blanks.

1. Yo no tomo tantas vacaciones _____ (como, que) tú.

2. Tú vas a ver las ciudades más grandes _____ (de, que) Europa.

3. Los alimentos cuestan _____ (menos, la menos) aquí que allí.

4. Este año gastarás más dinero _____ (como, que) antes.

5. Yo pasaré más _____ (que, de) una semana en Madrid.

6. Visitaré los museos _____ (más, los más) famosos.

7. Los edificios son más antiguos _____ (de, que) los de Chicago.

8. Me sentiré _____ (tan, tanto) afortunado como nadie.

9. Comeré en _____ (mejores, los mejores) restaurantes europeos.

10. Este hotel es el más moderno _____ (de, en) Madrid.

11. Más que _____ (algo, nada) quiero comprar recuerdos típicos.

12. En California no hay tantas guitarras buenas como _____ (de, en) Valencia.

13. Alemania tiene más tránsito_____ (como, que) España.

14. España tiene tanto tránsito _____ (como, que) Italia.

15. Los europeos son _____ (tan, más) corteses que los americanos.

16. No hay parques más bonitos _____ (de, que) los de París.

17. La industria del norte es mayor _____ (de, que) la del sur.

18. La música del sur es _____ (tan, más) bonita que la del norte.

19. Tijuana tiene más plazas de toros_____(como, que) Guadalajara.

20. Yo voy a visitar más _____ (que, de) ocho países en un mes.

21. Mi esposa leyó _____ (tantos, más) folletos sobre Lisboa como yo.

22. Saldremos para Lisboa en el avión más moderno _____ (como, que) hay.

General review

➤ Select the correct form and write it in the blanks.

1. Empezamos _____ (estudiar, a estudiar) la historia de México.

2. Guadalupe Victoria fue el _____ (primer, primero) presidente de México.

3. _____ (Las, Los) problemas del gobierno eran difíciles.

4. Victoria tuvo _____ (de, que) unificar el país.

5. México trató _____ (de, a) evitar más guerras.

6. _____ (Algún, Alguna) día viajaré a Venezuela.

7. _____ (El, La) clima de Caracas es muy agradable.

8. Visitaré _____ (un primo, a un primo) que vive allí.

9. Él _____ (me, mi) prometió llevar a todas partes.

10. _____ (Conoceré, Sabré) muy bien Caracas.

11. Mi casa es más grande que _____ (el, la) de Federico.

12. Mi casa tiene más _____ (que, de) cuatro cuartos.

13. Tu casa tiene _____ (tan, tantos) pisos como la mía.

14. Las _____ (mejor, mejores) casas tienen tres baños.

15. La piscina no es tan importante _____ (que, como) la cocina.

16. Mi universidad ofrece _____ (muchos, muchas) deportes.

17. _____ (Había, Habrá) un juego de béisbol mañana.

18. _____ (Sé, No sé) nada de béisbol.

19. Yo _____ (asisto, asisto a) todos los juegos de fútbol.

20. Nuestro equipo ganará más juegos _____ (que, de) nunca.

21. Miguel salió del trabajo a _____ (eso, ese) de las tres.

22. Él trabaja en una tienda cerca _____ (del, al) estadio.

23. Yo sé muy poco _____ (cerca, acerca) de su trabajo.

24. _____ (Algún, Algunos) estudiantes necesitan trabajar.

25. A otros sólo _____ (los, les) interesa la experiencia.

Worksheet 7.8 The definite article

Some uses of the definite article differ from English.

ENGLISH:	*The book*	refers to a specific book
SPANISH:	**El** libro	refers to a book in general
EXAMPLES:	**La** madera es útil.	*Wood* (not *the wood*) *is useful.*
	El oro es caro.	*Gold* (not *the gold*) *is expensive.*

The definite article is used in telling time and in identifying days:

EXAMPLES:	Es **la** una.	*It is one o'clock.*
	Llegaron **el** martes.	*They arrived on Tuesday.*
	Les pagamos **los** viernes.	*We pay them on Fridays.*
(*but*)	La fiesta es (*fue, era, será*) el viernes.	*The party is* (*was, will be*) *Friday.*

➤ In the blanks, supply the necessary article. If no article is required, simply place an X in the blank.

1. Según el calendario, hoy es _____ domingo.

2. Yo paso _____ domingos con mi familia.

3. Mi hermano siempre llega a _____ dos.

4. ¿Qué piensas hacer _____ domingo que viene?

5. Hoy me desperté a _____ cinco de la mañana.

6. No me levanté porque hoy es_____ sábado.

7. Yo nunca trabajo _____ sábados.

8. Me dormí otra vez y me despertaron a _____ ocho.

9. El despertador sonó a _____ siete y media.

10. Fue _____ lunes de la Semana Santa.

11. A _____ ocho y cuarto estaba en el coche.

12. A _____ una de la tarde empecé a pescar en el Lago Superior.

13. Más que nada me gusta _____ chocolate mexicano.

14. También me gustan _____ frijoles.

15. Yo cubro los frijoles con _____ queso.

16. Así es _____ almuerzo mexicano.

17. _____ oro es un metal precioso.

18. Personalmente, prefiero _____ plata.

19. Ayer me compré un anillo de _____ plata.

20. Ayer fue _____ viernes, ¿verdad?

21. La paloma es el símbolo de _____ paz.

22. La paloma es más tímida que _____ águila.

23. Parece que _____ paloma siempre tiene sueño.

24. _____ búho en cambio simboliza la sabiduría.

Worksheet 7.9 More on the definite article

Two other uses of the definite article that differ from English usage are:

1. The definite article is used with the names of languages, except after the verbs such as **aprender, estudiar, hablar, saber,** and after the preposition **en:**

   EXAMPLE: El español es fácil, pero el ruso es difícil.
               Ya saben español, ahora quieren aprender francés.

2. Certain countries, cities and states require the definite article:

la Argentina	el Canadá	la Florida	el Japón	el Perú
el Brasil	el Ecuador	La Habana	el Paraguay	la República Dominicana
el Cairo	los Estados Unidos	la India	La Paz	El Salvador

➤ In the blanks, supply the definite article. Where no article is required, place an X in the blank.

1. Buenos Aires es la capital de _____ Argentina.

2. Pasaste cuatro meses en _____ Habana.

3. Vamos a hacer un viaje a _____ México.

4. Vivieron en _____ Perú muchos años.

5. Dicen que _____ español es el idioma más bello del mundo.

6. Después de aprender _____ español, él piensa estudiar alemán.

7. Dicen que _____ inglés es más difícil de aprender que el francés.

8. _____ Brasil es el país más grande de Sudamérica.

9. Las cataratas del Niágara están en _____ Canadá.

10. Ellos vivían en Indiana; ahora viven en _____ Florida.

11. El señor Forti y su esposa siempre hablan en _____ italiano.

12. El año que viene van a hacer un viaje a _____ Italia.

13. El avión hace escala en _____ República Dominicana.

14. _____ inglés es un idioma práctico porque es muy comercial.

15. En cambio, _____ francés es el idioma diplomático.

16. _____ Japón se compone de varias islas.

17. Para muchos turistas _____ India es un país misterioso.

18. _____ Cairo es la capital de Egipto.

19. Los mayas aún viven en _____ Guatemala.

20. La unidad monetaria de _____ España era la peseta y ahora es el euro.

21. El sucre es la unidad monetaria en _____ Ecuador.

22. _____ chino es un idioma monosilábico.

Worksheet 7.10 More on the definite article

Three other special uses of the definite article include:

1. Before personal titles (except in direct address).

   EXAMPLE: Señora López, ¿conoce usted a **la** señora Medina?

2. To avoid repetition of an earlier word a definite article may become a pronoun.
   In English similar use is made of *that* and *those*.

   EXAMPLE: Tu novela es menos larga que **las** de Hemingway.

3. Instead of possessive adjectives (**mi, tu, su, nuestro**) with parts of the body or articles of clothing.

   EXAMPLES: El niño no quiere lavarse **las** manos.
   Los boxeadores se pusieron **los** guantes.

➤ In the blanks, supply the necessary definite article. If no article is required, place an X in the blank.

1. Buenos días, _____ señora Noguera.

2. Buenos días. ¿Está en casa _____ señora Ríos?

3. Tu coche es muy bonito, _____ tío Luis.

4. Sí, pero _____ de tu padre es más nuevo.

5. ¿Por qué te pusiste _____ impermeable?

6. _____ tía Mercedes dice que va a llover.

7. ¿No te quitas _____ guantes antes de comer?

8. ¿Sí, y tú, no te quitas _____ sombrero?

9. ¿Prefieres las manzanas de Ohio o _____ del estado de Washington?

10. La fruta que me gusta más es _____ de Washington.

11. ¿Es éste el libro que te prestó _____ senador Romero?

12. No, ya le devolví _____ del senador.

13. ¿Cómo te lastimaste _____ dedo pulgar?

14. Lo hice con el martillo. Voy a perder _____ uña.

15. Se escribieron muchos romances sobre _____ aventurero Casanova.

16. ¿Te manchaste _____ vestido nuevo con café?

17. Sí, también me quemé _____ rodilla.

18. ¿Es ésta la compañera de _____ hermanos García?

19. No, _____ de ellos está arriba en el primer piso.

20. ¿Te vas a poner _____ corbata que te regalé?

21. No, esta otra es más apropiada que _____ que me compraste tú.

Worksheet 7.11 Verbs ending in *-cer*

Verbs ending in *-cer* preceded by a vowel have **-zco** as the ending in the first person singular of the present indicative (**conozco, ofrezco**). **Hacer,** which uses **hago,** is a common exception. Useful **-cer** verbs include:

agradecer	*to thank*	**desaparecer**	*to disappear*	**obedecer**	*to obey*
aparecer	*to appear*	**enloquecer**	*to drive crazy*	**ofrecer**	*to offer*
carecer	*to lack*	**establecer**	*to establish*	**parecer**	*to seem*
complacer	*to please*	**fallecer**	*to die*	**parecerse a**	*to resemble*
conocer	*to know*	**merecer**	*to deserve*	**perecer**	*to perish*
crecer	*to grow*	**nacer**	*to be born*	**pertenecer**	*to belong*

➤ Supply the present tense of the verbs in parentheses.

1. Yo te _____ (agradecer) mucho este bonito libro.

2. Tú lo _____ (merecer) por ser estudioso.

3. Yo no _____ (conocer) al autor del libro.

4. Él _____ (pertenecer) al siglo pasado.

5. Yo siempre _____ (obedecer) a mis jefes.

6. Pero a veces yo _____ (enloquecerse) con tanta tarea.

7. Yo _____ (complacer) a mis amigos.

8. Me _____ (parecer) muy importante la educación.

9. Si hay trabajo, los perezosos_____ (desaparecer).

10. Piensan que nosotros _____ (nacer) para divertirnos.

11. En mi casa yo _____ (establecer) varias reglas.

12. La disciplina _____ (ofrecer) muchas ventajas.

13. Papá dice que yo _____ (parecerse) a mi abuelo.

14. Abuelito me _____ (parecer) mucho más alto.

15. Sin embargo, yo _____ (reconocer) el parecido.

16. Yo no _____ (carecer) de buenos libros en mi casa.

17. Algunos bomberos _____ (fallecer) en su trabajo.

18. Sus nombres _____ (aparecer) en el periódico.

19. Yo _____ (reconocer) el peligro de su trabajo.

20. Yo les _____ (agradecer) la protección que nos dan.

Worksheet 7.12 Verbs ending in -*cir*

Verbs ending in -**cir** preceded by a vowel have -**zco** as the ending in the first person singular of the present indicative. **Decir,** which uses **digo,** is a common exception.

EXAMPLES: yo produ**zco**, yo introdu**zco**

Some common -**cir** verbs include:

conducir	to conduct	**producir**	to produce
deducir	to deduce	**reducir**	to reduce
introducir	to introduce	**relucir**	to glow, glitter
inducir	to induce	**traducir**	to translate
lucir(se)	to look (*like*); to show off		

➤ Supply the correct present tense of the verbs in parentheses.

1. Cada idioma _____ (producir) este proverbio:

2. «No es oro todo lo que _____ (relucir).»

3. Yo _____ (traducir) la poesía española al inglés.

4. Yo _____ (producir) ahora el segundo tomo de poesías.

5. Juana _____ (lucir) su anillo de compromiso.

6. Ella _____ (introducir) el dedo en la jaula del pájaro.

7. Los testigos _____ (deducir) tu inocencia.

8. Ellos dicen que tú _____ (conducir) muy bien el autobús.

9. Los ejercicios _____ (producir) un cuerpo más sano.

10. Con ejercicio yo _____ (reducir) el riesgo de un ataque cardíaco.

11. Hace veinte años que él _____ (conducir) un taxi.

12. ¿Cómo _____ (lucir, yo) con este sombrero?

13. ¿Cómo se _____ (traducir) el verbo *inducir*?

14. Yo lo _____ (traducir) con el verbo *to induce*.

15. Los lugares altos me _____ (producir) vértigo.

16. Yo _____ (reducir) el efecto con un medicamento.

17. Yo siempre _____ (introducir) un producto nuevo en la feria.

18. Nosotros _____ (producir) algo nuevo anualmente.

19. ¿Por qué _____ (relucir) tanto estos diamantes?

20. Yo los _____ (lucir) sólo en las grandes ocasiones.

21. Por la evidencia, yo _____ (deducir) que no eres culpable.

22. Además, ya sabes que yo siempre _____ (decir) la verdad.

Worksheet 7.13 *Conocer/saber*

Conocer and **saber** both mean *to know*. **Conocer** means to know in the sense of being familiar with a person or place—in other words, to be acquainted with. **Conocer** in the preterite tense means *met*. **Saber** means *to know* in the sense of knowing how to do something or to know as a fact.

EXAMPLES: **Conozco** Cuba.   *I know (am familiar with) Cuba.*
             Conozco a Sara.   *I know (am acquainted with) Sara.*
             Yo **sé** nadar.   *I know how to swim.*

➤ In the blanks, supply the correct form of **saber** or **conocer**, whichever is required for proper meaning.

1. Mis tíos _____ bien la ciudad de La Habana.

2. ¿ _____ ellos también llegar a las pirámides?

3. Yo _____ muy bien a tu padre.

4. ¿ _____ usted que él fue piloto durante la guerra?

5. Mi hermana _____ a muchos estudiantes mexicanos.

6. Es porque ella _____ hablarles en español.

7. Yo viví en Inglaterra, pero yo no _____ Irlanda.

8. ¿Tú _____ que Irlanda está muy cerca de Inglaterra?

9. Ayer yo _____ al senador de Arizona en una fiesta.

10. Yo no _____ que ibas a fiestas tan importantes.

11. Yo no _____ a aquel muchacho cerca del escritorio.

12. Yo tampoco _____ su nombre.

13. En mi juventud yo _____ muy bien el estado de Colorado.

14. Nosotros no _____ que viviste allí.

15. Mañana _____ al novio de mi hermana.

16. Tú pronto _____ la fecha de la boda.

17. ¿Cómo se llama ella? Yo no la _____.

18. Se llama Susana. Yo no _____ su apellido.

19. ¿Cómo _____ tú al director de la escuela?

20. Pues, ¿no _____ tú que mis hijos estudian allí?

21. ¿ _____ usted quién es esa secretaria tan bonita?

22. Sí, la _____ bien. Es mi esposa.

Worksheet 7.14 Command form (imperative mood)—familiar

The affirmative familiar commands in the singular, familiar (**tú**)* form are the same as the third person singular of the present indicative tense: **habla, come, escribe.**

There are eight frequently used exceptions (all monosyllabic):

decir	di	salir	sal
hacer	haz	ser	sé
ir	ve	tener	ten
poner	pon	venir	ven

Although **tú** is always the subject of these verbs, it is usually omitted.

➤ Supply the singular imperative familiar command.

1. _____ (Hacer) las tareas en casa.

2. _____ (Estudiar) bien todos estos ejercicios.

3. _____ (Leer) los ejercicios en voz alta.

4. _____ (Escribir) una composición para mañana.

5. _____ (Esperar) hasta mañana.

6. _____ (Venir) lo más temprano posible.

7. _____ (Comprar) hoy los billetes.

8. _____ (Cerrar) la puerta al salir, por favor.

9. _____ (Ir) con ellos a la fiesta.

10. _____ (Prestar) este libro a Margarita, por favor.

11. _____ (Decir) siempre la verdad.

12. _____ (Poner) estas cosas en la gaveta de mi escritorio.

13. _____ (Tener) cuidado al cruzar la calle.

14. _____ (Escribir) a la compañía sobre ese asunto.

15. _____ (Llevar) cuenta de los gastos de viaje.

16. No _____ (permitir) fumar a los alumnos.

17. _____ (Comprar) otro escritorio igual para la otra oficina.

18. _____ (Tomar) un taxi si hay que llegar pronto.

19. _____ (Caminar) más despacio porque el piso está mojado.

20. _____ (Llevar) este paquete al correo.

21. Juan, _____ (poner) más atención a mi explicación.

22. No _____ (mezclar) tus libros con los de Miguel.

* The plural affirmative familiar commands (**hablad, comed, escribid**) are not used in Latin America.

Worksheet 7.15 Command form (imperative mood)—polite

Both affirmative and negative polite commands in the singular form are based on the **usted** form in the present tense, except that the **-a** and **-e** endings trade places (use the first person singular stem of all present tense irregular verbs ending in **-o**):

PRESENT TENSE	ENDING EXCHANGE	POLITE COMMAND
usted habla	a to e	**hable**
usted come	e to a	**coma**
usted escribe	e to a	**escriba**
usted trae (traigo)	e to a	**traiga**
usted pone (pongo)	e to a	**ponga**
usted conduce (conduzco)	e to a	**conduzca**
usted es (soy)*	*Does not apply*	**sea**
usted está (estoy)*	*Does not apply*	**esté**
usted da (doy)*	*Does not apply*	**dé**
usted va (voy)*	*Does not apply*	**vaya**
usted sabe (sé)*	*Does not apply*	**sepa**

*There is no rule for the five irregular verbs whose first person singular does not end in **-o.** These five polite commands must be memorized.

➤ Supply the singular imperative polite command.

1. _____ (Ir) a la biblioteca para leer sobre los dinosaurios.

2. _____ (Comer) más despacio.

3. _____ (Dar) estos libros a la maestra, por favor.

4. _____ (Escribir) su nombre y dirección.

5. _____ (Cerrar) la puerta con llave al salir de casa.

6. _____ (Ser) siempre lo más aplicado posible en sus clases.

7. _____ (Traer) sus documentos mañana.

8. _____ (Estar) aquí el sábado a la una en punto de la tarde.

9. _____ (Poner) su chaqueta en el ropero.

10. _____ (Hablar) más alto al leer su informe.

11. _____ (Conducir) con más cuidado o chocará con otro coche.

12. _____ (Ir) a la farmacia con esta receta, por favor.

13. _____ (Salir) a tiempo para no llegar tarde al aeropuerto.

14. _____ (Pedir) un aumento de sueldo.

15. _____ (Decir) la verdad y no tiene que preocuparse.

16. _____ (Venir) a mi casa el domingo y hablaremos más.

17. _____ (Llevar) estos platos sucios a la cocina.

18. _____ (Vivir) más económicamente y ahorrará más.

19. _____ (Volver) pronto a Los Ángeles e iremos a Disneylandia.

20. _____ (Hacer) menos ruido o nos echarán de la biblioteca.

21. _____ (Seguir) con esas lecciones y cantará como Plácido Domingo.

22. _____ (Pintar) su casa y lucirá mucho mejor.

Worksheet 7.16 Command form (imperative mood)—plural

In Latin America, familiar and polite commands are the same in the plural. Simply add **-n** to the singular polite command [see page 160]:

SINGULAR FAMILIAR	SINGULAR POLITE	PLURAL FAMILIAR AND POLITE
Habla más despacio.	Hable más despacio.	**Hablen** más despacio.
Come estas uvas.	Coma estas uvas.	**Coman** estas uvas.
Escribe menos cartas.	Escriba menos cartas.	**Escriban** menos cartas.
Ve a la tienda.	Vaya a la tienda.	**Vayan** a la tienda.
Ten cuidado.	Tenga cuidado.	**Tengan** cuidado.
Sé bueno.	Sea bueno.	**Sean** buenos.

➤ In the blanks, supply the polite plural command of the verb in parentheses.

1. _____ (Ir) a la pizarra con la tarea para hoy.

2. _____ (Escribir) las respuestas correctas.

3. _____ (Devolver) estos libros a la biblioteca mañana.

4. _____ (Saludar) a la bibliotecaria de mi parte.

5. _____ (Venir) con nosotros al cine esta noche.

6. _____ (Traer) bastante dinero para cenar después del cine.

7. _____ (Tomar) más café o té si quieren.

8. _____ (Pedir) un refresco para los niños.

9. _____ (Abrir) los libros de ejercicios en la página 72.

10. _____ (Tener) mucho cuidado al hacer estos ejercicios.

11. _____ (Vender) su automóvil al mejor precio posible.

12. _____ (Usar) el dinero para comprarse otro mejor.

13. _____ (Poner) los vasos en la mesa.

14. _____ (Tener) cuidado. Se rompen fácilmente.

15. _____ (Recordar) que mañana es la fiesta de cumpleaños.

16. _____ (Invitar) a sus novias también. Hay lugar para todos.

17. _____ (Limpiar) bien la madera antes de pintarla.

18. _____ (Dar) una segunda mano de pintura a toda la casa.

19. _____ (Abrir) primero el regalo más grande.

20. _____ (Agradecer) a los invitados su generosidad.

Worksheet 7.17 Command form (imperative mood)— with one object pronoun

If a direct object pronoun is used in an affirmative command, it is attached to the verb, forming a single word:

EXAMPLES: Cierra la puerta. **Ciérrala.**   Cierre la puerta. **Ciérrela.**
Trae los libros. **Tráelo.**   Traiga los libros. **Tráigalos.**

➤ In the blanks, copy the verb (familiar and polite commands) and replace the italicized phrase by attaching the appropriate pronoun. Be sure to add, if needed, a written accent mark.

1. Lleve *estos libros* al otro cuarto. _____

2. Espere *al señor Gómez* arriba en su oficina. _____

3. Haga *el trabajo* como le enseñé ayer. _____

4. Lea *el artículo* en voz alta. _____

5. Ponga *este cuaderno* en la gaveta de mi escritorio. _____

6. Pida *la cuenta* al regreso del mesero. _____

7. Limpie *las ventanas* antes de la fiesta del sábado. _____

8. Traiga *las maletas* a mi cuarto. _____

9. Ponga *los refrescos* sobre la mesa. _____

10. Espere a *la señora de Pérez* dentro de la tienda. _____

11. Compre *el anillo* para su novia. _____

12. Revise *la cuenta* antes de pagarla. _____

13. Eche *esta carta* al buzón. _____

14. Manda *las cartas* en seguida. _____

15. Cierra *la puerta* al salir del apartamento. _____

16. Lava *las cortinas y la persianas* otra vez. _____

17. Vende *los automóviles* lo más pronto posible. _____

18. Escriban *sus composiciones* con tinta, por favor. _____

19. Preparen *sus tareas* con más cuidado. _____

20. Compren *los billetes* en el centro. _____

21. Lleven *estas revistas* a sus amigos en la sala. _____

22. Lleven *al niño* con ustedes al circo. _____

Worksheet 7.18 Command form (imperative mood)— with two object pronouns

If a command has both an indirect and a direct object pronoun, the indirect object will always precede the direct, and both will be attached to the verb. Be sure to place written accent marks properly. If both pronouns begin with the letter **l**, change the first pronoun to **se**:

EXAMPLES: Traiga **el café** (a nosotros) ahora.   Tráiga**noslo** ahora.
Lea **el artículo** (a mí) en voz alta.   Léa**melo** en voz alta.
Manda **esta carta** (a ella) enseguida.   Mánda**sela** enseguida.

➤ Change the noun and the words in parentheses to object pronouns and attach them properly to the verb.

1. Traiga _____ (a mí) (el periódico).

2. Lleva _____ (a él) (estos libros) ahora.

3. Lean _____ (a mí) (sus composiciones) en voz alta.

4. Escriba _____ (a él) (la carta) esta tarde.

5. Traiga _____ (a nosotros) (agua mineral) con la comida.

6. Envíe _____ (a ella) (el mensaje) enseguida.

7. Dé _____ (a mí) (esos papeles) ahora mismo.

8. Devuelve _____ (a mí) (esos papeles) hoy, si puedes.

9. Lleven _____ (a ella) (estas revistas), por favor.

10. Repita _____ (a él) (la dirección de su oficina).

11. Diga _____ (a ellas) (la verdad).

12. Lleve _____ (a ellos) (las maletas) a sus cuartos.

13. Abra _____ (para ella) (este paquete).

14. Diga _____ (a nosotras) (lo que ocurrió ayer).

15. Cuente _____ (a mí) (su chiste favorito).

16. Venda _____ (a él) (el coche) enseguida.

17. Enseña _____ (a nosotros) (tu vestido nuevo).

18. Cante _____ (para nosotros) (su nueva canción).

19. Mande _____ (a mí) (la cuenta de ellos).

20. Construya _____ (para ellos) (una casa original).

21. Diga _____ (a los soldados) (las órdenes del día).

22. Lee _____ (a mi tía) (el telegrama que recibiste).

Worksheet 7.19 Command form (imperative mood)—negative familiar/polite

Although object pronouns are attached to the end of affirmative commands, these same object pronouns precede the negative command and are detached from the verb. The same applies to reflexive pronouns. Note that the familiar verb form also changes in the negative, becoming the same as the affirmative polite command plus **-s**. The polite verb form, however, remains exactly the same in both affirmative and negative forms:

EXAMPLES:	AFFIRMATIVE	NEGATIVE		AFFIRMATIVE	NEGATIVE
	Tómelo ahora.	No lo tome ahora.		Dínoslas.	No nos las digas.
	Tómalo ahora.	No lo tomes ahora.		Levántate.	No te levantes.
	Díganoslas.	No nos las diga.		Dáselo.	No se lo des.

➤ Change the following affirmative commands to the negative form. Write the word **no**, the object pronoun(s), and the negative command in the spaces to the right.

1. Hágalos en la clase. _____

2. Llévalo a tu casa. _____

3. Escríbale la carta ahora. _____

4. Tráigame esa revista vieja. _____

5. Pónganlos sobre la mesa. _____

6. Enséñeselas a ella. _____

7. Quítese la chaqueta. _____

8. Ciérralas antes de salir. _____

9. Pónganselos ahora. _____

10. Espérenme después de la clase. _____

11. Dígame lo que pasó. _____

12. Cuéntamelo ahora. _____

13. Véndemelos a buen precio. _____

14. Dígame la verdad. _____

15. Piénsalo antes de hacerlo. _____

16. Píntela de negro. _____

17. Enciéndamela ahora. _____

18. Inscríbete en ese curso. _____

19. Quítatelos antes de comer. _____

20. Repítesela al chofer. _____

21. Llévalo al cine esta tarde. _____

22. Désela al niño. _____

Worksheet 7.20 Adjectives without -*o* ending

As we know, adjectives ending in a consonant remain the same in both genders (**un libro fácil, una canción fácil, cursos fáciles**). Some adjectives that end in **-an, -ón,** or **-or** add **-a** to the feminine form.

EXAMPLES: burl**ón**   burlon**a**
             trabajad**or**   trabajador**a**
             hablad**or**   hablador**a**

Most adjectives of nationality must end in **-a** in the feminine regardless of the masculine ending.

EXAMPLES: francés   frances**a**
             español   español**a**

➤ In the blanks, supply the correct form of the adjectives in parentheses.

1. Elena es una muchacha muy _____ (trabajador).

2. Estos alumnos _____ (alemán) son muy aplicados.

3. La bandera _____ (español) es muy bonita.

4. Ella siempre tiene una expresión _____ (burlón).

5. En la bahía había muchos barcos _____ (inglés).

6. A mí me gusta mucho la lengua_____ (español).

7. En cambio, el idioma _____ (portugués) parece difícil.

8. Aquella muchacha alta es _____ (holandés).

9. La señora Chávez es muy _____ (hablador).

10. Mi hermana menor es muy _____ (juguetón).

11. La señora García es una mujer _____ (encantador).

12. En frente de nosotros vive una familia _____ (irlandés).

13. Tú tienes muchas amigas _____ (turco).

14. Los dos hermanos son muy _____ (trabajador).

15. Los dos alumnos nuevos son _____ (finlandés).

16. Su máquina de coser es _____ (japonés).

17. La criada es muy _____ (hablador).

18. La película que vimos es _____ (francés).

19. La perrita es muy _____ (juguetón).

20. En esa tienda venden artículos _____ (español).

21. Ella es una artista _____ (escocés).

22. Dicen que la cerveza _____ (alemán) es mejor que ésta.

Buscapalabras grande

➤ Find 66 nouns by searching in all eight possible directions. Many spaces are used two or three times; nine are not used at all. See how many you can find before checking the list on the next page:

```
A  P  O  L  L  O  S  R  A  Q  U  E  T  A  C
R  U  I  D  O  A  N  I  L  O  C  A  Z  N  O
T  E  D  I  T  O  R  O  L  O  M  N  D  A  R
I  N  F  E  E  O  U  F  I  L  A  O  O  L  R
C  T  E  R  M  I  N  O  M  D  A  R  L  A  I
U  E  L  E  I  N  G  E  N  I  E  R  O  I  D
L  L  M  A  S  G  R  U  M  M  O  A  R  P  A
O  E  O  L  T  L  E  O  I  E  L  C  U  S  R
A  F  P  M  E  E  A  R  L  T  L  A  M  E  T
E  O  O  A  R  S  P  L  A  O  A  R  T  E  E
S  N  E  M  I  R  C  C  G  D  C  R  I  E  L
P  O  T  R  O  S  O  O  R  O  O  E  R  O  M
E  C  A  R  E  R  B  M  O  N  R  R  O  A  O
J  O  A  I  A  O  R  I  T  M  O  A  R  R  T
O  L  L  M  C  D  E  D  U  T  N  L  O  R  O
C  A  O  A  A  M  A  A  L  M  A  C  E  N  R
```

Worksheet 7.21 Rodeo de palabras

If you failed to circle all 66 nouns in the previous lesson, check the following list, then return to the puzzle to look for the words still missing. As each of those words is located, write its meaning in the blank to the right. If you do not know the meaning, check the vocabulary.

alma _____	espía _____	olla _____
almacén _____	fila _____	onza _____
arpa _____	guitarra _____	oro _____
arte _____	idea _____	oso _____
artículo _____	ingeniero _____	poeta _____
boca _____	inglés _____	pollo _____
cama _____	lana _____	primero _____
carrera _____	letra _____	puente _____
carro _____	loro _____	raqueta _____
cobre _____	lote _____	refrigerador _____
cola _____	luto _____	riel _____
colina _____	mar _____	rima _____
color _____	memoria _____	río _____
comida _____	metal _____	risa _____
coro _____	método _____	ritmo _____
corrida _____	milagro _____	ruido _____
crimen _____	milla _____	silla _____
danza _____	misterio _____	taco _____
dolor _____	motor _____	teléfono _____
editor _____	nombre _____	tema _____
entrada _____	norte _____	término _____
espejo _____	ola _____	torre _____

Part 8

Contents

Worksheet 8.1 Use of *hace*

In expressions involving time, besides the present perfect, Spanish has another method for identifying an action, a state, or condition that began in the past and continues in the present. Compare the English and Spanish approaches:

EXAMPLE: *I have been studying Spanish for three years.* (Present progressive tense)
He estudiado español por tres años. (Present perfect)
Hace tres años que estudio español. (Simple present tense)
(Literally: *It makes three years that I study Spanish.*)

➤ Supply the present tense form of the verbs in parentheses.

1. *Hace* más de un mes que ella _____ (estar) enferma.

2. *Hace* dos años que él _____ (vivir) en Caracas.

3. *Hace* muchos años que nosotros _____ (ser) buenos amigos.

4. *Hace* un mes que Enrique _____ (estar) en el hospital.

5. *Hace* diez años que ellos _____ (vivir) en esta casa.

6. *Hace* solamente un mes que nosotros nos _____ (conocer).

7. *Hace* tres años que él _____ (ser) presidente de la compañía.

8. *Hace* más de dos semanas que tú no _____ (venir) a tus clases.

9. *Hace* varios años que mi vecino _____ (dar) clases de español.

10. *Hace* media hora que los niños _____ (jugar) en el parque.

11. *Hace* casi dos meses que mi tío no nos _____ (escribir).

12. *Hace* once años que tú _____ (vivir) en el Perú.

13. *Hace* mucho tiempo que su padre _____ (buscar) trabajo.

14. *Hace* dos años que él _____ (tocar) la flauta.

15. *Hace* más de un mes que yo no _____ (ver) a Raquel.

16. *Hace* menos de un año que ella _____ (bailar) profesionalmente.

17. *Hace* tres años que él _____ (estudiar) español.

18. *Hace* más de un mes que nosotros no _____ (ir) al cine.

19. *Hace* tiempo que yo no _____ (cenar) fuera de casa.

20. *Hace* tres días que tú _____ (tener) el mismo dolor de cabeza.

21. ¿Cuánto tiempo *hace* que Juan no _____ (venir) a vernos?

22. *Hace* mucho tiempo que nosotros no _____ (salir) de noche.

Worksheet 8.2 Present perfect tense (*pretérito perfecto*)

The present perfect tense is formed with the present tense of the auxiliary verb **haber** followed by the past participle of the main verb.

The present tense of the verb **haber** is conjugated:

Regular past participles are formed from the infinitive. Change the -**ar** ending to -**ado** (**hablado, contestado**). Change the -**er** and -**ir** endings to -**ido** (**comido, traído, vivido, recibido**). The past participle, as a verb, never changes form.

haber			
yo	he	nosotros(as)	hemos
tú	has	vosotros(as)	habéis
él, ella, usted	ha	ellos, ellas, ustedes	han

EXAMPLE: **he hablado**   **hemos hablado**
          has hablado   **habéis hablado**
          ha hablado   **han hablado**

➤ Change the following verbs from the present tense to the present perfect tense.

1. Yo estudio _____

2. Él habla _____

3. Ella viene _____

4. Vivimos _____

5. Regresan _____

6. Tú viajas _____

7. Ella busca _____

8. Te acuestas _____

9. Se levanta _____

10. Yo traigo _____

11. Usted gana _____

12. Julio da _____

13. Tú vas _____

14. Nadie sabe _____

15. Juan toma _____

16. Me cepillo _____

17. Él cierra _____

18. Tú vives _____

19. Ellos van _____

20. Él aprende _____

21. Yo tengo _____

22. Ellos salen _____

23. Tú eres _____

24. Ella está _____

25. Él puede ir _____

26. Ana estudia _____

27. Tú duermes _____

28. Ella canta _____

29. Usted baila _____

30. Me gusta _____

31. Él empieza _____

32. Tú compras _____

33. Yo leo _____

34. Yo insisto _____

35. Yo conozco _____

36. Él quiere _____

37. Trabajan _____

38. Tú preparas _____

39. Yo sé _____

40. Él se viste _____

Worksheet 8.3 More on the present perfect tense

The present perfect tense in Spanish is used to describe a recently completed action or one that began in the past and continues in the present:

EXAMPLES: **He comprado** un coche nuevo.   (Recently completed action)
I have bought a new car.
Bolivia **ha producido** mucho estaño.   (Continuing action)
Bolivia has produced much tin.

➤ Supply the present perfect tense of the verbs in parentheses.

1. Alguien me _____ (robar) el coche.

2. Yo _____ (hablar) con la policía.

3. Ellos me _____ (prometer) buscar mi auto.

4. Yo _____ (tener) que usar el tranvía.

5. Yo _____ (conocer) a muchos músicos.

6. Ellos _____ (practicar) mucho sus instrumentos.

7. Le _____ (comprar) a mi hijo una guitarra eléctrica.

8. Hasta ahora yo _____ (aprender) una sola canción.

9. Mi tía nos _____ (llamar) desde Costa Rica.

10. Ella _____ (vivir) allí tres meses.

11. Nosotros _____ (hablar) de visitarla en la primavera.

12. Aquel país siempre me _____ (interesar) mucho.

13. La maestra me _____ (dar) mucha tarea para mañana.

14. Yo _____ (tratar) de hacerla pero es muy difícil.

15. Mi compañero _____ (tener) tiempo para ayudarme.

16. Con su ayuda yo _____ (poder) completarla.

17. Yo _____ (ser) vendedor por trece años.

18. Yo _____ (comer) en muchos restaurantes finos.

19. Todos los camareros me _____ (tratar) bien.

20. Ellos siempre _____ (contar) con una buena propina.

21. Tú _____ (estar) muy enferma toda la semana.

22. ¿Por qué no _____ (ir) al médico?

23. La medicina _____ (curar) muchas enfermedades.

24. Mi primo _____ (aliviarse) de los mismos síntomas.

Worksheet 8.4 More on the present perfect tense

➤ Change these sentences from the simple present tense to the present perfect tense. Be aware of each change in meaning.

1. Los soldados *se entrenan* por ocho semanas.

   _____

2. El sargento los *enseña* muy bien.

   _____

3. Por muchos años nosotros *gozamos* de paz.

   _____

4. En tiempos de guerra nuestros soldados *son* muy valientes.

   _____

5. Nosotros siempre *contamos* con ellos.

   _____

6. Yo *admiro* mucho a los maestros de mi escuela.

   _____

7. Ellos siempre *tratan* de enseñarnos y educarnos bien.

   _____

8. Sus alumnos siempre *aprenden* lecciones valiosas.

   _____

9. Gracias a ellos yo *soy* bien educado.

   _____

10. Yo *pienso* a veces en ser maestro también.

    _____

11. El cartero siempre *llega* a la misma hora.

    _____

12. Hoy me *trae* una carta muy importante.

    _____

13. Dice que me *aceptan* en la Universidad de Salamanca.

    _____

14. Por muchos años yo *sueño* en estudiar allí.

    _____

15. Es por eso que *estudio* mucho español.

   _____

16. Yo nunca *voy* a ese cine.

   _____

17. Siempre *tienen* películas de vaqueros.

   _____

18. A mí me *interesan* más las películas históricas.

   _____

19. Mi favorita *es* «Novela de dos ciudades».

   _____

20. El actor Ronald Coleman me *impresiona* mucho.

   _____

21. A mí me *encantan* los poemas de Bécquer.

   _____

22. Yo *leo* todas sus poesías varias veces.

   _____

23. Nadie *entiende* mejor la rima y el color.

   _____

24. Cada obra suya *es* una joya de la literatura.

   _____

25. Sus cuentos también le *traen* mucha fama.

   _____

26. Mi tío siempre *fuma* demasiado.

   _____

27. Recientemente él *empieza* a toser muchísimo.

   _____

28. Los médicos *declaran* que el tabaco es peligroso.

   _____

29. Yo siempre *estoy* de acuerdo con los médicos.

   _____

30. ¡Qué bueno! Mi tío *promete* que no fumará más.

   _____

Worksheet 8.5 More on the present perfect tense

➤ Change these sentences from **yo** to **él** and then to **tú**. Write the forms in the blanks. (For additional oral practice, change the subjects also to **nosotros** and **ustedes**.)

1. Yo *he estudiado* español un año. _____

2. Yo *he estado* enfermo últimamente. _____

3. Yo *he viajado* mucho por Sudamérica. _____

4. Yo *he hablado* con ellos de esto. _____

5. Yo *he ido* a España tres veces. _____

6. Hoy yo *he tomado* mucho café. _____

7. También yo *he comido* demasiado postre. _____

8. Yo *he preparado* muy bien las tareas. _____

9. Yo *he conversado* con ellos en inglés. _____

10. Yo *he vivido* diez años en esta ciudad. _____

11. Yo *he trabajado* aquí ocho meses. _____

12. Yo *he sido* siempre un buen empleado. _____

13. Yo la *he esperado* dos horas. _____

14. Yo *he visitado* a Felipe en su casa. _____

15. Yo *he recibido* dos cartas de Elena. _____

16. Yo ya *he conocido* a los Sánchez. _____

17. Yo *he leído* esa novela por primera vez. _____

18. Yo *he traído* a casa todos mis libros. _____

19. Yo *he prometido* visitarlos esta noche. _____

20. Yo *he llamado* a la compañía varias veces. _____

21. Yo nunca *he tenido* dolor de cabeza. _____

22. Yo *he aprendido* mucho en esta clase. _____

Worksheet 8.6 Past perfect (pluperfect) tense

The past perfect tense is formed the same in both languages: the past tense (imperfect) of the helping verb *to have* (**haber**) plus the past participle of the main verb:

EXAMPLE: Ella **había estudiado** francés en la escuela.   había estudiado
She had studied French in school.   *had studied*

➤ Supply the past perfect tense form of the verbs in parentheses.

1. Él insistió en decir que _____ (echar) la carta al buzón.

2. Yo le dije que no la _____ (recibir).

3. Fuimos a su casa, pero Juan y María _____ (salir).

4. Después dijeron que nos _____ (esperar) dos horas.

5. Yo le _____ (preguntar) algo al profesor.

6. Él dijo que no _____ (entender) mi pregunta.

7. Ellos _____ (vivir) en Francia por varios años.

8. Allí ellos _____ (aprender) a hablar francés.

9. Tú sabías que yo _____ (estar) enfermo toda la semana.

10. Fue por eso que yo no te _____ (invitar) a la fiesta.

11. Ella _____ (manejar) más lentamente que nunca.

12. Ella creyó que _____ (llegar) tarde.

13. Oímos decir que tú padre _____ (vivir) en Italia.

14. Sí, pero yo nunca _____ (estar) allí.

15. Yo nunca _____ (comer) en un restaurante tan elegante.

16. Siempre me _____ (asustar) los precios.

17. Mi primo _____ (ganar) mucho dinero en el boxeo.

18. Desgraciadamente, él no _____ (ahorrar) nada.

19. Yo _____ (dormir) una siesta a mediodía.

20. El bebé de mi hermana _____ (llorar) toda la noche.

21. En su juventud él _____ (tener) demasiadas ambiciones.

22. Él no _____ (realizar) ni la mitad.

Worksheet 8.7 Irregular past participles

The following past participles are irregular.

abierto (abrir)	**cubierto (cubrir)**	**hecho (hacer)**	**roto (romper)**	**visto (ver)**
dicho (decir)	**escrito (escribir)**	**muerto (morir)**	**puesto (poner)**	**vuelto (volver)**

The addition of a prefix does not alter the irregular form of the past participle. Can you give the past participles for **descubrir, deshacer, componer,** and **devolver**?

A number of regular past participles require written accent marks: **leer (leído), creer (creído), traer (traído), oír (oído), reír (reído).**

➤ Supply the correct past participle of the verbs in parentheses.

1. Han _____ (abrir) una nueva zapatería en Los Ángeles.

2. Me han _____ (decir) que está en una de las mejores esquinas.

3. Ya habían _____ (poner) un anuncio en los periódicos.

4. Es sólo el primer día, pero ya han _____ (hacer) buenas ventas.

5. No hemos _____ (ver) nuestro florero de cristal.

6. A lo mejor, la criada nos lo había _____ (romper).

7. Ella no nos ha _____ (decir) nada sobre el asunto.

8. Pero yo he _____ (descubrir) los pedazos en la basura.

9. El dictador de aquel país se ha _____ (morir).

10. Un periodista ha _____ (escribir) sobre el nuevo gobierno.

11. Yo he _____ (leer) sus reportes con mucho interés.

12. El nuevo presidente ya ha _____ (traer) muchas reformas al país.

13. Los pintores habían _____ (abrir) todas las ventanas.

14. Mucho polvo ha entrado y ha _____ (cubrir) todos los muebles.

15. También hace frío. Yo me he _____ (poner) el suéter.

16. Han _____ (decir) que en la noche podremos cerrarlas.

17. Yo he _____ (escribir) una carta en español.

18. He _____ (descubrir) algunas palabras que no parecen correctas.

19. Papá se ha _____ (reír) de mis errores de ortografía.

20. ¿Ha _____ (ver) usted mi diccionario inglés-español?

21. Nosotros hemos _____ (volver) a la iglesia del padre Hidalgo.

22. El padre Hidalgo había _____ (morir) durante la guerra.

23. Él todavía no había _____ (ver) la independencia de México.

24. Pero nadie había _____ (hacer) más para ganarla.

Worksheet 8.8 Past participles as adjectives

Past participles as verbs never change forms:

> EXAMPLES: Él ha **hablado**. Ellas han **hablado**.

As adjectives, past participles observe the same agreements in number and gender as other adjectives:

> EXAMPLE: El libro está **abierto**.
> La revista **abierta** es la última.

➤ Supply the past participle form of the verbs given in parentheses and used here as adjectives.

1. La novela «La barraca» fue _____ (escribir) por Blasco Ibáñez.

2. Un famoso retrato de él fue _____ (pintar) por Picasso.

3. Sus libros son _____ (leer) por millones de españoles.

4. También han sido _____ (traducir) a muchos idiomas.

5. En California las casas están _____ (construir) de estuco.

6. Las casas _____ (hacer) totalmente de madera son bonitas.

7. En Boston vi muchos edificios _____ (cubrir) de hiedra.

8. Los rascacielos son _____ (construir) de acero y hormigón.

9. La música está _____ (componer) por Albéniz.

10. Fue uno de los compositores más _____ (conocer) de España.

11. Sus composiciones son _____ (oír) en todas partes.

12. También han sido _____ (grabar) por las mejores orquestas.

13. El niño tiene la camisa _____ (cubrir) de lodo.

14. Estaba _____ (distraer) y se cayó jugando en el parque.

15. Ese niño _____ (atrever) nunca tiene cuidado cuando juega.

16. Ya tiene _____ (lastimar) las dos rodillas.

17. Me gustan las comidas _____ (preparar) al estilo español.

18. Me encantan los mariscos _____ (combinar) con pollo y arroz.

19. Las frutas _____ (cultivar) en España son deliciosas.

20. El pescado _____ (cocer) con aceitunas es mi favorito.

21. La fiesta más _____ (celebrar) en mi familia es la Navidad.

22. El aspecto religioso siempre es _____ (observar).

23. También es una temporada _____ (dedicar) a las compras.

24. El año _____ (pasar) gastamos mucho en regalos navideños.

Past participles

➤ In the blanks, supply the past participle of the following verbs.

1. hablar _____

2. escribir _____

3. abrir _____

4. preferir _____

5. ir _____

6. comer _____

7. vivir _____

8. estudiar _____

9. empezar _____

10. salir _____

11. leer _____

12. construir _____

13. traducir _____

14. romper _____

15. gustar _____

16. preparar _____

17. ser _____

18. estar _____

19. tener _____

20. coger _____

21. hacer _____

22. llevar _____

23. traer _____

24. oír _____

25. morir _____

26. telefonear _____

27. pedir _____

28. reír _____

29. dirigir _____

30. pagar _____

31. volver _____

32. cubrir _____

33. haber _____

34. ofrecer _____

35. llamar _____

36. recibir _____

37. poner _____

38. creer _____

39. dar _____

40. ver _____

41. prestar _____

42. levantar _____

43. saber _____

44. cerrar _____

45. venir _____

46. decir _____

47. desaparecer _____

48. conocer _____

Worksheet 8.9 Future perfect tense

The future perfect tense describes an action that will already have taken place with reference to another action. It uses the future tense of **haber** plus the past participle.

> EXAMPLE: Si llegamos a las seis, ellos **habrán cenado.**
> *If we arrive at six o'clock, **they will have eaten** dinner.*

➤ Supply the future perfect tense of the verbs in parentheses.

1. Si vamos allí ahora, ellos _____ (ver) la televisión.

2. Mañana a esta hora el avión _____ (volar) sobre el mar.

3. Él dice que tú _____ (nadar) en la piscina todo el día.

4. Si llegamos antes de las dos, ellos no _____ (almorzar).

5. Se enojará si le molestamos porque no _____ (terminar).

6. ¿Qué _____ (hacer) usted esta noche hasta las siete?

7. El lunes, a estas horas, nos _____ (divertir) en el río.

8. Ve a las cinco porque Isabel ya _____ (terminar) la clase de piano.

9. Esta tarde sólo _____ (estar) descansando en su hamaca.

10. A esta hora mañana _____ (llegar) a nuestro destino.

11. Comprendo que él ya lo _____ (hacer).

12. El lunes ya él _____ (recibir) la carta.

13. Al llegar a casa seguramente que él _____ (contestar).

14. Estoy convencido que él ya _____ (escribir) la carta.

15. Nos dicen que ellos _____ (terminar) el trabajo al fin de mes.

16. No sabemos si para esa fecha lo _____ (hacer) todo.

17. Antes de comprar alguna casa, nosotros _____ (ver) muchas otras.

18. Creo también que _____ (pagar) mucho más de lo que pensamos.

Worksheet 8.10 Passive voice (*la voz pasiva*)

In both English and Spanish, the passive voice is a sentence pattern in which the subject receives the action of the verb rather than performing that action.

EXAMPLES: *active*

El cocinero **usa** mucha sal.

El médico **curó** la enfermedad.

Tomás **escribirá** la carta.

passive

Mucha sal es **usada** por el cocinero.

La enfermedad fue **curada** por el médico

La carta **será** escrita por Tomás.

Note that the past participle must agree with the noun it refers to (as in the previous exercise). Note also that the subject in the active voice becomes the object of **por** in the passive voice, also that **sal, enfermedad,** and **carta** become the subjects in the passive voice.

➤ Supply the past participles of the verbs in parentheses.

1. «El pensador» fue _____ (esculpir) por Rodin.

2. «La Mona Lisa» fue _____ (pintar) por Da Vinci.

3. «Don Quijote» fue _____ (escribir) por Cervantes.

4. «La Traviata» fue _____ (componer) por Verdi.

5. El trigo es _____ (cultivar) por un agricultor.

6. La seda es _____ (producir) por un gusano.

7. Los cacahuetes son semillas _____ (producir) por las raíces de una planta.

8. Las comidas son _____ (preparar) por los cocineros.

9. El viaje será _____ (planear) por la agencia.

10. La ruta será _____ (escoger) por mis padres.

11. Las escalas serán _____ (incluir) en el precio total.

12. La propina será _____ (incluir) en la cuenta.

13. Mi reloj ha estado _____ (romper) por seis meses.

14. Muchos relojes han sido _____ (reparar) por el joyero.

15. Tengo otro reloj que me fue _____ (regalar) por mis abuelos.

16. Fue _____ (comprar) por ellos cuando yo cumplí diez años.

17. El pararrayos fue _____ (descubrir) por Benjamín Franklin.

18. La luz eléctrica fue _____ (inventar) por Tomás Edison.

19. El primer antiséptico fue _____ (usar) por José Lister.

20. El autogiro fue _____ (inventar) por Juan de la Cierva.

21. La boda fue _____ (arreglar) por los padres de los novios.

22. Los músicos fueron _____ (contratar) por los padres de él.

23. El fotógrafo fue _____ (pagar) por los padres de ella.

24. El brindis fue _____ (hacer) por el hermano del novio.

Worksheet 8.11 More on the passive voice

The true passive voice is used much less frequently in Spanish than in English. The preterite passive tense is used much more than the other passive tenses.

➤ Rewrite the following sentences using the preterite passive voice.

1. *Él escribió* ese libro hace muchos años. ___El libro fue escrito hace muchos años.___

2. Tú *cerraste* las ventanas. _____

3. *Terminaron* el trabajo en enero. _____

4. *Construyeron* ese edificio en 1954. _____

5. *Hicieron* esos muebles en La Habana. _____

6. Todos *admiraron* al gran artista. _____

7. Nos *recibieron* con muchas atenciones. _____

8. *Pusieron* a todos los alumnos nuevos en la misma clase. _____

    _____

9. Un buen arquitecto *planeó* ese edificio. _____

10. Hasta Colón, los europeos *desconocían* América. _____

    _____

11. A ti te *escucharon* con mucha atención mientras hablabas. _____

    _____

12. La población *recibió* a los visitantes con honores. _____

    _____

13. Ayer *aprobaron* los planos para el nuevo edificio. _____

    _____

14. *Sentenciaron* al acusado a dos años de cárcel. _____

15. *Enviaron* los muebles por barco. _____

16. *Castigaron* a los niños por jugar a la pelota en la calle. _____

    _____

17. *Multaron* al chofer por exceso de velocidad. _____

    _____

18. *Pintaron* la casa dos veces este año. _____

Worksheet 8.12 Passive voice—future

➤ Rewrite the following future tense sentences in the future passive voice.

1. Elena *preparará* la comida. _____La comida será preparada por Elena._____

2. Un arquitecto colombiano *hará* los planos. _____

3. La secretaria *escribirá* las cartas a máquina. _____

4. Lo *recibirán* a usted con muchas atenciones. _____

   _____

5. La *tratarán* a ella con mucho respeto. _____

6. Pablo *pondrá* todos los papeles en orden. _____

7. Rosario y Cecilia *traerán* todas las cosas necesarias. _____

   _____

8. *Sentenciarán* al hombre a dos años de cárcel. _____

9. *Terminarán* el trabajo en enero. _____

10. Pronto *usarán* este nuevo aparato eléctrico en todas partes. _____

    _____

11. Los artistas siempre *estudiarán* los cuadros de Velázquez. _____

    _____

12. De Italia *traerán* todos los mosaicos para el edificio nuevo._____

    _____

13. *Publicarán* el libro el mes que viene. _____

14. Una compañía alemana *construirá* el nuevo puente. _____

    _____

15. *Anunciarán* la exhibición de obras de arte en el periódico. _____

    _____

16. El director *dará* los premios a los mejores alumnos. _____

    _____

17. El 2 de enero *inaugurarán* la nueva escuela._____

    _____

18. Raquel *enviará* los paquetes por avión._____

    _____

Worksheet 8.13 Passive voice—present perfect

➤ The following sentences are in the present perfect tense, active voice. Rewrite them in the present perfect tense, passive voice. Remember to add the helping verb **ser.**

1. Por fin *han vendido* su casa. _____Por fin su casa ha sido vendida._____

2. Todo el mundo *ha admirado* mucho a nuestro presidente. _____
   _____

3. *Han dicho* muchas cosas buenas acerca de él. _____
   _____

4. *Han terminado* la carretera nueva. _____

5. Muchos artistas *han copiado* los cuadros de Velázquez. _____
   _____

6. *Ya han aprobado* los planos para el nuevo edificio. _____

7. *Han entregado* los muebles que ordenamos hace tanto tiempo. _____
   _____

8. El incendio *ha destruido* toda la cocina. _____

9. *Han recibido* a nuestro embajador con muchos honores. _____
   _____

10. *Han capturado* a muchos ladrones. _____

11. Los policías *han arrestado* a mucha gente culpable. _____
    _____

12. *Han liberado* a varios inocentes. _____

13. *Hemos escrito* todas las cartas. _____

14. Ya *han despachado* por avión todos los paquetes grandes. _____
    _____

15. La criada *ha llevado* a los niños al parque. _____

16. *Han vacunado* a todos los estudiantes contra la gripe. _____
    _____

17. No *han encontrado* todavía al autor del delito. _____

18. *Han puesto* al niño en una escuela militar. _____

19. Ya *han anunciado* en el periódico la nueva exhibición de obras de arte. _____
    _____

20. *Han traído* flores de todas partes del mundo para la exposición. _____
    _____

Worksheet 8.14 Reflexive verbs in place of the passive voice

Reflexive structures are used much more frequently in Spanish, especially where the subject is impersonal, inanimate, or relatively unimportant. The literal translations may seem strange, but are helpful in understanding the agreements:

EXAMPLES: **Se vende** el periódico aquí.   *The newspaper is sold here.*
                                                        (Literally: The newspaper sells itself here.)

            Se venden los periódicos aquí.   *The newspapers are sold here.*
                                                        (Literally: The newspapers sell themselves here.)

➤ Supply the reflexive form of the verbs in parentheses.

1. _____ (Venderse) las legumbres muy frescas en este mercado.

2. _____ (Ofrecerse) las frutas a precio reducido.

3. Pero aquí no _____ (venderse) carne.

4. La carne _____ (comprarse) en otro mercado.

5. En la Argentina la elle y la y griega _____ (pronunciarse) diferente.

6. _____ (Decirse) que el gaucho es un tipo pintoresco.

7. La música _____ (oírse) por todas partes.

8. El tango y la samba _____ (bailarse) en las fiestas.

9. En ese edificio _____ (alquilarse) apartamentos económicos.

10. Los apartamentos de lujo _____ (encontrarse) en otra calle.

11. Desde algunos apartamentos _____ (verse) las montañas.

12. Los más caros _____ (hallarse) frente al océano.

13. El béisbol _____ (considerarse) el deporte nacional.

14. El béisbol _____ (jugarse) mucho en la América Latina.

15. En México _____ (jugarse) hasta en los pueblos chicos.

16. Allí _____ (descubrirse) peloteros famosos como Fernando Valenzuela.

17. La comida italiana _____ (prepararse) con mucho ajo.

18. Mucho cari _____ (agregarse) en las recetas indias.

19. En México _____ (ponerse) el cilantro en muchos platos.

20. La nacionalidad _____ (reconocerse) por los condimentos.

21. En México, la guitarra _____ (tocarse) mucho.

22. El bandoleón _____ (oírse) mucho en la Argentina.

23. El arpa _____ (usarse) mucho en Veracruz.

24. En Chiapas _____ (preferirse) la marimba.

Worksheet 8.15 Present participles

Present participles (**participios presente**) are mostly used as in English. Like verbs, they may have objects, but they are used as adjectives, as adverbs, or in combination with *to be* (**estar**) to form the progressive tenses, which will be reviewed later. In Spanish, they are known as **gerundios.** Present participles are formed by adding **-ando** to the stem of **-ar** verbs and **-iendo** to the stem of **-er** and **-ir** verbs:

EXAMPLES: **habla   hablando**   **comer   comiendo**   **vivir   viviendo**

Note: Gerunds in English are equivalent to infinitives in Spanish:

EXAMPLE: ***Swimming** is good (for you).*   **Nadar** es bueno.

➤ In the blanks, supply the present participle of the following verbs.

1. vender _____
2. estudiar _____
3. terminar _____
4. hacer _____
5. poner _____
6. escribir _____
7. firmar _____
8. decorar _____
9. rezar _____
10. indicar _____
11. echar _____
12. pegar _____
13. llover _____
14. tocar _____
15. nadar _____
16. volar _____
17. beber _____
18. servir _____
19. crecer _____
20. usar _____
21. admirar _____
22. atacar _____

23. abrir _____
24. cerrar _____
25. comprar _____
26. esperar _____
27. acabar _____
28. necesitar _____
29. asistir _____
30. tener _____
31. trabajar _____
32. pasar _____
33. saber _____
34. conocer _____
35. recibir _____
36. querer _____
37. andar _____
38. lavarse _____
39. levantarse _____
40. dar _____
41. perder _____
42. llevar _____
43. nevar _____
44. patinar _____

Busсapalabras

Palabras revueltas

The following strange-looking words are actually two common words scrambled together. Look for the clue, then unscramble the words, and write them in the blank spaces.

1. **T E R A G R O P O**   (animals) _____
2. **E U G A C H A L E**   (beverages) _____
3. **A V A P U R E**   (fruits) _____
4. **V A S O C R A L L E**   (flowers) _____
5. **O B A J O C O**   (body parts) _____
6. **S U F L A B A L D A**   (apparel) _____
7. **E S O C H I S O**   (numbers) _____
8. **H I M O J I P R A**   (relatives) _____
9. **C A B R A T O N T E O L** (buildings) _____
10. **M O G R A L A**   (water) _____
11. **S O N A L A B A**   (rooms) _____
12. **T E N C H O C R E**   (vehicles) _____
13. **L L A N U S O**   (heavenly bodies) _____
14. **R E T O P A L D E N T O** (eating) _____
15. **P O L O T A R A**   (metals) _____
16. **M A L A C I S L A**   (furniture) _____
17. **P R O M O B E L I A** (reading) _____
18. **R E A L O A N A**   (beach) _____
19. **Z O R R A G R I T O** (grains) _____
20. **T A C R O N D O D O** (titles) _____

Worksheet 8.16 Present progressive tense

The present progressive tense uses the present tense of the helping verb **estar** plus the present participle **(hablando, comiendo, viviendo)**. The helping verb must agree in person and number with its subject. The participle does not change:

	singular			plural	
yo	estoy hablando		nosotros(as)	estamos hablando	
tú	estás hablando		vosotros(as)	estáis hablando	
él, ella, usted	está hablando		ellos, ellas, usted	están hablando	

➤ Supply the present progressive tense of the verbs in parentheses.

1. Yo _____ (hablar) con acento americano.

2. Tú _____ (pronunciar) el español como los madrileños.

3. Ella _____ (estudiar) un vocabulario de mejicanismos.

4. Todos _____ (practicar) el habla de una manera u otra.

5. De esta manera _____ (aprender) a hablar mejor.

6. El perro _____ (ladrar).

7. El gato _____ (maullar).

8. El burro _____ (rebuznar).

9. Las ovejas _____ (balar).

10. Los caballos _____ (relinchar).

11. Yo _____ (pintar) un cuadro muy bonito.

12. Tú _____ (componer) una canción alegre.

13. Ella _____ (escribir) un poema romántico.

14. Ustedes _____ (leer) una novela de Unamuno.

15. Nosotros _____ (escuchar) el Himno nacional.

16. Los niños _____ (pedir) dinero a sus papás.

17. Ellos _____ (planear) ir juntos al cine.

18. Ellos _____ (escoger) una película que no han visto antes.

19. El más joven _____ (insistir) en ver una comedia musical.

20. La mayor le _____ (explicar) que cierta comedia es la mejor.

21. El zapatero _____ (trabajar) en la zapatería.

22. Los alumnos _____ (estudiar) en la biblioteca.

23. El jardinero _____ (plantar) rosas y claveles.

24. La criada _____ (barrer) el patio.

Worksheet 8.17 More on the present progressive tense

Note carefully that, contrary to English usage, Spanish restricts the present progressive tense to what is happening at the moment the speaker is speaking. You may not say literally in Spanish, for example, *I'm flying to New York next week*. If you say you *are flying*, you must be doing it now, not anticipating doing it later. The simple present tense, by contrast, can refer to repeated or anticipated actions:

EXAMPLES: **Juan come uvas.**   *later, often, regularly, always, sometimes…*
           Juan está comiendo uvas.   *right now (at this moment only)*

➤ Rewrite the verbs in the following sentences in the present progressive tense.

Todos los días … Ahora

1. Yo estudio gramática. _____

2. Yo aprendo conceptos un poco complicados. _____

3. Yo aplico las reglas gramaticales. _____

4. Tú me ayudas con las reglas más difíciles. _____
   _____

5. Amalia toca el piano en un restaurante. _____

6. Los clientes piden sus canciones favoritas. _____

7. Ella gana mucho dinero en el restaurante. _____

8. También conoce a mucha gente interesante. _____

9. Llueve mucho en la selva. _____

10. Nieva en las montañas. _____

11. Hace calor en el desierto. _____

12. La neblina se forma cerca del mar. _____

13. El carpintero construye un garaje. _____

14. La bibliotecaria arregla los libros. _____

15. Las enfermeras dan inyecciones. _____

16. Los soldados se entrenan para la defensa. _____

17. Mi hijo va a la escuela. _____

18. Mi esposa trabaja en un banco. _____

19. Mi hija escucha sus discos favoritos. _____

20. Nos divertimos de una manera u otra. _____

Worksheet 8.18 Present participle—irregular forms

Every present participle ends in **-ndo.** Irregularities in some stems of present participles may be classified as follows:

1. **-ir** verbs with stem changes in the third person of the preterite will have the same stem change in the present participle:
   EXAMPLES: servir → **sir**viendo   dormir → **dur**miendo

2. Whenever the addition of a verb ending results in an **-i-** between vowels, change the **-i-** to **-y**
   EXAMPLES: creer (cre+**ie**ndo) → creyendo   oir (o+**ie**ndo) → oyendo

   The verb **ir**, which has no stem, also changes **i** to **y**, resulting in **yendo.**

3. **Poder, morir,** and **dormir** have the same stem vowel as in the preterite tense:
   EXAMPLES: poder → **pu**diendo   morir → **mu**riendo

➤ Supply the present progressive tense of the verbs in parentheses.

1. Yo sé que él _____ (decir) la verdad.

2. Ellos_____ (leer) unas revistas mejicanas.

3. Él _____ (traer) la medicina directamente de Washington.

4. Dicen que el padre de Manuel _____ (morirse).

5. Todas las hojas de ese árbol _____ (caerse).

6. Los niños_____ (divertirse) mucho en el parque.

7. Tú _____ (repetir) las palabras de tu hermano.

8. Yo sé que su vecino _____ (mentir).

9. ¿De qué_____ (reírse) ellos tanto?

10. El niño_____ (pedir) dulces a su abuelo.

11. No haga tanto ruido. El niño _____ (dormir).

12. ¿Cuál de esos camareros nos_____ (servir)?

13. Todos_____ (oír) por radio el discurso del presidente.

14. Nosotros _____ (repetir) el curso como repaso.

15. Tú _____ (vestirse) para el baile.

16. Esa casa_____ (caerse).

17. Pedro_____ (pedir) un aumento de sueldo.

18. Todo el mundo _____ (reírse) del chiste de Luis.

19. Hace días que Rafael no_____ (sentirse) bien.

20. El perro _____ (dormir) debajo del sofá.

Worksheet 8.19 Participles as adjectives and adverbs

Present participles may also function as adverbs (describing how an action is performed) or as adjectives (modifying the subject of the sentence), but their **-ndo** ending never changes. They may be modified by an adverb (**corriendo rápidamente**) or may have an object (**reconociendo a Juana**).

> EXAMPLES: **Hablando francamente**, yo no tengo ningún interés en ir allí.
> No **teniendo nada** más interesante que hacer, nos fuimos al cine.

➤ Supply the present participles of the verbs in parentheses.

1. Se lo regalé, _____ (pensar) que puede serle útil.

2. Agradeció el regalo _____ (abrazar) al amigo.

3. Vi al muchacho _____ (sonreír) con agrado.

4. _____ (Admirar) su obra, el pintor quedó satisfecho.

5. La firmó _____ (pensar) a quién se la vendería.

6. No _____ (tener) ningún comprador, la guardó.

7. Comencé _____ (ganar) un buen sueldo.

8. Ahorro mucho _____ (gastar) lo menos posible.

9. _____ (Invertir) cuidadosamente, crecerá mi capital.

10. _____ (Decir) qué se sentía mal, se fue a su casa.

11. _____ (Descansar) bien por unos días, sanará pronto.

12. No _____ (tener) nada qué hacer en casa, se aburrió.

13. _____ (Disculparse) mucho por su demora, al fin lo entregó.

14. _____ (Examinar) detenidamente el informe, decide aceptarlo.

15. _____ (Pagar) pronto y bien, consigo lo mejor.

16. _____ (Ver) que el autobús no llegaba, decide tomar un taxi.

17. Vi a un amigo _____ (cruzar) la calle en dirección opuesta.

18. Lo llama _____ (pensar) que pueden ir juntos en taxi.

19. _____ (Ser) rico y guapo, Juanito tiene muchas admiradoras.

20. _____ (Tener) de todo, aún no está conforme.

21. _____ (Conocer) bien el caso, el matrimonio le hará bien.

22. _____ (Presentir) que algo pasaba, la llamé.

23. _____ (Llorar) amargamente, me contó lo que había pasado.

24. No _____ (saber) yo qué aconsejarle, simplemente le escuché pacientemente.

General review

➤ Choose the correct form and write it in the blank.

1. No se _____ (vende, venden) periódicos en esa tienda.

2. Hay _____ (tantos, tantas) hombres como mujeres en esta clase.

3. La casa ha sido _____ (rodeado, rodeada) por la policía.

4. ¿Cómo se _____ (dice, decir) en español *dry cleaner's*?

5. Nosotros fuimos _____ (recibidos, recibidas) con entusiasmo.

6. Tú eres una persona muy _____ (trabajador, trabajadora).

7. ¿Cuánto tiempo _____ (hace, haces) que estudias español?

8. ¿Cuál es el _____ (tercer, tercero) día de la semana?

9. Todas las ventanas estaban _____ (abiertos, abiertas).

10. Al entrar, Raúl se quitó _____ (el sombrero, su sombrero).

11. Empezaron _____ (estudiar, a estudiar) español este año.

12. Tu padre _____ (levanta, se levanta) siempre a la misma hora.

13. La carne que sirvieron estaba mal _____ (cocinado, cocinada).

14. ¡Silencio! La niña _____ (dormida, está durmiendo).

15. La niña está aprendiendo _____ (caminar, a caminar).

16. Ella domina perfectamente la lengua _____ (francés, francesa).

17. El maestro _____ (sabe, conoce) las obras de Shakespeare.

18. ¿De qué país es _____ (Habana, La Habana) la capital?

19. Ahora tiene muy _____ (poco, poca) dificultad en entendernos.

20. Francisco _____ (parece, se parece) mucho a su madre.

21. Ayer me acompañó _____ (señor González, el señor González).

22. Ella es la alumna más inteligente _____ (de, en) la clase.

23. Dicen que el amigo de Pilar _____ (es, está) muy enfermo.

24. Mañana tengo que _____ (levantar, levantarme) muy temprano.

Part 9

Contents

Worksheet 9.1 Past progressive tense

The past progressive tense describes an action that took place or was taking place with reference to some point in the past. It combines the imperfect of **estar** and the present participle:

Singular		Plural	
yo	estaba hablando	nosotros(as)	estabámos hablando
tú	estabas hablando	vosotros(as)	estabais hablando
él, ella, usted	estaba hablando	ellos, ellas, ustedes	estaban hablando

➤ Supply the past progressive tense of the verbs in parentheses.

1. Cuando yo llegué, tú ya me _____ (esperar).

2. Te expliqué que yo _____ (trabajar).

3. Ella dijo que _____ (morirse) de hambre.

4. A las ocho, ya _____ (comer) en el restaurante.

5. Ana se enfermó cuando _____ (viajar) en México.

6. Ella nos dijo que _____ (tomar) el agua del grifo.

7. No sé por qué ella no _____ (tomar) más precauciones.

8. Sus amigas en cambio sólo _____ (usar) agua filtrada.

9. A las siete de la mañana, me _____ (bañar).

10. A las siete y media, _____ (preparar) el desayuno.

11. A las ocho _____ (saludar) a mi jefe.

12. A las cinco de la tarde _____ (regresar) a casa.

13. Durante las fiestas yo _____ (reparar) mi coche.

14. El lunes, yo _____ (reemplazar) las bujías.

15. El martes, yo _____ (cambiar) el aceite.

16. El miércoles, yo _____ (ajustando) los frenos.

17. En marzo, yo _____ (viajar) en el Oriente.

18. En mayo, yo _____ (buscar) trabajo como intérprete.

19. En junio, yo _____ (trabajar) en las Naciones Unidas.

20. En julio, yo _____ (buscar) casa en Nueva York.

21. Cuando me caí, _____ (jugar) al fútbol en el parque.

22. Cuando chocaste, _____ (manejar) sin mucha práctica.

23. Cuando se casó, ella _____ (vivir) en Chihuahua.

24. Cuando ustedes salieron, nosotros _____ (dormir).

Worksheet 9.2   More on the past progressive tense

The past progressive tense is used similarly to the imperfect tense but it seems to place more emphasis on the feeling that an action already in motion is interrupted by a shorter action of briefer duration (indicated by a preterite). In both of the following examples, one action was interrupted by another.

EXAMPLE: IMPERFECT: Cuando Juan llegó, yo **preparaba** mis lecciones.
           PAST PROGRESSIVE: Cuando Juan llegó, yo **estaba preparando** mis lecciones

➤ Change the verbs in italics to the past progressive tense.

1. Los niños *jugaban* en el parque cuando pasé por allí. _____

2. Él *viajaba* por Francia cuando empezó la guerra. _____

3. Tú *dormías* profundamente cuando sonó el teléfono. _____

4. *Comíamos* tranquilamente cuando llegó el telegrama. _____

5. El accidente ocurrió mientras *viajaban* a Chicago. _____

6. Mientras *esperábamos* un taxi, tú pasaste en coche. _____

7. Cuando los vi en la tienda, ustedes *conversaban*. _____

8. El ladrón *trataba* de entrar cuando vino la policía. _____

9. *Llovía* a cántaros cuando salí de casa esta mañana. _____

10. Mientras él *actuaba* en París, contrajo matrimonio. _____

11. Mientras *jugaba* a la pelota, Eduardo se lastimó. _____

12. Cuando el jefe entró, ya *trabajábamos*. _____

13. Yo no entendí ni una palabra de lo que me *decías*. _____

14. Fernando dijo que *hacía* más viajes que antes. _____

15. ¿Qué *hacían* los alumnos cuando llegó el maestro? _____

16. Me di cuenta de que Dolores no *comía* casi nada. _____

17. Mientras me *hablaba*, reconocí la mentira. _____

18. Cuando por fin llegué, el profesor *pasaba* lista. _____

19. El padre de Ramón *discutía* contigo en ese momento. _____

20. La lavandera *lavaba* ropa en el río cuando la vi. _____

21. Supe que él *tenía* dificultad en obtener el préstamo. _____

22. El acusado confesó cuando lo *interrogaban*. _____

23. Mientras *veía* las caricaturas, me eché a reír a carcajadas. _____

24. Durante la cena los mariachis *cantaban* «La golondrina.» _____

Worksheet 9.3 Present perfect progressive tense

The present perfect progressive tense describes an action that has been in progress with reference to another action. It uses the present perfect tense of **estar** plus the present participle.

EXAMPLE: Él **ha estado trabajando** muy bien últimamente.
He has been working very well lately.

➤ Supply the present perfect progressive tense of the verbs in parentheses.

1. Él _____ (dormir) toda la tarde.

2. Ellos _____ (ver) televisión desde el mediodía.

3. Los niños _____ (jugar) en el parque toda la tarde.

4. Tú _____ (hablar) más de una hora sin parar.

5. Hoy tú _____ (estudiar) las formas de la voz pasiva.

6. Yo _____ (buscar) mis llaves por todas partes.

7. Carmen _____ (bailar) con el mejicano toda la noche.

8. La pobre criada _____ (limpiar) todo el día.

9. Tú _____ (hacer) mucho ruido con tus tambores.

10. Sus padres los _____ (llamar) repetidamente.

11. Yo lo _____ (pensar) seriamente.

12. El humo de esos fumadores me _____ (molestar).

13. Se lo _____ (decir) desde hace tiempo.

14. Nosotros _____ (buscar) apartamento por aquí.

15. Ellos _____ (ahorrar) lo más posible.

16. Tú y yo _____ (trabajar) desde muy temprano.

17. El tiempo _____ (pasar) sin darnos cuenta.

18. ¡Ese perro _____ (ladrar) casi una hora!

19. Yo _____ (tratar) de dormir.

20. No pudimos salir porque _____ (llover).

21. Usted lo _____ (esperar) pacientemente.

22. Ellos lo _____ (llamar) al número equivocado.

Worksheet 9.4 Present participles with object pronouns

In the progressive tenses, object pronouns may be placed in front of the helping verb and unattached, or they may be attached to the end of the present participle, creating the need for a written accent mark.

EXAMPLE: Él **nos estaba dando** el regalo.   Él **estaba dándonos** el regalo.

The same rules apply when two object pronouns are used together, bearing in mind that the indirect object always precedes the direct object.

EXAMPLE: Él **nos lo** estaba dando.   Él estaba **dándonoslo.**

➤ Attach the object pronouns to the present participle and write the complete progressive tense of the verb.

1. Yo le estaba explicando la lección. _____

2. Él no me estaba escuchando. _____

3. Yo te estoy mostrando una revista. _____

4. Tú la estás leyendo con mucho interés. _____

5. Ellos me están contestando las preguntas. _____

6. Usted no me las está contestando correctamente. _____

7. Juana nos está resolviendo un problema. _____

8. Ella lo está haciendo perfectamente. _____

9. Juan me está escribiendo una carta en inglés. _____

10. Lola me la está escribiendo en español. _____

11. Ricardo me estaba diciendo las respuestas. _____

12. Yo se las estaba repitiendo claramente. _____

13. Tú me estabas revisando los papeles. _____

14. Después me los estabas arreglando. _____

15. Yo me estaba limpiando los zapatos. _____

16. Mañana temprano me los estaré limpiando otra vez. _____

17. Te estoy copiando la tarea de hoy. _____

18. ¿Por qué no lo estabas haciendo tú? _____

19. La directora me estaba felicitando. _____

20. ¡Qué suerte! A mí me estaba regañando. _____

21. ¿Usted nos estará dando el examen mañana? _____

22. No, el Sr. Ortíz les estará dando el examen mañana. _____

Worksheet 9.5 More on present participles with object pronouns

In the previous exercise we practiced moving object pronouns from left to right of the verb, attaching them to the present participles. In this exercise we shall do the opposite, detaching them from the present participle and placing them before the helping verb.

EXAMPLE: Estaba explicándo**noslos.**
Nos los estaba explicando.

➤ Supply the object pronoun(s), followed by the complete verb of the sentence.

1. Papá, Tito está robándome el lápiz. _____

2. ¡Mentira! Yo no estoy robándotelo. _____

3. Yo estoy explicándote las reglas de ortografía. _____

4. Anoche estaba explicándomelas el profesor. _____

5. Ayer estaba escribiéndome los ejemplos. _____

6. Hoy está enseñándomelos. _____

7. Tu asistente está preparándonos los contratos. _____

8. Mañana estaremos firmándolos. _____

9. Ella está preparándomelos en la computadora. _____

10. Más tarde estará imprimiéndomelos. _____

11. ¿Por qué no estás comprándome la bicicleta? _____

12. Estaré comprándotela para tu cumpleaños. _____

13. Raúl está afinándome la guitarra. _____

14. ¡Qué milagro si está afinándotela bien! _____

15. ¿Por qué estabas comprándote esos guantes? _____

16. Estaré poniéndomelos para esquiar. _____

17. ¿Has estado construyéndote un garaje? _____

18. Sí, he estado construyéndomelo de estuco. _____

19. ¿Quién está pintándote la casa? _____

20. Mi cuñado está pintándomela. _____

21. Miguel está escribiéndonos una bonita canción. _____

22. Claro. Estará cantándonosla en nuestra boda. _____

23. María anda diciéndonos mentiras. _____

24. Y tú sigues repitiéndonoslas. _____

Worksheet 9.6 *Para* and *por*

Although both have other meanings, the most common meaning of both **para** and **por** is *for*. To avoid making the wrong selection, remember that **para** looks ahead and **por** looks back:

EXAMPLES:

para	***looking ahead*** [*for, toward, future action or purpose*]
La taza es **para** café.	*The cup is for coffee (but it's empty at present).*
El libro es **para** Juan.	*The book is for John (but he doesn't have it yet).*
Está aquí **para** aprender español.	*He's here to learn Spanish (but he hasn't learned it yet).*
Salió **para** Madrid.	*He left for Madrid (but he's not there yet).*

por	***looking back*** [*for, in exchange for*]
Lo hago **por** Mamá.	*I'm doing it for Mother (due to a preexisting need).*
Trabajo **por** Miguel.	*I work for Michael (in his place, because he's sick).*
Le di un dólar **por** la revista.	*I gave him a dollar for the magazine (not yet mine).*

por	***looking back*** [*through, by, per*]
El ladrón entró **por** la ventana.	*The thief entered by the window (already done).*
Viajamos **por** tren.	*We traveled by train (past activity).*
Fue pintado **por** Picasso.	*It was painted by Picasso (the painting is finished).*
Los impuestos representan el diez **por** ciento.	*Taxes represent ten per cent (of already established amount).*

➤ Supply **para** or **por**, as needed, for the completion of the sentence.

1. Blanca salió ayer _____ Santiago.

2. Ellos compraron todos estos libros _____ mí.

3. Tenemos que enviar estas cartas _____ correo aéreo.

4. Nunca he leído ningún libro _____ segunda vez.

5. Tienes que comprar varias lámparas _____ tu nuevo apartamento.

6. Estando cerrada la puerta, tuvimos que entrar _____ la ventana.

7. Fui al Centro Gallego _____ ver la exposición de automóviles.

8. El presidente fue aclamado _____ la multitud.

9. Este edificio tiene una piscina pequeña _____ los niños.

10. Recibimos la noticia _____ la tarde.

11. Me multaron veinte _____ ciento del costo.

12. El canario salió _____ la puerta entreabierta.

13. Vino aquí de Colombia _____ trabajar como dibujante técnico.

14. El puente fue diseñado _____ un arquitecto alemán.

15. Durante el fin de semana me quedé en casa _____ estudiar.

16. Jaime compró un diamante _____ su esposa.

Worksheet 9.7 More on *para* and *por*

Set expressions require **para** or **por:**

EXAMPLES:
estar listo **para**	*to be ready to…*
servir **para**	*to be worth…, to be useful for…*
estudiar **para**	*to study to be a…*
para vivir	*in order to live*
pequeño **para** su edad	*small for his age*
por la mañana	*in the morning*
por lo general	*in general*
por eso, **por** lo tanto, **por** consiguiente	*therefore, accordingly*

The concept of looking ahead (**para**) or looking back (**por**) still applies.

➤ Supply **para** or **por,** as needed, to complete each sentence.

1. Ella nunca está en casa _____ la noche.

2. Ella nunca está en casa _____ cenar.

3. Esta pluma no sirve _____ nada.

4. No cambio esta pluma _____ nada.

5. Catalina compró un reloj _____ su padre.

6. Ella compró un reloj _____ ochenta dólares.

7. Tú fuiste a Honduras _____ tres meses.

8. Tú fuiste a Honduras _____ una fiesta religiosa.

9. Las flores son _____ su amabilidad.

10. Las flores son _____ la profesora.

11. Mi vecino está enfermo. Voy a trabajar _____ él.

12. Mi vecino es el patrón. Yo trabajo _____ él.

13. El dólar es _____ la camarera.

14. El otro dólar es _____ la cajera.

15. Mamá no puede ir a la tienda. Yo voy _____ ella.

16. Mamá está en el aeropuerto. Yo voy _____ ella.

17. Habrá una elección _____ presidente.

18. Habrá una elección _____ los miembros del gabinete.

19. Yo he trabajado _____ muchos años.

20. Yo he trabajado _____ muchos patrones.

21. Tú recibes veinte _____ ciento de las ganancias.

22. El veinte por ciento de las ganancias son _____ ti.

23. La canasta es _____ las manzanas.

24. Las compré _____ tres dólares.

25. Te debo una carta; _____ eso te estoy escribiendo.

26. El muchacho escribe muy bien _____ tener sólo once años.

Worksheet 9.8 Present tense of -*uir* verbs

Verbs ending in -**uir** such as **incluir, huir, destruir, construir, distribuir**, (but not -**guir**, -**quir**), add -**y** to the present tense before all endings, except endings which begin with **i*** (first and second person plural):

huir			
yo	huyo	nosotros(as)	huimos*
tu	huyes	vosotros(as)	huis*
él, ella, usted	huye	ellos, ellas, ustedes	huyen

incluir			
yo	incluyo	nosotros(as)	incluimos*
tú	incluyes	vosotros(as)	incluis*
él, ella, usted	incluye	ellos, ellas, ustedes	incluyen

➤ Supply the correct present tense of the verbs in parentheses.

1. Usted _____ (construir) frases muy interesantes.

2. Me gusta sobre todo como usted _____ (concluir) el párrafo.

3. Ese escritor _____ (atribuir) su éxito a sus estudios en Madrid.

4. Lope de Vega y Calderón de la Barca lo _____ (influir) mucho.

5. Mucha agua _____ (fluir) en ese río.

6. Los ríos _____ (contribuir) agua a las lluvias.

7. El maestro nos _____ (instruir) sobre la poesía romántica.

8. La tarea _____ (incluir) un poema de Rosalía de Castro.

9. En España se _____ (construir) catedrales enormes.

10. Ni los siglos _____ (destruir) esas obras arquitectónicas.

11. Cerrando la ventana, yo _____ (disminuir) el ruido de afuera.

12. El silencio _____ (contribuir) a mi descanso.

13. ¿A qué _____ (atribuir) usted su gran talento de bailarina?

14. La maestra me _____ (instruir) en cada aspecto de mi carrera.

15. ¿Cómo _____ (distribuir) ustedes los periódicos?

16. Nosotros los _____ (distribuir) en nuestros coches.

17. Los antisépticos _____ (destruir) muchos microbios.

18. Muchas curas se _____ (atribuir) al uso de antisépticos.

19. Los venados _____ (huir) de los cazadores.

20. El número de venados _____ (disminuir) anualmente.

21. El concierto _____ (incluir) una obra de Albéniz.

22. El pianista se _____ (distinguir) mucho en este concierto.

Worksheet 9.9 Preterite/progressive tenses of -*uir* verbs

Verbs ending in -**uir** (but not -**guir**, -**quir**) add **y** before the ending of preterite tense forms, in the third person only.*

huir			
yo	huí	nosotros(as)	huimos
tú	huiste	vosotros(as)	huisteis
él, ella, usted	huyó*	ellos, ellas, ustedes	huyeron*

incluir			
yo	incluí	nosotros(as)	incluimos
tú	incluiste	vosotros(as)	incluisteis
él, ella, usted	incluyó*	ellos, ellas, ustedes	incluyeron*

➤ Supply the preterite tense of the verbs in parentheses.

1. Los conquistadores _____ (destruir) mucho arte azteca.

2. El capitán Alvarado _____ (huir) de Tenochtitlán.

3. Los aztecas _____ (construir) pirámides y acueductos.

4. Los españoles los _____ (instruir) en su religión.

5. El éxito de Cortés se _____ (atribuir) en parte a La Malinche.

6. La conquista se _____ (concluir) con la ayuda de ella.

7. Moctezuma _____ (incluir) mucho oro entre sus tesoros.

8. Los indios _____ (distribuir) el oro entre los caciques.

9. El número de indios _____ (disminuir) después de la conquista.

10. Las enfermedades europeas _____ (contribuir) a muchas muertes.

An -**y**- is also introduced in the present participle of those same -**uir** verbs that change in the present and preterite.

EXAMPLES: INFINITIVE   PRESENT PARTICIPLE
          atribuir   **atribuyendo**
          huir   **huyendo**

Verbs ending in -**eer** and -**aer** also follow this pattern.

EXAMPLES: INFINITIVE   PRESENT PARTICIPLE
          poseer   **poseyendo**
          traer   **trayendo**

➤ Supply the present participle of the verbs in parentheses.

1. La medicina está _____ (contribuir) mucho a nuestra salud.

2. La Cruz Roja la está _____ (distribuir) mundialmente.

3. Estaba _____ (huir) del perro cuando me mordió.

4. Ahora estoy _____ (instruir) al perro a no morder.

5. La poetisa está _____ (incluir) algunas obras románticas.

6. Ella está _____ (concluir) la conferencia con un chiste.

7. Roberto se está _____ (distinguir) mucho en la política.

8. Gracias a él, estamos _____ (construir) una biblioteca nueva.

9. En su plato estoy _____ (incluir) maíz.

10. Porque usted lo pidió, estoy _____ (sustituir) los guisantes.

Worksheet 9.10 Preterite tense and commands of -*gar* verbs

A silent -**u**- is placed between the stem of -*gar* verbs and the -**e** ending of the first person singular, preterite tense. This silent -**u** is necessary to retain the hard quality of the **g**. Otherwise the Spanish **g** is pronounced the same as Spanish **j** before **e** or **i** (**general, ginebra**). The same applies to the -**e** and -**en** polite command endings. Spelling adjustments to verbs are often called *orthographical changes*.

EXAMPLE: pagar

Preterite	Polite Command	Familiar Command
pa**gué**, pagaste, pagó	pa**gue**	no pa**gues**
pagamos, (pagasteis), pagaron	pa**guen**	no pa**guen**

➤ Supply the preterite tense or command form of the verbs in parentheses.

1. Señor Ruiz, pida y _____ (pagar) la cuenta, por favor.

2. Ayer varios estudiantes _____ (llegar) tarde a clase.

3. Yo _____ (jugar) al tenis contra mi vecino, Ricardo.

4. La policía _____ (investigar) las circunstancias del robo.

5. Yo _____ (fregar) casi todos los cristales ayer.

6. Nosotros_____ (regar) el césped anoche.

7. María, _____ (entregar) un dólar al cartero y pida un recibo.

8. Yo _____ (investigar) las causas por tres horas ayer.

9. ¿Cuánto _____ (pagar) usted por su diccionario?

10. Benito, no _____ (pegar) a los otros niños en la escuela.

11. Los soldados _____ (vengar) la captura del coronel.

12. Yo _____ (colgar) mi chaqueta en el ropero de tu casa.

13. Señor Cisneros, _____ (pagar) lo que le prestó el banco.

14. Cuando dijiste que soy pobre, yo no lo _____ (negar).

15. Lorca escribió sobre un niño que se_____ (ahogar) en un pozo.

16. Yo _____ (castigar) muy ligeramente a mi hijo.

17. Señora, no _____ (entregar) sus ahorros a esos señores.

18. Nosotros_____ (llegar) más temprano que de costumbre.

19. Yo _____ (pagar) la cuenta cuando comimos en el restaurante.

20. ¿Por qué no _____ (investigar) tú la causa del accidente?

21. Buena inversión o no, yo no _____ (arriesgar) mi dinero.

22. Niños, _____ (apagar) las luces.

Worksheet 9.11 Preterite tense and commands of *-car* verbs

The letter **c** is pronounced the same as **s** before the letters **i** and **e**. To retain the hard [**k**] sound in **-car** verbs, **c** is changed to **qu** before **e** or **i** endings:

EXAMPLE: sacar

Preterite	Polite Command	Familiar Command
sa**qué**, sacaste, sacó	sa**que**	no sa**ques**
sacamos, (sacasteis), sacaron	sa**quen**	no sa**quen**

➤ Supply the preterite or command form of the verbs in parentheses.

1. Yo _____ (sacar) buenas notas en todas mis asignaturas.

2. Los marineros _____ (identificar) a muchos piratas.

3. La niña _____ (brincar) con sus amigas en el parque.

4. Muchachos, no _____ (pescar) en este lado del río.

5. Todas las fotos que yo _____ (sacar) ayer salieron mal.

6. Por favor, _____ (indicar) el camino para el aeropuerto.

7. Anteayer yo me _____ (dislocar) el hombro jugando a pelota.

8. La grúa _____ (remolcar) tu coche hasta el garaje.

9. Señor, _____ (comunicar) sus quejas directamente al gerente.

10. Evita, no _____ (colocar) más cosas ahí.

11. Los Pérez _____ (embarcarse) el mes pasado para Chile.

12. Mi hermana lavó los platos y yo los _____ (secar).

13. Yo me _____ (educar) muy bien en las escuelas públicas.

14. Ella _____ (roncar) tanto anoche que yo no pude dormir.

15. El caballo _____ (brincar) las dos cercas con gran agilidad.

16. Tomasito, no _____ (tocar) el pastel que hice para la fiesta.

17. El testigo _____ (identificar) en seguida al acusado.

18. ¿Maestra, qué _____ (significar) el verbo *saquear*?

19. Yo _____ (sacar) buenas notas cuando estudié en la Argentina.

20. Maestro, _____ (tocar) la guitarra en la fiesta, por favor.

21. Yo _____ (masticar) esa carne con gran dificultad.

22. Los muchachos ya _____ (cascar) todas las nueces.

Worksheet 9.12 Present tense and commands of -ger, -gir, -guir verbs

As in English, the letter **g** is pronounced differently before the letters **-e** and **-i**. In Spanish, this **g** is pronounced the same as Spanish **j**. To preserve this **j** sound throughout the conjugation of **-ger** and **-gir** verbs, Spanish changes the **g** to **j** before verb endings that begin with **a** or **o**.

EXAMPLES: recoger

Preterite	Polite Command	Familiar Command
reco**jo**, recoges, recoge	reco**ja**	no reco**jas**
recogemos, (recogéis), recogen	reco**jan**	no reco**jan**

dirigir

| diri**jo**, diriges, dirige | diri**ja** | diri**jas** |
| dirigimos, (dirigís), dirigen | diri**jan** | no diri**jan** |

Because the letter **u** would not be silent in the **-o** and **-a(n)** endings of **-guir** verbs, the **u** is dropped:

EXAMPLE: seguir

| si**go**, sigues, sigue | si**ga** | no si**gas** |
| seguimos, (seguís), siguen | si**gan** | no si**gan** |

➤ Supply the present tense or the command form of the verb in parentheses.

1. Yo siempre _____ (escoger) a mis amigos con mucho cuidado.

2. El capitán _____ (dirigir) el barco hacia el muelle.

3. Según el optometrista, yo no _____ (distinguir) bien los colores.

4. ¿Dónde _____ (conseguir) usted estas manzanas tan sabrosas?

5. En vez de contestarme, ella se _____ (encoger) de hombros.

6. Sí, _____ (seguir) usted por esta carretera hasta la capital.

7. El niño _____ (fingir) tener hambre para pedir dulces.

8. Olivier se _____ (distinguir) mucho en el papel de Hamlet.

9. Muchachos, _____ (corregir) sus exámenes antes de salir.

10. Yo _____ (recoger) todas las hojas que cayeron del árbol.

11. Los gemelos _____ (escoger) bicicletas idénticas.

12. Yo casi nunca _____ (coger) resfriado en el verano.

13. Ella _____ (seguir) asistiendo a las clases de francés.

14. ¿En qué mes del año _____ (recoger) ellos las cerezas?

15. Algunos dictadores _____ (perseguir) a sus críticos.

16. Yo _____ (dirigir) la orquesta cuando el maestro estaba ausente.

17. Niños, _____ (recoger) los juguetes que no usan.

18. Mi hija, no _____ (fingir) compasión si no es genuina.

Worksheet 9.13 Preterite tense and commands of *-zar* verbs

Although **z** is pronounced the same as **c** before **e** or **i,** Spanish prefers to change **z** to **c** before verb endings beginning with **e** or **i:**

EXAMPLE: lanzar

Preterite	Polite Command	Familiar Command
lan**cé**, lanzaste, lanzó	lan**ce**	no lan**ces**
lanzamos, (lanzasteis), lanzaron	lan**cen**	no lan**cen**

➤ Supply the preterite tense or command form of the verbs in parentheses.

1. La orquesta _____ (empezar) a tocar a las ocho de la noche.

2. Nosotros _____ (lanzar) un nuevo producto.

3. Cuando yo _____ (bostezar), decidimos acostarnos.

4. Salí de casa a las dos y _____ (alcanzar) el autobús de las tres.

5. Yo _____ (cruzar) gran parte de la ciudad antes de llegar.

6. Cuando abriste la puerta, nos _____ (abrazar).

7. Yo _____ (comenzar) a jugar al béisbol en abril del año pasado.

8. Yo _____ (realizar) mis sueños de ser lanzador.

9. Ayer yo _____ (lanzar) muy bien, pero el otro equipo ganó.

10. Los indios _____ (cazar) animales con flechas o cuchillos.

11. Los pioneros _____ (utilizar) sus rifles para cazar.

12. Alicia _____ (avanzar) al primer lugar en su graduación.

13. Su madre le _____ (rizar) el pelo antes de la ceremonia.

14. Alicia _____ (gozar) mucho de tanta atención.

15. Muchos científicos se _____ (especializar).

16. Los inventores _____ (industrializar) nuestra civilización.

17. La maquinaria _____ (pasteurizar) los productos de la leche.

18. Sanford Cluett _____ (sanforizar) nuestra ropa.

19. Los sicólogos nos _____ (hipnotizar) y nos curaron de muchos miedos.

20. Los historiadores _____ (dramatizan) esos descubrimientos.

21. Si usted va a la iglesia, por favor _____ (rezar) por nosotros.

22. Cuando juegas al béisbol, _____ (lanzar) lo mejor posible.

23. En tiempo de guerra, no _____ (fraternizar) ustedes con nuestros enemigos.

Vocabulary check-up—opposites

➤ Supply the opposites of the following words and phrases.

1. alegre _____

2. antes _____

3. pesado _____

4. delante _____

5. por encima _____

6. duro_____

7. caro _____

8. dentro _____

9. despierto _____

10. abrir_____

11. entrar _____

12. agradable _____

13. culpable _____

14. preguntar _____

15. tragedia_____

16. grueso _____

17. subir _____

18. cerca _____

19. ancho _____

20. dulce _____

21. lentamente _____

22. aumentar _____

23. admitir _____

24. cortés _____

25. cuidadoso _____

26. recordar _____

27. temprano _____

28. feo_____

29. fácil _____

30. suave_____

31. mayor _____

32. tranquilo _____

33. seco_____

34. apretado _____

35. complicado_____

36. vacío _____

37. cómodo _____

38. útil _____

39. alto _____

40. todo el mundo _____

41. fuerte _____

42. sucio _____

43. ausente _____

44. mejor_____

45. debajo de _____

46. perder_____

47. oscuro _____

48. a menudo _____

49. futuro _____

50. joven_____

Laberinto de palabras

➤ Las palabras de este laberinto representan quince ocupaciones.

ENGLISH

SPANISH

1. actress ___ ___ ___ ___ ___ ___

2. athlete ___ ___ ___ ___ ___

3. baker ___ ___ ___ ___ ___ ___ ___ ___

4. cook ___ ___ ___ ___ ___ ___ ___ ___

5. doctor ___ ___ ___ ___ ___ ___

6. lawyer ___ ___ ___ ___ ___ ___ ___

7. nurse ___ ___ ___ ___ ___ ___ ___ ___ ___

8. painter ___ ___ ___ ___ ___ ___ ___

9. pilot ___ ___ ___ ___ ___ ___

10. poet ___ ___ ___ ___ ___

11. police officer ___ ___ ___ ___ ___ ___ ___ ___

12. salesman ___ ___ ___ ___ ___ ___ ___

13. tailor ___ ___ ___ ___ ___ ___

14. waiter ___ ___ ___ ___ ___ ___ ___

15. writer ___ ___ ___ ___ ___ ___ ___ ___ ___

Indefinite articles

➤ Supply the correct definite article [**el, la, los, las**].

1. Él duerme _____ siesta todas las tardes.

2. Tú vas a _____ iglesia casi diariamente.

3. Siempre vamos a la playa _____ domingos.

4. Yo prefiero estos ejercicios a _____ del otro libro.

5. Ayer hablé con _____ señor González sobre ese asunto.

6. Nuestro profesor de geometría es _____ señor Varona.

7. Todo el mundo debe lavarse _____ manos antes de comer.

8. _____ café es el producto principal de exportación de Colombia.

9. Vamos a pasar nuestras vaciones en _____ Paz.

10. Tú pasaste seis meses en _____ Japón con tu familia.

11. Llegamos a Santiago de Chile a _____ dos y media.

12. Nuestra lección de dibujo empieza a _____ una y cuarto.

13. Después de aprender español, yo quiero estudiar _____ francés.

14. Dicen que _____ ruso es un idioma muy difícil de aprender.

15. En Tijuana hablan en _____ acento de esa región.

16. Me gustan todas las flores, pero especialmente _____ rosas.

17. Dicen que _____ vino estimula el apetito en muchas personas.

18. Ellos piensan pasar el mes de abril en _____ Argentina.

19. _____ Canadá se encuentra al norte de los Estados Unidos.

20. Ayer vi en la calle a _____ señora de Salas con sus hijos.

21. En general, _____ lana da más calor que el algodón.

22. Siempre venimos a _____ la clase en coche.

23. En _____ clase hablamos solamente en español.

24. _____ policía patrulla esa sección todas las noches.

25. _____ gramática española es más difícil que la inglesa.

26. Cuando visité el palacio real no vi a su majestad _____ reina Isabel.

General review

➤ Choose the correct form and write it in the blank.

1. Compré estos dos libros _____ (por, para) un peso.

2. Ésta es una colección de poemas _____ (para, por) tu cumpleaños.

3. Voy a regalarle este otro _____ (a, al) señor Rodríguez.

4. Al entrar en el restaurante me quité _____ (mi, el) abrigo.

5. Lo _____ (colgué, colgó) al lado de la mesa.

6. Volví a_____ (ponerlo, ponérmelo) al salir.

7. Fui a tu casa, pero tú ya _____ (saliste, habías salido).

8. Ahora te ando _____ (buscado, buscando) en casa de tu hermana.

9. _____ (Tampoco, también) te encontré allí.

10. Papá se _____ (enoja, enojó) cuando vio mis notas.

11. Tuve _____ (de, que) prometerle mejores notas en el futuro.

12. En junio _____ (había, habré) cumplido la promesa.

13. La decisión fue_____ (hecho, hecha) por la directora.

14. Los graduados tendrán _____ (un, una) baile tradicional.

15. Muchos estudiantes no estaban_____ (de, en) acuerdo.

16. Tengo que _____ (levantar, levantarme) muy temprano mañana.

17. Será mi _____ (primer, primero) día de trabajo en el banco.

18. Usted no sabe cuánto me importa_____ (esto, este) trabajo.

19. No tuve_____ (ningún, ninguna) dificultad en conocer a Luisa.

20. Ella y yo íbamos _____ (a, en) la misma iglesia.

21. Yo la había _____ (visto, vista) allí todos los domingos.

General review

➤ Underline the correct forms or answers.

1. Si yo hago algo enseguida, lo hago (más tarde, con poco interés, inmediatamente, lentamente).

2. De vez en cuando quiere decir (temprano, nunca, ocasionalmente, con frecuencia).

3. A mediados de mayo quiere decir (al principio de mayo, al final de mayo, alrededor del 15 de mayo).

4. Una de estas palabras es un participio pasado: (decir, puso, hecho, saliendo, estudiando).

5. Una de estas palabras puede ser un gerundio: (venir, estudiado, poniendo, leído, estudiante).

6. Una de estas palabras es femenina: (libro, mano, cuento, baile, autobús).

7. Una de estas palabras es masculina: (mapa, mesa, lección, carne, novela).

8. El negativo de «también» es (siempre, ninguno, tampoco, nada).

9. Uno de estos países requiere el artículo definido—la (Cuba, Venezuela, Argentina, Ecuador).

10. Uno de estos verbos es reflexivo: (echar, escribir, casarse, vivir, preferir).

11. Uno de estos verbos tiene el participio pasado irregular: (llamar, tratar, decir, salir).

12. Uno de estos verbos tiene el gerundio irregular: (ser, hacer, ir, estar).

13. Si tengo ganas de hacer una cosa, yo (quiero hacerla, tengo que hacerla, la haré más tarde).

14. Si compro algo al contado, yo (pago más tarde, dejo un depósito, pago enseguida, regateo).

15. Si alguien se disgusta, (se enferma, se enoja, se acuesta, se queda).

16. Si tengo sueño, deseo (tomar algo, comer, dormir, salir).

17. Una de estas frases significa «por supuesto» (no importa, desde luego, a propósito, a veces).

18. Una de estas frases significa «sin embargo» (por eso, sin duda, no obstante, para siempre).

19. Lo opuesto de «grueso» es (grande, angosto, haragán, delgado).

20. Si dejo de fumar, (sigo fumando, no fumo más, estaré fumando, nunca fumaba, fumaré a veces).

Part 10

Contents

Worksheet 10.1 Possessive adjectives/pronouns

Short possessive adjectives precede the nouns they modify; long ones follow them.

BEFORE (SHORT FORM)

mi, mis
tu, tus
su, sus
nuestro, nuestra, nuestros, nuestras
(vuestro, vuestra, vuestros, vuestras
su, sus

AFTER (LONG FORM)

mío, mía, míos, mías
tuya, tuya, tuyos, tuyas
suyo, suya, suyos, suyas
nuestro, nuestra, nuestros, nuestras
vuestro, vuestra, vuestros, vuestras)
suyo, suya, suyos, suyas

EXAMPLES: Es **mi libro.**   Es **mío.**

Note from the preceding examples that the long form may perform a double function (both adjective and pronoun). It modifies (and must agree with) the noun, while it may also replace the noun. Note also that it always agrees with the thing possessed, never with the person possessing it.

➤ Replace the italicized words with the correct form of the long possessive adjective.

1. *Este lápiz* es *mi lápiz.* _____

2. *Esta pluma* es *mi pluma.* _____

3. *Estos juguetes* no son *sus juguetes.* _____

4. *Esta sombrilla amarilla* es *mi sombrilla.* _____

5. ¿De quién es este cuaderno? ¿Es *de usted*? _____

6. *Estos dos automóviles* son *de Carlos.* _____

7. ¿*Esta composición* es *su composición*, verdad? _____

8. ¿De quién son estos libros? No son *nuestros libros.* _____

9. *Este cuarto y el cuarto de al lado* son *de nosotros.* _____

10. ¿*Esta aula* es *nuestra aula de clase*, no? _____

11. Parece que *estos anteojos* son *tus anteojos.* _____

12. *Las dos casas, la blanca y la verde,* son *de mi tío.* _____

13. *Este abrigo* no es *mi abrigo.* Es *de Elena.* _____

14. *Aquel dinero que está en el armario* es *de ellos.* _____

15. ¿De quién son estas monedas? ¿Son *mis monedas*? _____

16. ¿De quién son estos asientos? No son *de ustedes.* _____

17. Yo creo que *esta revista* es *mi revista.* _____

18. *La oficina de arriba* es *tu oficina.* _____

19. *Los planos para el rascacielos* son *del arquitecto.* _____

20. *La bufanda encima del sofá* es *de la señora Chávez.* _____

Worksheet 10.2 More on possessive adjectives

➤ Substitute the verb **ser** for the verb **pertenecer**. Add the necessary possessive adjective (**mío**) to replace the prepositional pronoun (**a mí**).

1. Esta pluma *me pertenece a mí.* _____

2. Esos dos automóviles *le pertenecen a él.* _____

3. Ese abrigo elegante *le pertenece a la profesora.* _____

   _____

4. Estas bicicletas *nos pertenecen a nosotros.* _____

5. Creo que esta cartera *te pertenece a ti.* _____

6. Estas llaves *le pertenecen al señor Gómez.* _____

7. Estos cuadernos *les pertenecen a ellos.* _____

8. Este lapicero *me pertenece a mí.* _____

9. Ese par de guantes *le pertenece a ella.* _____

10. Este par *me pertenece a mí.* _____

11. Estas dos sombrillas *nos pertenecen a nosotros.* _____

    _____

12. ¿Esa cajetilla de cigarrillos *te pertenece a ti?* _____

13. ¿No *le pertenece a Teresa* esta pluma? _____

14. ¿No *les pertenecen* estos libros *a ustedes?* _____

15. Aquellos cuadernos *les pertenecen a ustedes.* _____

16. Esas dos bicicletas *les pertenecen a Rosa y a Elena.* _____

    _____

17. Este abrigo no *te pertenece a ti.* _____

18. Este escritorio *le pertenece al director.* _____

19. Aquella casa verde *le pertenece al señor Rojas.* _____

    _____

20. El automóvil inglés *le pertenece a él* también. _____

21. El espejo que rompiste *me pertenecía a mí.* _____

    _____

22. Las maletas perdidas *nos pertenecían a nosotros.* _____

    _____

Worksheet 10.3 Possessive pronouns

Mío, tuyo, suyo, nuestro, (vuestro), when preceded by the definite article, are always possessive pronouns. In reality, there is no difference; they are both "double antecedent" pronouns, which replace both the thing possessed and the person who possesses it. Example: In **nosotros tenemos la nuestra**, for example, **nuestra** stands for *us*, which is plural, but also replaces something we own, which is singular.

The long forms of the possessive pronoun are used for emphasis, since the short forms (**mi, tu, su, etc.**) must never be uttered strong.

EXAMPLE: No es **tu** (*weak*) libro.
            Es el **mío** (*strong, emphasis for disputed ownership*).
            El **tuyo** es rojo; el **mío** es verde (*emphasis for contrast*).

When used emphatically, they are preceded by the definite article:

el mío	la mía	los míos	las mías	*mine*
el tuyo	la tuya	los tuyos	las tuyas	*yours*
el suyo	la suya	los suyos	las suyas	*yours, his, hers*
el nuestro	la nuestra	los nuestros	las nuestras	*ours*
(el vuestro	la vuestra	los vuestros	las vuestras	*yours*)
el suyo	la suya	los suyos	las suyas	*yours, theirs*

➤ Substitute the corresponding possessive pronoun for the words in italics.

1. Él quiere usar *mi libro*. _____

2. Yo tengo mis libros. Julio tiene *sus libros*. _____

3. Esta casa es más grande que *nuestra casa*. _____

4. Esta es mi cartera. ¿Dónde está *la cartera de usted*? _____

5. El maestro siempre lee *nuestros poemas* en clase. _____

6. Me pongo nervioso cuando lee *mi poema*. _____

7. Ellos tienen que respetar *tus derechos*. _____

8. Él nunca respeta *mis opiniones*. _____

9. Yo siempre respeto *sus opiniones de él*. _____

10. Siempre respeto *sus opiniones de ella* también. _____

11. Necesito una pluma. ¿Me prestas *tu pluma*? _____

12. *Mi cuarto* y *tu cuarto* son idénticos. _____

13. La cartera de Isabel se parece a *la cartera de usted*. _____

14. Yo encontré mi lápiz, pero tú no encontraste *tu lápiz*. _____

15. Tú compraste tu reloj donde yo compré *mi reloj*. _____

16. Tengo mis billetes. ¿Dónde pusiste *tus billetes*? _____

17. Compro mi ropa aquí. ¿Dónde compra usted *su ropa*? _____

18. La sala de ustedes tiene más sillas que *nuestra sala*. _____

19. Su computadora funciona mejor que *mi computadora*. _____

20. El apartamento de ellos es mayor que *tu apartamento*. _____

Worksheet 10.4 Possessive pronouns—*suyo*

El suyo (la suya, los suyos, las suyas) could mean *yours, his, hers, or theirs*. To make clear who the possessor is, Spanish speakers frequently use **de usted, de ustedes, de él, de ella, de ellos,** and **de ellas.**

EXAMPLES: *Tengo la dirección de Juan, pero no tengo* **la suya.**   *Unclear:* *yours, his, hers, theirs*
                                   la de usted.   *yours*
                                   la de ustedes.   *yours, pl.*
                                   la de él.   *his*
                                   la de ella.   *hers*
                                   la de ellos.   *theirs*

➤ Supply the appropriate definite article.

1. Me gusta la casa de ustedes tanto como _____ de ellos.

2. Pero el baño de ellos es más grande que _____ de ustedes.

3. Las rosas de ella tienen más fragancia que _____ de usted.

4. Las rosas de usted son más grandes que _____ de ella.

5. Ya envié el paquete de Luis y _____ de Pedro.

6. No recibí ni la carta de Luis ni _____ de Pedro.

7. Probé las galletas de María pero no _____ de usted.

8. La receta de ella y _____ de usted son idénticas.

9. Mi coche tiene dos puertas; _____ de ella tiene cuatro.

10. La radio de mi coche funciona mejor que _____ de ella.

11. Ningún perro es más feroz que _____ de usted.

12. Su perro tiene la cola más corta que _____ nuestro.

13. Los poetas de Chile son más conocidos que _____ de Bolivia.

14. El estaño de Bolivia es más valioso que _____ de Chile.

15. ¿Has visto las botas de los chicos? Sólo están _____ del profesor.

16. Ellos tienen sus bufandas. ¿Tiene Rita _____ de ella?

17. Tengo los guantes de Nora, pero no tengo _____ de Pepe.

18. Encontré mi paraguas, pero no sé dónde está _____ de Ana.

19. Las fotos que ella saca son mejores que _____ de ustedes.

20. Su cámara costó mucho menos que _____ de ella.

Worksheet 10.5 Conditional

The conditional tense, like the future tense, uses the entire infinitive as a stem. The endings for *all* conditional tense verbs are as follows:

hablar		
yo	hablaría	*I would speak*
tú	hablarías	*you would speak*
él, ella, usted	hablaría	*he, she, you would speak*
nosotros(as)	hablaríamos	*we would speak*
vosotros(as)	hablaríais	*you would speak*
ellos, ellas, ustedes	hablarían	*they, you would speak*

➤ Change these verbs to the future tense first and then to the conditional tense. Remember to use the proper stem.

PRESENT TENSE	FUTURE TENSE	CONDITIONAL TENSE
1. yo escribo		
2. ella compra		
3. nosotros vivimos		
4. él va		
5. yo conozco		
6. él estudia		
7. tú prometes		
8. él saca		
9. le gusta		
10. el tren llega		
11. yo repito		
12. tú pides		
13. ella recibe		
14. tú preparas		
15. usted lee		
16. yo escojo		
17. tú te levantas		
18. él se acuesta		
19. la clase empieza		
20. ustedes trabajan		
21. ella gasta		
22. yo como		
23. nosotros vamos		
24. mis primos bailan		
25. tú respondes		
26. tu hermana vive		

Worksheet 10.6 Conditional in noun clauses

In indirect speech using a noun clause, when the main verb of a sentence is in the past tense, the verb in the noun clause (denoting future action or intention in the past) will be in the conditional tense.

EXAMPLES: *Noun Clause*

Luis **dice** que **hablará** con ella.   *present tense + future tense*

Luis **dijo** que **hablaría** con ella.   *past tense + conditional tense*

➤ Supply the conditional tense of the verb in parentheses.

1. Mi padre dijo que me _____ (comprar) un perro.

2. Yo le prometí que lo _____ (cuidar) muy bien.

3. El dijo que me _____ (ayudar) a pintar la casa.

4. Yo sabía que él _____(cumplir) su palabra.

5. El insistió en que_____ (regresar) el miércoles.

6. Yo creía que no _____ (llegar) hasta el jueves.

7. Ella mencionó que le _____ (gustar) viajar a Chicago.

8. Yo le dije que_____ (pagar) su boleto.

9. El jefe dijo que nosotros _____ (trabajar) los sábados.

10. Yo le aseguré que yo _____ (cooperar) con los otros.

11. Le dije a mi esposa que _____ (buscar) un buzón.

12. Un señor dijo que nosotros _____ (ver) un buzón en la esquina.

13. Tú prometiste que _____ (aprender) francés.

14. Él te aseguró que lo _____ (lograr) con una maestra.

15. Ellos insistieron en que yo _____ (ganar) el torneo.

16. Yo les dije que eso me _____ (sorprender).

17. La maestra dijo que el examen _____ (ser) muy largo.

18. Yo le prometí a ella que lo _____ (terminar) a tiempo.

19. Yo creí que_____ (llover) muy pronto.

20. Tú dijiste que ellos no _____ (cancelar) el desfile.

21. La policía indicó que _____ (cerrar) nuestra calle.

22. Yo no sabía donde yo _____ (estacionar) mi coche.

Worksheet 10.7 More on conditional in noun clauses

➤ Change the first verb of each sentence to the past tense, preterite, or imperfect; then change the second verb to the conditional tense.

1. Juan dice que les escribirá mañana. _____

2. Ellos dicen que estudiarán más tarde. _____

3. Él piensa que el negocio será un éxito. _____

4. En su carta dicen que llegarán mañana. _____

5. Su secretaria dice que él volverá dentro de poco. _____

6. Tú dices que nos pagarás pronto. _____

7. El niño insiste en que cumplirá ocho años. _____

8. Él piensa que usted le ayudará. _____

9. Elena dice que ella preparará toda la cena. _____

10. El periódico dice que lloverá mañana. _____

11. Creo que Elena y Felipe llegarán hoy. _____

12. Yo le prometo a usted que iré con ellos. _____

13. Le aseguro a usted que pagaré pronto. _____

14. El arquitecto dice que terminará la obra. _____

15. Crees que tu padre te regalará un coche. _____

16. El pintor dice que empezará a pintar la casa. _____

17. Los empleados creen que les darán más sueldo. _____

18. Ella dice que volverá pronto a nuestra casa. _____

19. Tú insistes en que sacarás buenas notas. _____

20. Todos creen que nosotros nos casaremos. _____

21. Él indica que la comida estará lista. _____

22. Creo que la huelga terminará pronto. _____

23. ¿No adivinas que yo te escogeré a ti? _____

Worksheet 10.8 Conditional of irregular verbs

Those verbs that have irregular stems in the future tense will have identical stems in the conditional tense:

EXAMPLE:
caber	cabría, etc.	poder	podría, etc.	salir	saldría, etc.
decir	diría, etc.	poner	pondría, etc.	tener	tendría, etc.
haber	habría, etc.	querer	querría, etc.	valer	valdría, etc.
hacer	haría, etc.	saber	sabría, etc.	venir	vendría, etc.

➤ Change each verb first to the future tense, then to the conditional.

PRESENT TENSE	FUTURE TENSE	CONDITIONAL TENSE
1. yo salgo		
2. él tiene		
3. tú dices		
4. esto vale		
5. ella viene		
6. nadie sabe		
7. esto cabe		
8. yo sé		
9. ellos hacen		
10. yo quiero		
11. yo pongo		
12. tú tienes		
13. ellos salen		
14. yo puedo		
15. hay		
16. tú sabes		
17. nosotros hacemos		
18. Fernando puede		
19. ustedes vienen		
20. él dice		
21. Elena sale		
22. tú pones		
23. nadie tiene		
24. yo vengo		

Worksheet 10.9 More on conditional of irregular verbs

➤ Supply the conditional tense of the verbs in parentheses.

1. El dueño dijo que nos _____ (pagar) hoy.

2. Yo pensaba que no lo _____ (hacer).

3. Él dijo que no _____ (poder) vivir sin ella.

4. Ella creía que él pronto_____ (tener) otra novia.

5. Tú dijiste que nos _____ (decir) todo lo que pasa.

6. Yo sabía que tú no _____ (saber) nada del asunto.

7. Carmen indicó que posiblemente _____ (querer) aprender francés.

8. Nosotros le dijimos que _____ (tener) que practicar mucho.

9. Me parecía que _____ (haber) más azúcar en esta receta.

10. Yo pensaba que tú le _____ (poner) un poco más.

11. Me imaginaba que nosotros no_____ (caber) en este cochecito

12. El chofer dijo que él _____ (hacer) dos viajes.

13. El artista prometió que la pintura pronto _____ (valer) más.

14. Yo, en cambio, pensaba que _____ (tener) menos valor.

15. El embajador dijo que _____ (venir) a Washington en marzo.

16. Yo creía que_____ (hacer) el viaje a mediados de febrero.

17. Ustedes sabían que nosotros _____ (salir) temprano del cine.

18. Adivinaron bien que nosotros no _____ (querer) quedarnos.

19. ¿Cómo sabías tú que ella nos_____ (decir) la verdad?

20. Pues, ella me aseguró que yo_____ (poder) confiar en ella.

21. ¿Por qué piensas que yo_____ (saber) afinar su guitarra?

22. Evita me dijo que tú _____ (poder) hacérmelo.

23. Yo sabía que ella nunca me _____ (decir) su secreto.

24. Creo que _____ (valer) la pena preguntárselo

   una vez más.

Worksheet 10.10 Corresponding verb and noun forms

Note the noun forms that correspond to each verb:

EXAMPLES: nacer → nacimiento   contar → cuento   pescar → pesca

➤ Supply the appropiate noun form for each verb.

VERB	NOUN	VERB	NOUN
1. repetir		26. aburrir	
2. bailar		27. discutir	
3. regañar		28. explicar	
4. regalar		29. desear	
5. proteger		30. imaginar	
6. remediar		31. invitar	
7. prometer		32. jugar	
8. recibir		33. limpiar	
9. satisfacer		34. pelear	
10. terminar		35. trabajar	
11. cambiar		36. preparar	
12. bromear		37. llamar	
13. beber		38. testificar	
14. reservar		39. confiar	
15. besar		40. conversar	
16. alegrar		41. aprender	
17. abrazar		42. describir	
18. conocer		43. viajar	
19. decidir		44. celebrar	
20. descubrir		45. preguntar	
21. excitar		46. permitir	
22. sospechar		47. pasar	
23. robar		48. pagar	
24. castigar		49. gastar	
25. observar		50. gustar	

Worksheet 10.11 Verbs requiring prepositions

Note the prepositions that accompany the following verbs:

acostumbrarse a	acabar de (*just ...*)	confiar en	contar con
aprender a	acordarse de	constar en	chocar con
comenzar a	dejar de (*stop*)	entrar en	soñar con
empezar a	olvidarse de	insistir en	estar para
invitar a	salir de	pensar en	estudiar para
principiar a	sorprenderse de	quedar en	salir para
volver a (*...again*)	tratar de (*try*)	tardar en	tener que

➤ Supply the preposition needed to complete the meaning of each sentence.

1. Yo dejé _____ leer ese libro porque me parecía aburrido.

2. Mi esposa empezó _____ leer el libro cuando yo lo abandoné.

3. Ella dijo que volvería _____ llover.

4. Por eso insistió _____ ponerse el impermeable.

5. Mis tíos me invitaron _____ viajar con ellos en Europa.

6. Yo nunca soñé _____ tanta suerte.

7. Su hermano tardó mucho _____ buscar trabajo.

8. Mi padre y yo quedamos _____ ofrecerle empleo.

9. Tengo _____ representar mi compañía en Roma.

10. Mañana empezaré _____ estudiar italiano.

11. Mi camión chocó _____ la camioneta del vecino.

12. No vi su vehículo cuando salí _____ mi garaje.

13. Un día de estos trataré _____ visitar a sus abuelos.

14. No quiero dejar _____ verlos de vez en cuando.

15. Mi hermana ya salió _____ Nueva York donde espera ser modelo.

16. Yo acabo _____ despedirme de ella en el aeropuerto.

17. Trataremos _____ llegar al concierto a tiempo.

18. Más vale salir ahora. No te olvides _____ llevar los boletes.

19. ¡Mira qué bonita! La niña se vistió _____ payasito.

20. Afortunadamente, me acordé _____ traer mi cámara.

21. Cuando entré, el perro empezó _____ ladrar.

22. El animal dejó _____ ladrar cuando me reconoció.

23. Tengo _____ pagarle con un cheque de viajeros.

24. Está bien. Yo siempre confío _____ esa forma de pagar.

Prepositions

➤ Supply the preposition needed to complete the meaning of each sentence.

1. Tratamos varias veces _____ ponernos en contacto con él.

2. Dijo que iba _____ llamarme, pero no lo ha hecho.

3. Tú no tienes ningún interés _____ visitar a tus tíos.

4. Es bueno que ellos vienen aquí de vez _____ cuando.

5. Soñé toda la noche _____ unos amigos de mi infancia.

6. Me desperté con ganas _____ visitarlos.

7. Mi esposa acaba _____ salir de casa.

8. Dijo que iba a volver _____ enseguida.

9. A ella le gusta mucho ir _____ compras en el centro.

10. Ayer gastó más _____ cien dólares de ropa nueva.

11. Él se parece mucho _____ su padre.

12. Hasta empieza _____ hablar como él.

13. Nadie le ha dado _____ comer al pobre perro.

14. No sé por qué nos olvidamos tanto _____ él.

15. Este bolígrafo nuevo no sirve _____ nada.

16. _____ lo mejor se secó la tinta.

17. Yo voy a quedarme _____ casa todo el día.

18. Después _____ descansar un día, espero sentirme mejor.

19. Ellos vienen aquí muy _____ menudo.

20. Un día _____ éstos, nosotros vamos a visitarlos a ellos.

21. Ahora tenemos que despedirnos _____ ustedes.

22. Muchas gracias _____ habernos invitado.

23. Elena asiste _____ una universidad venezolana.

24. No sé por qué le gusta tanto _____ Habana.

25. Estos papeles no tienen nada que ver _____ mi trabajo.

26. Mi hijo necesita llevar estos papeles _____ la escuela.

27. Mi tienda está _____ frente del banco.

28. También está al lado _____ la clínica.

29. _____ pesar de la lluvia, Carlos tiene que salir de casa.

30. El patrón cuenta _____ él en la fábrica.

General review

➤ Choose the correct form and write it in the blank.

1. Vasco Núñez de Balboa _____ (descubrió, descubría) un océano.

2. El océano _____ (llama, se llama) el Pacífico.

3. Lo _____ (había, estaba) descubierto en el año 1513.

4. Hernán Cortés salió _____ (de, por) Cuba con 500 soldados.

5. En 1519 _____ (desembarcaron, desembarcarán) en la isla de Cozumel.

6. Después _____ (que, de) conquistar a los aztecas, los gobernó.

7. Pedro de Alvarado acompañó _____ (Cortés, a Cortés) en México.

8. Él exploró _____ (muchos, muchas) partes de la América Central.

9. Hasta el Perú _____ (llegado, llegó) Alvarado.

10. Cabeza de Vaca fue un _____ (gran, grande) explorador de ríos.

11. Él _____ (descubrió, descubrió a) varios ríos en tres continentes.

12. _____ (Escribió, Escrito) el libro «Naufragios y comentarios».

13. Hernando de Soto _____ (fue, estuvo) gobernador de Cuba.

14. Antes _____ (había, habrá) estado con Pizarro en el Perú.

16. Ponce de León descubrió _____ (Florida, la Florida) en 1512.

17. Fue el _____ (primer, primero) gobernador de Puerto Rico.

18. Cuando fue a Cuba ya se _____ (estaba, está) muriendo.

19. Francisco Pizarro _____ (fue, iba) con Balboa a Panamá.

20. Fue el explorador _____ (más, el más) conocido del Perú.

21. Se apoderó _____ (del, al) emperador Atahualpa en Cajamarca.

22. Sebastián de Benalcázar era compañero _____ (de, con) Pizarro.

23. En _____ (Ecuador, el Ecuador) fundó Quito y Guayaquil.

24. Estaba _____ (explorado, explorando) esa región en 1534.

Part 11

Contents

Worksheet 11.1 Subjunctive mood—present tense

There are three moods. The *indicative mood* is used for statements of fact, the *imperative mood* is the command form, and the *subjunctive mood* is for statements that are not necessarily true. The *subjunctive mood* has not been seen in any of the preceding exercises.

In English, we may say: *I hope she sings*. This sounds strange in Spanish, because *she sings* is a statement of fact. She will not necessarily sing just because I hope she will. Spanish therefore says *I hope she may sing*, with *may sing* being a single verb in the subjunctive mood. This verb form will be required in dependent clauses after such verbs as *want, wish, hope, doubt, fear*, and also in impersonal expressions, such as *It is important (necessary, probable) that*. It also appears after verbs of emotion, like *I am delighted that*.

Indicatives and subjunctives trade endings. The endings for **-ar** verbs in the subjunctive mood are the same as the endings for **-er** verbs in the indicative mood, except that the third person and first person singular* forms are the same:

INDICATIVE		SUBJUNCTIVE	
hablo	hablamos	*hable	hablemos
hablas	habláis	hables	habléis
habla	hablan	hable	hablen

➤ Supply the present subjunctive form for each of the following verbs.

1. yo estudio _____
2. ellos compran _____
3. ella habla _____
4. yo me lavo _____
5. él se levanta _____
6. él toma _____
7. tú miras _____
8. usted paga _____
9. nosotros usamos _____
10. él pregunta _____
11. ellos llegan _____
12. tú cuentas _____
13. nosotros atamos _____
14. él se enferma _____
15. tú estudias _____
16. ustedes hablan _____
17. tú te peinas _____
18. Pablo anda _____
19. él explica _____
20. ella cambia _____

21. él enseña _____
22. nadie roba _____
23. ella contesta _____
24. usted pregunta _____
25. él saluda _____
26. ella recuerda _____
27. tú escuchas _____
28. él regala _____
29. tú trabajas _____
30. ella espera _____
31. usted enseña _____
32. ella compra _____
33. yo me canso _____
34. nosotros damos _____
35. ellos miran _____
36. yo empiezo _____
37. ustedes hablan _____
38. yo necesito _____
39. Ana manda _____
40. nosotros ganamos _____

Worksheet 11.2 More on subjunctive mood—present tense

Both -**er** and -**ir** verbs trade endings with -**ar** verbs. The first person singular, however, will have the same ending as the third person singular:

INDICATIVE		SUBJUNCTIVE		INDICATIVE		SUBJUNCTIVE	
como	comemos	com**a**	com**amos**	vivo	vivimos	viv**a**	viv**amos**
comes	coméis	com**as**	com**áis**	vives	vivís	viv**as**	viv**áis**
come	comen	com**a**	com**an**	vive	viven	viv**a**	viv**an**

➤ Supply the present subjunctive for each of the following verbs.

1. él escribe _____
2. ellos insisten _____
3. tú crees _____
4. yo rompo _____
5. ellos cometen _____
6. él bebe _____
7. tú asistes _____
8. usted vende _____
9. yo debo _____
10. él reparte _____
11. yo cojo _____
12. ella escoge _____
13. nosotros metemos _____
14. tú temes _____
15. yo prefiero _____
16. ellos descubren _____
17. yo comprendo _____
18. ustedes suben _____
19. yo me sorprendo _____
20. todos responden _____

21. ella asiste _____
22. él corre _____
23. tú prefieres _____
24. nosotros cosemos _____
25. él cubre _____
26. tú te aburres _____
27. nosotros debemos _____
28. él se mete _____
29. ellos recogen _____
30. tú aprendes _____
31. yo recibo _____
32. ellos comen _____
33. él vive _____
34. tú comes _____
35. nosotros leemos _____
36. ellas venden _____
37. él abre _____
38. yo cometo _____
39. nadie vende _____
40. tú vives _____

Worksheet 11.3 Subjunctive mood—present tense of irregular verbs

If an irregular present indicative verb ends in **-o** in the first person singular, its stem will also be used for the present subjunctive:

VERB	INDICATIVE	SUBJUNCTIVE	VERB	INDICATIVE	SUBJUNCTIUE
caer	caigo	**caiga,** etc.	poner	pongo	**ponga,** etc.
caber	quepo	**quepa,** etc.	salir	salgo	**salga,** etc.
decir	digo	**diga,** etc.	tener	tengo	**tenga,** etc.
oír	oigo	**oiga,** etc.	valer	valgo	**valga,** etc.

➤ Supply the present subjunctive of each of the following verbs.

1. él hace __que él haga_____
2. ella oye _____
3. yo salgo _____
4. usted viene _____
5. él dice _____
6. tú ves _____
7. ustedes pierden _____
8. yo me siento _____
9. ustedes hacen _____
10. tú cierras _____
11. yo traduzco _____
12 nadie tiene_____
13. él cabe _____
14. nada sirve _____
15. él produce _____
16. usted hace _____
17. tú oyes _____
18. él duerme _____
19. yo puedo _____
20. tú traes _____

21. ellos tienen _____
22. él conoce_____
23. ella merece _____
24. tú ofreces_____
25. ellos valen _____
26. yo almuerzo _____
27. nosotros decimos _____
28. ellos salen _____
29. nosotros oímos _____
30. yo entiendo_____
31. ellos ponen _____
32. ellos se mueren_____
33. nada sale _____
34. ellos oyen _____
35. tú vuelves _____
36. nosotros traemos _____
37. nosotras venimos _____
38. ustedes tienen_____
39. él se cae_____
40. nosotros dormimos _____

El presente del subjuntivo

➤ Find the subjunctive form of each verb in the list, then locate it in the puzzle. As you find and circle the word, write it in the blank spaces provided.

L	O	N	F	I	N	J	A	N	O	S
T	E	E	C	T	E	M	A	O	S	T
E	H	A	Y	A	A	B	R	A	H	O
N	R	U	S	U	I	O	L	E	U	Q
G	B	E	O	R	U	G	V	I	E	U
A	A	L	C	T	A	H	A	B	L	E
N	J	S	U	E	L	A	Y	M	A	N
D	E	O	P	O	N	G	A	M	O	S
I	N	Q	U	E	P	A	R	I	O	S
G	I	C	O	N	D	U	Z	C	A	R
A	H	O	G	U	E	N	O	V	U	I
S	O	M	E	D	A	S	I	G	A	A
I	P	A	G	U	E	V	E	A	N	S

PRESENT	SUBJUNCTIVE	PRESENT	SUBJUNCTIVE	PRESENT	SUBJUNCTIVE
sale	_____	conduce	_____	huele	_____
ponemos	_____	pago	_____	bajan	_____
temo	_____	tocan	_____	come	_____
lees	_____	da	_____	ven	_____
son	_____	caemos	_____	sigue	_____
voy	_____	dices	_____	ahogan	_____
damos	_____	rezan	_____	ríes	_____
habla	_____	cabe	_____	suelo	_____
escriben	_____	fingen	_____	lees	_____
vives	_____	he	_____	abre	_____
hace	_____	tienen	_____		

Worksheet 11.4 Subjunctive mood to express uncertainty

It is not a certainty that something will happen just because someone *wants, wishes, asks, commands, insists, prefers, hopes, begs,* or *prays* that it will happen. If the main clause of a sentence features such a verb, the verb in the dependent clause, which expresses the uncertain action, will be in the subjunctive mood and will be preceded by the word **que.**

EXAMPLES: **Quiero que ella cante.**   *I want her to sing.*   (*I want that she sing[s].*)
          Ella espera que vengas. *She hopes you'll come.* (*She hopes that you come.*)

➤ Supply the present subjunctive form of the verbs in parentheses.

1. Mamá quiere que nosotros (*lavar*) los platos. _____

2. Espero que mi hermanita me (*ayudar*) a lavarlos. _____

3. El profesor exige que yo (*leer*) cincuenta páginas. _____

4. Él desea que yo (*terminar*) el libro en cuatro días. _____

5. Susana espera que Tomás la (*invitar*) al baile. _____

6. Tomás espera que Susana (*querer*) aceptar su invitación. _____

7. Es importante que tú (*ahorrar*) la mitad de tu sueldo. _____

8. Es necesario que tú (*tener*) el dinero para pagar tus estudios. _____

9. Insistimos en que ellos (*llegar*) antes de las ocho. _____

10. Quieren que nos (*sentar*) antes de la primera escena. _____

11. Espero que toda la familia (*caber*) en tu coche. _____

12. Es preferible que (*usar*) dos coches para el viaje. _____

13. Sólo quiero que me (*decir*) siempre la verdad. _____

14. En cambio, quiero que tú no me (*hacer*) tantas preguntas. _____

15. Dígale a su hermano que (*volver*) a casa enseguida. _____

16. Dile a Mamá que no se (*preocupar*). Regreso muy pronto. _____

17. Espero que te (*aliviar*) pronto de la gripe. _____

18. El médico insiste en que yo no (*trabajar*) mañana. _____

19. El dueño exige que ustedes se (*poner*) corbata. _____

20. Me alegro que él se (*preocupar*) tanto de la seguridad. _____

21. El entrenador quiere que nosotros (*practicar*) una hora más. _____

22. Con tanta práctica, espero que nosotros (*empezar*) a ganar. _____

Worksheet 11.5 More on the subjunctive mood to express uncertainty

The subjunctive mood is used only when there is a change of subject in the dependent clause.

EXAMPLE: **Yo quiero que tú vuelvas.**   *I want you to return.*

If there is no change in subject, the infinitive will be used.

EXAMPLE: **Yo quiero volver.**   *I want to return.*

➤ In the following sentences, introduce **usted** as a second subject, and change the verb to the subjunctive.

1. Yo quiero *estudiar* francés. _____*que usted estudie*_____

2. Espero *empezar* mañana. _____

3. Ella desea *cantar* el papel de Carmen en Milán. _____

4. Yo prefiero *cantar* el papel de Dalila en Nueva York. _____

5. Nosotros queremos *conocer* San Francisco en el verano. _____

6. Sobre todo deseamos *pasear* en los tranvías. _____

7. Yo insisto en *leer* las instrucciones otra vez. _____

8. Yo quiero *armar* la bicicleta correctamente. _____

9. El quiere *pasar* el día escribiendo cartas. _____

10. Ella prefiere *usar* el tiempo para limpiar la casa. _____

11. En Tijuana insisto en *regatear* con los comerciantes. _____

12. Mi amigo insiste en *aceptar* los precios fijos. _____

13. Yo espero *tocar* el piano mejor que ella. _____

14. Su mamá espera *aprender* a tocarlo mejor que nadie. _____

15. Tomás desea *organizar* una huelga de los obreros. _____

16. El jefe quiere *seguir* negociando con la compañía. _____

17. Yo espero *sacar* buenas notas este semestre. _____

18. Yo quiero *conseguir* una beca universitaria. _____

19. Nosotros insistimos en *apoyar* al presidente. _____

20. Ellos prefieren *ayudar* al otro candidato. _____

21. Yo quiero *revisar* las reglas de nuestro club. _____

22. El tesorero insiste en *cambiarlas.* _____

Worksheet 11.6 Subjunctive mood—*ser, estar, dar, ir*

You will recall that there are no rules for knowing the subjunctive stems of verbs whose first person singulars do not end in **-o**. There are six such verbs; four end in **-oy** and two end in **-e** (see the following exercise). This exercise provides practice with the four **-oy** verbs (**voy, doy, estoy, soy**).

ser	sea	seas	sea	seamos	seáis	sean
estar	esté	estés	esté	estemos	estéis	estén
dar	dé	des	dé	demos	deis	den
ir	vaya	vayas	vaya	vayamos	vayáis	vayan

➤ Supply the present subjunctive form of the verbs in parentheses.

1. Mis padres no quieren que yo _____ (ir) a Europa.

2. Ellos prefieren que yo _____ (estar) siempre en Chicago.

3. Espero que ella me _____ (dar) su número telefónico.

4. ¡Ojalá que algún día nosotros _____ (ser) buenos amigos!

5. Es necesario que usted me _____ (dar) su pasaporte.

6. Esperamos que todo _____ (estar) en orden.

7. Sospecho que usted _____ (ser) el culpable.

8. Espero que los testigos me _____ (dar) una mejor descripción.

9. El médico recomienda que tú _____ (ir) a las montañas.

10. Él quiere que tú _____ (estar) allí a lo menos un mes.

11. A mí no me gusta que nadie me _____ (dar) consejos.

12. Espero que nadie me _____ (ir) a aconsejar.

13. Sus padres se oponen a que él _____ (ser) boxeador.

14. Yo tampoco quiero que su cara _____ (estar) desfigurada.

15. Espero que ese autobús _____ (ir) a mi calle.

16. No me gusta que mi trabajo _____ (estar) tan lejos de mi casa.

17. El profesor exige que nosotros _____ (dar) informes más largos.

18. También insiste en que nadie _____ (estar) ausente.

19. Todos deseamos que la huelga no _____ (ser) muy larga.

20. Los obreros quieren que pronto _____ (estar) de acuerdo.

21. Te recomiendo que no le _____ (dar) de comer a ese gato.

22. Sería mejor que usted _____ (irse) a su casa.

Worksheet 11.7 Subjunctive mood—*saber* and *haber*

The other two verbs whose first person singulars do not end in **-o** are **saber** (*se*) and **haber** (*he*). This means that there are no rules regarding formation of their irregular subjunctive stems. As with those verbs practiced in the preceding exercise, their stems must be memorized without benefit of clues.

| **saber** | sepa | sepas | sepa | sepamos | sepáis | sepan |
| **haber** | haya | hayas | haya | hayamos | hayáis | hayan |

➤ Supply the present subjunctive of the verbs in parentheses.

1. Dudo que me _____ (haber) dicho la verdad.

2. Es posible que ellos no la _____ (haber) sabido.

3. Espero que todos mis amigos me _____ (haber) respaldado.

4. ¡Ojalá que ellos _____ (saber) la importancia de esta elección!

5. Espero que usted se _____ (haber) especializado en frenos.

6. No tenga cuidado. No hay nadie que los_____ (saber) arreglar mejor.

7. Espero que los músicos _____ (haber) aprendido algunos valses.

8. Es una lástima que no_____ (saber) la música de Strauss.

9. Sospechan que ustedes _____ (haber) escrito al senador.

10. Es importante que el senador _____ (saber) la verdad.

11. María duda que nosotros _____ (haber) encontrado las perlas.

12. Deseamos que ella _____ (saber) las horas que pasamos en esto.

13. No es cierto que la policía lo _____ (haber) identificado.

14. No obstante, insisto en que ellos _____ (saber) su nombre.

15. ¿Es cierto que te _____ (haber) inventado esta receta?

16. Es posible que nadie más que yo_____ (saber) los ingredientes.

17. Espero que el candidato_____ (haber) estudiado informática.

18. Ojalá que él _____ (saber) usar nuestra computadora.

19. Nunca creeré que ellas nos _____ (haber) dicho mentiras.

20. Lo que importa es que nosotros _____ (saber) la verdad.

21. Esperamos que ustedes _____ (haber) invitado a los vecinos.

22. Prefiero que algunos ni _____ (saber) que habrá una fiesta.

Worksheet 11.8 Subjunctive mood required by change in subject

➤ In the following sentences, introduce **ustedes** as the second subject, then repeat the exercise with **tú**, **nosotros**, and **ustedes.**

1. Yo prefiero *ir* allí hoy. _____ que ustedes vayan _____

2. Él quiere *saber* la fecha de mi cumpleaños._____

3. Desean *llegar* temprano al concierto. _____

4. Él quiere *ser* presidente de nuestro club de español. _____

5. Insisten en *darle* esta responsabilidad a Carlos. _____

6. Él no quiere *saber* nada de mis negocios. _____

7. Insisten en *ir* a la playa con nosotros esta tarde. _____

8. Yo prefiero *ir* con ustedes al cine esta noche. _____

9. Desean *ir* a estudiar a los Estados Unidos. _____

10. Él quiere *estar* contento en su nuevo puesto. _____

11. Ella quiere *darle* un regalo a la profesora. _____

12. ¿Por qué quieren ellos *ir* allí tan tarde? _____

13. Quiero *darle* a ella las gracias por su regalo. _____

14. Él quiere *ser* siempre lo mejor de la clase. _____

15. Yo quiero *darle* a ella lecciones de español. _____

16. Ellos insisten en *saber* exactamente lo que pasó. _____

17. Ella no quiere *ir* al baile esta noche. _____

18. Yo no quiero *montar* a caballo con ellos en el parque. _____

19. Él prefiere *estar* siempre con los estudiantes. _____

20. Él espera *saber* las palabras de la lista. _____

21. Nosotros esperamos *conocer* a los vecinos. _____

22. Ellas insisten en *ayudar* con la comida. _____

23. Mis abuelos quieren *contribuir* a la Cruz Roja. _____

24. Quiero *darles* de comer a las palomas en la plaza. _____

Worksheet 11.9 Subjunctive mood after verbs of emotion

The subjunctive mood is used in Spanish after all verbs of emotion (**sentir, alegrarse, lamentar, temer, extrañarse, sorprenderse**), provided there is a change of subject in the dependent clause.

EXAMPLES: CHANGE OF SUBJECT   NO CHANGE
              Siento mucho que tú **hayas** fracasado.   Siento haber fracasado.
              Tengo miedo que ella **salga** sola.   Tengo miedo salir solo.

➤ Supply the present subjunctive form of the verbs in parentheses.

1. Lamento mucho que tú no _____ (poder) acompañarnos al cine.

2. Siento que tu abuela _____ (estar) enferma.

3. Me sorprende que él _____ (hablar) español sin acento.

4. Me alegro que él _____ (tener) oportunidades de practicar.

5. A mí no me importa lo que la gente _____ (decir).

6. Me extraña que ellos no _____ (tratar) de conocerme mejor.

7. Él teme que alguien lo _____ (reconocer) en el restaurante.

8. Siento que su fama no le _____ (permitir) salir de casa.

9. Nos interesa que tú _____ (invertir) tanto en ese negocio.

10. Siento que tú _____ (arriesgar) demasiado en tu inversión.

11. Me sorprende que ese producto no _____ (tener) más venta.

12. Lamento que él _____ (perder) tanto dinero en desarrollarlo.

13. Me preocupa que ella _____ (estar) tan delgada.

14. Me extraña que ella nunca _____ (aumentar) ni una libra.

15. Él se alegra de que ustedes _____ (ser) tan buenos amigos.

16. ¿Le sorprende que ella se _____ (parecer) a su madre?

17. ¿Le extraña que yo _____ (saber) esquiar mejor que usted?

18. Me extraña que _____ (encontrar) el tiempo para practicar.

19. ¿Por qué lamentas tanto que yo _____ (vender) mi casa?

20. Temo que una persona menos simpática la_____ (comprar).

21. ¿Te molesta que este coche no_____ (tener) cuatro puertas?

22. No, pero lamento que no _____ (caber) toda la familia.

Worksheet 11.10 Subjunctive mood after impersonal expressions

Uncertainty is also established by such impersonal expressions as **es necesario que, es importante que, es sorprendente que, es una lástima que, no importa que,** etc. If there is a change in subject following such expressions, the verb will be in the subjunctive mood.

EXAMPLES: Es importante que usted **vaya** allí enseguida.
Es una lástima que tú no **aprendas** a bailar.

➤ Supply the present subjunctive form of the verbs in parentheses.

1. Es sorprendente que ellos _____ (querer) hacerlo.

2. Es mejor que ellos _____ (esperar) afuera.

3. Es muy dudoso que ella _____ (viajar) sin su familia.

4. Es importante que nosotros les _____ (dar) la bienvenida.

5. Es indispensable que los niños _____ (hacer) ejercicio físico.

6. Es casi seguro que ellos _____ (pasar) el día viendo televisión.

7. Es necesario que usted _____ (alcanzar) el estante más alto.

8. ¡Qué lástima que usted no _____ (ser) más alta!

9. Es importante que nosotros _____ (ir) al banco esta tarde.

10. Es una lástima que _____ (estar) lloviendo a cántaros.

11. Más vale que ustedes _____ (ahorrar) su dinero para el futuro.

12. Es probable que el costo de la vida _____ (seguir) subiendo.

13. Es preciso que nosotros _____ (interrogar) a los testigos.

14. Es importante que nosotros _____ (establecer) su inocencia.

15. Es necesario que los alumnos _____ (obedecer) a la maestra.

16. Si no, es probable que ella _____ (llamar) a algunos padres.

17. Es justo que tú _____ (recibir) las ganancias de esa inversión.

18. Es increíble que el dinero ya se _____ (haber) duplicado.

19. Es dudoso que yo _____ (asistir) a los juegos olímpicos.

20. Es más probable que yo los _____ (ver) en televisión.

21. Es sorprendente que tú _____ (dejar) de fumar tan fácilmente.

22. Es probable que te _____ (aliviar) completamente de esa tos.

Worksheet 11.11 Subjunctive mood after expressions of doubt or uncertainty

A degree of uncertainty is present in every subjunctive or imperative verb. The need for the subjunctive mood should be immediately evident following actual expressions of doubt or uncertainty.

EXAMPLE: No creo que **conozcas** a una señorita más simpática.
Dudo que **haya** otra como ella.

The expressions **quizá** and **tal vez** also use the subjunctive. If, however, the clause expresses fact rather than doubt, the indicative mood will be used.

EXAMPLE: Nadie duda que ellos son ricos.
Creo que tienen una buena herencia de sus famosos padres.

➤ Supply the present subjunctive form of the verbs in parentheses.

1. Yo dudo que ella _____ (ir) a la feria con nosotros.

2. No creo que a ella le _____ (interesar) las ferias.

3. ¿Tú niegas que _____ (pensar) invertir dinero en esa empresa?

4. No, pero no espero que la inversión me _____ (hacer) rico.

5. Ellos niegan que _____ (ser) de origen nicaragüense.

6. Yo dudo que el inspector de inmigración lo _____ (creer).

7. Yo temo que Pablo _____ (morir) muy pronto.

8. ¡Qué disparate! No creo que _____ (poder) morir de gripe.

9. El acusado niega que _____ (usar) un cómplice en sus robos.

10. El juez duda que él _____ (haber) cometido los robos solo.

11. Yo no creo que Consuelo nos _____ (decir) la verdad.

12. Yo dudo que ella _____ (tener) más de veinte años.

13. No creo que tú _____ (necesitar) cuatro cartas de referencia.

14. Dudo que esa compañía _____ (exigir) tantos documentos.

15. El padre de Luis duda que él _____ (pasar) los exámenes.

16. Luis niega que nunca _____ (preparar) sus lecciones.

17. Lola teme que el perro de los vecinos tal vez _____ (morder).

18. Yo dudo que ese perro no _____ (hacer) más que ladrar.

19. Quizá ellos _____ (volver) el año próximo.

20. Temo que ellos no se _____ (divertir) mucho aquí.

21. Su madre niega que Alicia _____ (oír) con dificultad.

22. Temo que la señora no _____ (desear) creer a la enfermera.

Worksheet 11.12 Subjunctive mood in adverbial clauses

The subjunctive is used in Spanish in adverbial clauses introduced by certain conjunctions expressing a future condition or event, purpose or result, concession or supposition: **cuando, antes (de) que, hasta que, tan pronto como, mientras, para que, a fin de que, de manera que, sin que, aunque, a menos que, con tal (de) que.** Uncertainty, as with all subjunctives, is an obvious factor, since the future is always uncertain.

EXAMPLES: Yo le preguntaré cuando él **venga.**   *He may not come at all.*
 Le doy este libro para que lo **lea.**   *He may prefer not to read it.*
 Iremos allí a menos que **haga** mal tiempo.   *Future weather is uncertain.*

If, however, an accomplished fact is indicated, the indicative mood will be used.

EXAMPLE: Nosotros siempre comemos tan pronto como llega Juan.
 John will definitely be there; we never eat later.

➤ Supply the present subjunctive form of the verbs in parentheses.

1. Tenemos que llamar a Rosa antes de que ella _____ (salir).

2. No iremos a menos que usted_____ (ir) también.

3. Él dice que nos llamará aunque _____ (ser) muy tarde.

4. Tú podrás entender esto con tal que lo _____ (estudiar).

5. Saldré para Europa tan pronto como _____ (recibir) mi visa.

6. Ella no saldrá hasta que nosotros _____ (regresar).

7. Iremos a la playa mañana a menos que _____ (llover).

8. Hablaré con él otra vez de eso cuando lo_____ (ver).

9. Hágame el favor de esperar aquí hasta que yo _____ (venir).

10. No puedes apreciar mi voz a menos que me _____ (oír) cantar.

11. No puedo pagarles hasta que yo _____ (cambiar) este cheque.

12. Te avisaré tan pronto como_____ (llegar) el senador.

13. Tenemos que limpiar la casa antes de que ella _____ (volver).

14. Yo esperaré aquí hasta que tú me_____ (llamar).

15. Te habla en español para que tú_____ (tener) más práctica.

16. No saldremos hasta que _____ (terminar) las clases.

17. No iré a la ópera a menos que tú me _____ (acompañar).

18. Ella no entrará hasta que yo _____ (anunciar) su llegada.

19. Yo te traeré la camisa para que tú me la_____ (planchar).

20. No le pagaré sin que usted me _____ (dar) un recibo.

21. Usted podrá salir tan pronto como _____ (pagar) la multa.

22. Te prestaré el mío con tal que un día me _____ (prestar) el tuyo.

Worksheet 11.13 Subjunctive mood in adjective clauses

The subjunctive is used in Spanish in all adjective clauses where the relative pronoun **que** has a negative antecedent or where the antecedent represents some indefinite person or thing. Note the following changes according to mood:

EXAMPLE: **Busco a alguien aquí que hable español.**
I do not know if anyone here speaks Spanish, but I am looking for such a person.

Busco a alguien aquí que habla español.
I know someone here speaks Spanish, and I am looking for that specific person.

➤ Supply the present subjunctive form of the verbs in parentheses.

1. No hay ninguna región que_____ (tener) paisajes más hermosos que ésta.

2. Busco un libro que _____ (tratar) de la historia del Perú.

3. Deseamos una casa que _____ (dar) al parque.

4. ¿Hay alguien aquí que _____ (saber) bien la gramática?

5. No hay nadie que _____ (conocer) la historia de ese asunto mejor que el señor Carrillo.

6. Queremos visitar un país donde los precios_____ (ser) bajos.

7. No hay nadie en la clase que_____ (estudiar) con más afán que Enrique.

8. Yo necesito un libro que me _____ (dar) una explicación más clara de la gramática.

9. ¿Hay alguien aquí que _____ (poder) decirme dónde se vende ese libro?

10. Él necesita una secretaria que _____ (saber) bien los dos idiomas.

11. Necesitamos una casa que _____ (tener) por lo menos tres dormitorios.

12. Yo no conozco a nadie que _____ (ser) más seria en su trabajo que Elena.

13. Nosotros no hemos encontrado a nadie que _____ (ser) experto en esa materia.

14. Preferimos un chofer que _____ (ser) venezolano.

15. Solicitan a dos hombres jóvenes que _____ (saber) bien el negocio de exportación.

16. La compañia prefiere a candidatos que _____ (tener) mejores referencias.

17. Se solicita un guía que_____ (conocer) bien la ciudad.

18. Quiero ir a una universidad que _____ (tener) una buena facultad de medicina.

Uses of the subjunctive

➤ Supply the present subjunctive form of the verbs in parentheses.

1. Dígale al carnicero que _____ (traer) sus cuchillos.

2. Es necesario que _____ (estar) bien afilados.

3. Él desea que yo _____ (ir) a ver su nueva casa.

4. Yo iré a verla tan pronto como _____ (ser) posible.

5. La maestra quiere que nosotros _____ (leer) cuatro libros.

6. Más vale que yo _____ (empezar) a leer el primero hoy mismo.

7. Voy a esperar aquí hasta que ella _____ (venir).

8. Ojalá que ella no _____ (llegar) tarde.

9. Me extraña mucho que ese niño _____ (portarse) mal.

10. Yo le diré que _____ (dejar) de ser tan travieso.

11. Es posible que Mamá nos _____ (llevar) al zoólogico.

12. Quizá nos _____ (permitir) dar de comer a los monos.

13. No quiero que mis empleados _____ (malgastar) el tiempo.

14. Es importante que la fábrica _____ (producir) mucho más.

15. Escríbeme tan pronto como _____ (desembarcar) allí.

16. Espero que me _____ (decir) tus impresiones de la isla.

17. No hay nadie en la clase que _____ (entender) ese problema.

18. Creo que este libro nos lo _____ (explicar) mejor.

19. Es dudoso que _____ (llover) esta tarde.

20. Me alegro que nosotros _____ (poder) salir sin mojarnos.

21. Es increíble que tú _____ (haber) construido este garaje.

22. Es imposible que tú _____ (tener) tiempo para hacer tanto.

23. Esperamos que el viaje _____ (ser) más agradable este año.

24. Es improbable que el tren _____ (chocar) por segunda vez.

More on uses of the subjunctive

➤ In the following sentences, introduce **usted** as the subject of the subordinate clause. Repeat the exercise with **tú** and **ustedes.**

1. Yo prefiero *estudiar* geografía. _____
2. Es necesario *tener* un atlas corriente. _____
3. Es casi imposible *saber* la capital de cada nación africana. _____
4. Yo *insisto* en leer correctamente los mapas. _____
5. Es posible *identificar* las cordilleras de Estados Unidos. _____
6. Yo quiero *memorizar* también los ríos principales. _____
7. Yo limpiaré la casa antes de *salir*. _____
8. No quiero *verla* tan sucia. _____
9. Espero *lavar* las ventanas y los espejos. _____
10. Insisto en *barrer* los suelos del segundo piso. _____
11. Es importante *llevar* estas botellas a la basura. _____
12. Me alegro mucho *volver* a tener limpia la casa. _____
13. Es bonito *recibir* regalos de cumpleaños. _____
14. No quiero *esperar* hasta pasado mañana. _____
15. Prefiero *abrir* ese misterioso paquete ahora mismo. _____
16. Es importante *saber* de quién es. _____
17. Me alegro *tener* otra carta de la tía Lupe. _____
18. Es necesario *agradecérsela* enseguida. _____
19. Nuestros primos quieren *ir* a la playa. _____
20. Me alegro mucho de *poder* ir con ellos. _____
21. Espero *nadar* en Varadero. _____
22. Es posible *caber* todos en la camioneta de ellos. _____
23. Es necesario *llevar* una botella de loción. _____
24. Nadie quiere *quemarse* del sol. _____
25. Siento mucho *estar* enfermo. _____
26. No quiero *tomar* esa horrible medicina. _____
27. Es posible *aliviarse* con el tiempo. _____
28. Más que nada es importante *descansar*. _____
29. Es mala suerte *tener* la gripe todos los años. _____
30. Lo peor es *faltar* al examen. _____

Part 12

Contents

Worksheet 12.1 Present perfect subjunctive

The present perfect subjunctive is formed the same as the present perfect indicative, except that the helping verb **haber** is in the present subjunctive mood.

PRESENT PERFECT INDICATIVE		PRESENT PERFECT SUBJUNCTIVE	
he hablado	hemos hablado	haya hablado	hayamos hablado
has hablado	habéis hablado	hayas hablado	hayáis hablado
ha hablado	han hablado	haya hablado	hayan hablado

EXAMPLE: Él **ha salido.**   Siento que él **haya salido.**

➤ Supply the present perfect subjunctive of the verbs in parentheses.

1. Dudo que ellos _____ (llegar) tan rápidamente.

2. Siento que ellos _____ (tener) que salir temprano.

3. Temo que el barco _____ (hundirse).

4. No creo que el capitán_____ (dirigirse) a otro puerto.

5. ¡Qué lástima que tú no _____ (poder) ver a Felipe!

6. Me extraña que ella no _____ (dejar) ni un recado.

7. Yo dudo que él_____ (ganar) mucho dinero allí.

8. Es improbable que tú _____ (perder) el concurso.

9. Me alegro que él _____ (aliviarse) del sarampión.

10. Siento que tú no _____ (ver) esa película tan graciosa.

11. Es una lástima que él no _____ (venir) conmigo.

12. Dudo que ellos_____ (tener) tiempo para ayudarme.

13. Es posible que ya _____ (despegar) el avión.

14. Me alegro de que por fin tú _____ (dejar) de fumar.

15. Nos alegramos de que Pepe _____ (graduarse) hoy.

16. Es posible que ellos me _____ (enviar) el paquete.

17. Es probable que ellos _____ (hacer) escala en Lisboa.

18. Sentimos mucho que su perro _____ (perderse).

19. No creo que el señor Ibarra_____ (volver).

20. Esperamos que tú _____ (llegar) sin dificultad.

21. Yo dudo que Raúl les _____ (hablar) de sus planes.

22. No creo que usted _____ (robar) a nadie.

Worksheet 12.2 Imperfect (past) subjunctive (-*ar* verbs)

The imperfect subjunctive is used in subjunctive clauses when the main verb is in the past tense.

EXAMPLE: Insistieron en que yo **hablara** español.

Although two sets of endings exist for this tense, we shall concentrate on the set that is used in Latin America:

hablar			
yo	hablara	nosotros	habláramos
tú	hablaras	vosotros	hablarais
él, ella, usted	hablara	ellos, ellas, ustedes	hablaran

➤ Change the verbs from the present subjunctive to the imperfect subjunctive.

PRESENT SUBJUNCTIVE	PAST SUBJUNCTIVE		PRESENT SUBJUNCTIVE	PAST SUBJUNCTIVE
1. yo estudie _____			19. él trabaje _____	
2. él gane _____			20. tú regales _____	
3. usted pague _____			21. ella espere _____	
4. tú hables _____			22. usted enseñe _____	
5. yo compre _____			23. él piense _____	
6. él tome _____			24. tú busques _____	
7. nosotros miremos _____			25. ella compre _____	
8. ella arregle _____			26. él se enferme _____	
9. ustedes hablen _____			27. ellos regañen _____	
10. tú preguntes _____			28. usted cuide _____	
11. ellos lleguen _____			29. yo adivine _____	
12. usted cuente _____			30. nosotros cenemos _____	
13. nosotros pasemos _____			31. él invite _____	
14. usted robe _____			32. yo indique _____	
15. tú contestes _____			33. ellos respeten _____	
16. él salude _____			34. nadie confie _____	
17. ella recuerde _____			35. nadie repite _____	
18. ustedes escuchen _____			36. tú pronuncies _____	

Worksheet 12.3 Imperfect (past) subjunctive (-*er*, -*ir* verbs)

Regular -**er** and -**ir** verbs have the same endings in the imperfect subjunctive:

comer			
yo	com**iera**	nosotros(as)	com**iéramos**
tú	com**ieras**	vosotros(as)	com**ierais**
él, ella, usted	com**iera**	ellos, ellas, ustedes	com**ieran**

➤ Change the verbs from the present subjunctive to the imperfect subjunctive.

PRESENT SUBJUNCTIVE	IMPERFECT SUBJUNCTIVE	PRESENT SUBJUNCTIVE	IMPERFECT SUBJUNCTIVE
1. yo escriba _____		19. tú insistas _____	
2. ellos insistan _____		20. él asista _____	
3. tú vivas _____		21. ellos prefieran _____	
4. yo rompa _____		22. nosotros vivamos _____	
5. ellos cometan _____		23. él cubra _____	
6. él beba _____		24. él se cubra _____	
7. usted venda _____		25. tú debas _____	
8. tú asistas _____		26. él se meta _____	
9. yo deba _____		27. ellos recojan _____	
10. él reparta _____		28. usted aprenda _____	
11. yo coja _____		29. yo reciba _____	
12. ella escoja _____		30. nosotros comamos _____	
13. tú metas _____		31. él viva _____	
14. yo tema _____		32. yo prefiera _____	
15. él rompa _____		33. ellos vendan _____	
16. ellos descubran _____		34. nadie venda _____	
17. yo aprenda _____		35. nadie viva _____	
18. usted suba _____		36. tú abras _____	

Worksheet 12.4 Imperfect (past) subjunctive—irregular verbs

Verbs that are irregular in the imperfect subjunctive do not have irregular endings. Their stems, however, will match those of the third person plural of irregular preterites:

INFINITIVE	PRETERITE	STEM	INFINITIVE	PRETERITE	STEM
caber	cupieron	cup-	poner	pusieron	pus-
dar	dieron	d-	querer	quisieron	quis-
decir	dijeron	dij-*	saber	supieron	sup-
estar	estuvieron	estuv-	ser	fueron	fu-*
hacer	hicieron	hic-	tener	tuvieron	tuv-
ir	fueron	fu-*	traer	trajeron	traj-
poder	pudieron	pud-	venir	vinieron	vin-

*For these verbs the **-i-** is dropped from the imperfect subjunctive ending.

EXAMPLES:
diera	diéramos	fuera	fuéramos	oyera	oyéramos
dieras	dierais	fueras	fuerais	oyeras	oyerais
diera	dieran	fuera	fueran	oyera	oyeran

➤ Change the verbs from the present subjunctive to the imperfect subjunctive.

PRESENT SUBJUNCTIVE	IMPERFECT SUBJUNCTIVE		PRESENT SUBJUNCTIVE	IMPERFECT SUBJUNCTIVE
1. él haga _____			19. ellos tengan _____	
2. nosotros oigamos _____			20. él conozca _____	
3. yo salga _____			21. nosotros demos _____	
4. ella venga _____			22. yo sea _____	
5. él diga _____			23. tú puedas _____	
6. yo vaya _____			24. ellos ofrezcan _____	
7. tú veas _____			25. ellos puedan _____	
8. yo pierda _____			26. yo haga _____	
9. tú sientas _____			27. ellos vayan _____	
10. ella sepa _____			28. usted traiga _____	
11. yo ponga _____			29. ustedes estén _____	
12. ellos hagan _____			30. nadie salga _____	
13. tú vengas _____			31. nosotros oigamos _____	
14. él se muera _____			32. ellas tengan _____	
15. nosotros vayamos _____			33. ustedes sean _____	
16. tú traduzcas _____			34. él se caiga _____	
17. usted oiga _____			35. usted quiera _____	
18. ellas quepan _____			36. tú estés _____	

Worksheet 12.5 Uses of the imperfect subjunctive

The same situations that trigger the subjunctive in the present tense will cause the imperfect subjunctive to be used in the past. If the meaning warrants, the imperfect subjunctive may also be used with main verbs that are in the present or the imperfect.

EXAMPLES:	MAIN VERB	*Past Subjunctive in the Dependent Clause*
	PRESENT	Yo dudo que Fernando **dejara** ayer los libros abandonados.
	PRETERITE	Fue necesario que él **tomara** parte en la discusión.
	IMPERFECT	Temíamos que ella no **llegara** a tiempo.

➤ Supply the imperfect subjunctive form of the verbs in parentheses.

1. Dudaron que mi amigo _____ (querer) verme.

2. Insistieron en que yo lo _____ (visitar) anoche.

3. Yo quería que tú no _____ (trabajar) ayer.

4. El médico te dijo que _____ (descansar) más.

5. Yo no quería que ellos le _____ (hacer) preguntas.

6. Yo temía que él no les _____ (decir) la verdad.

7. Yo preferiría que usted _____ (salir) con Maricarmen.

8. Era dudoso que ella _____ (aceptar) su invitación.

9. No querían que su hijo _____ (ser) comerciante.

10. Era improbable que él _____ (cambiar) de profesión.

11. Yo no creía que Juanita _____ (necesitar) anteojos.

12. Yo le aconsejé que _____ (consultar) a un buen optometrista.

13. No permitían que los estudiantes _____ (fumar) en clase.

14. Además prohibían que ellos _____ (mascar) chicle.

15. La bibliotecaria exigió que yo _____ (pagar) una multa.

16. Ella no deseaba que yo _____ (devolver) los libros con retraso.

17. Tú siempre insistías en que yo _____ (dormir) más.

18. Quería que tú no _____ (tener) que preocuparte de mí.

19. El camarero insistió en que yo _____ (dejar) una propina.

20. Yo dudaba que _____ (merecer) el veinte por ciento.

21. ¿No había nadie allí que _____ (saber) traducir mi carta?

22. Yo no pensaba que alguien _____ (hablar) inglés en ese pueblecito.

23. Siento mucho que tú no _____ (poder) contestar a la maestra.

24. Ella deseaba que nosotros _____ (entender) la lección.

Worksheet 12.6 Present or imperfect subjunctive?

➤ Supply either the present subjunctive or the imperfect subjunctive, whichever is required according to the main verb and meaning of the sentence.

1. Era necesario que ellos me _____ (avisar) de su llegada.

2. Insisten en que yo_____ (ir) con ellos al cine esta noche.

3. Insistieron en que yo _____ (ir) con ellos al cine anoche.

4. El profesor no permite que nosotros_____ (hablar) inglés en la clase.

5. Él insiste también en que todos los días nosotros _____ (tener) alguna práctica de

   conversación.

6. Ayer él insistió en que nosotros_____ (pasar) la hora entera conversando en español.

7. Era muy importante que tú _____ (tener) bastante dinero para cubrir

   los gastos del primer mes.

8. Temíamos que el avión_____ (llegar) con mucho atraso.

9. Fue muy justo que tú _____ (recibir) el primer premio.

10. Tú dudabas que ellos _____ (quedarse) allí más de un mes.

11. Yo dudo que ella _____ (tener) más de quince años.

12. No quieren que nadie _____ (mencionar) el asunto delante de ti.

13. No querían que nadie _____ (mencionar) el asunto delante de ti.

14. Temen que tú _____ (estar) un poco enferma.

15. Temían que tú _____ (estar) un poco enferma.

16. Llevé mi perro al parque esta mañana para que_____ (hacer) ejercicio.

17. El profesor dice que duda que Rodrigo_____ (pasar) sus exámenes.

18. El profesor dijo que dudaba que Rodrigo _____ (pasar) sus exámenes.

19. Dudo mucho que nosotros _____ (volver) aquí el año que viene.

20. Se solicita un guía que _____ (conocer) bien la ciudad.

21. Esa compañía exige que los empleados _____ (trabajar) los sábados.

22. Esa compañía exigía antes que los empleados_____ (trabajar) los sábados.

23. Mandaron a su hijo a Estados Unidos para que _____ (aprender) bien el inglés.

24. Van a mandar a su hijo a Estados Unidos para que _____ (aprender) bien el

   inglés.

Worksheet 12.7 Present subjunctive to imperfect subjunctive

➤ Change the main verb of each sentence to the past (preterite or imperfect) tense. Then change the verb in the subordinate clause from the present subjunctive to the imperfect subjunctive.

1. Yo *dudo* que ellos *lleguen* a tiempo. _____

2. Él *insiste* en que yo *vaya* con él. _____

3. Él *prefiere* que usted *haga* las decisiones. _____

4. *Es* necesario que tú *vengas* en seguida. _____

5. Yo *dudo* que él *tenga* bastante dinero para entrar en ese negocio. _____

   _____

6. Me *alegro* de que Eduardo *pueda* acompañarnos. _____

7. *Insisten* en que cada pasajero *enseñe* todos sus documentos. _____

   _____

8. Me *alegra* que tú *vayas* con nosotros. _____

9. *Temo* que usted se *canse* mucho en un viaje tan largo. _____

10. *Es* hora de que ustedes *empiecen* a leer algunos libros en español. _____

    _____

11. *Es* importante que todo el mundo *venga* a tiempo. _____

12. La policia *exige* que todo el mundo *cumpla* con las leyes de tránsito. _____

    _____

13. *Es* posible que tu *estés* enojada conmigo. _____

14. *Quieren* que su hija *haga* un viaje a Europa antes de casarse. _____

    _____

15. No *hay* nadie en la clase que *sepa* bien la gramática. _____

16. *Exigen* que el director *sea* un hombre de edad y experiencia. _____

17. *Exigen* también que todos los candidatos *tengan* más de cinco años de experiencia._____

    _____

18. *Preferimos* un guía que *hable* bien inglés. _____

19. *Necesitamos* una casa que *tenga* por lo menos tres dormitorios. _____

    _____

20. *Vamos* al parque todos los días para que los niños *hagan* ejercicio al aire libre. _____

    _____

21. Me *extraña* mucho que el jefe nos *dé* la tarde libre. _____

    _____

22. No *queremos* que usted *esté* solo el día de Navidad. _____

23. *Quiero* que ella *sepa* la verdad. _____

24. *Dudo* mucho que él *acepte* nuestra oferta. _____

Present and imperfect subjunctives

➤ Choose the form that corresponds with the meaning of the sentence.

1. Yo dudaba que el banco les _____ (preste, prestara) tal cantidad de dinero.

2. El médico me dijo que _____ (guarde, guardara) cama por lo menos una semana.

3. También me dijo que _____ (deje, dejara) de fumar.

4. Ella quiere que yo le _____ (ayude, ayudara) a empaquetar todos sus regalos de Navidad.

5. Insisten en que yo _____ (coma, comiera) en su casa esta noche.

6. Insistieron en que yo _____ (coma, comiera) en su casa anoche.

7. No permiten que nadie _____ (entre, entrara) allí.

8. El objeto de esta ley es que personas indeseables no _____ (entren, entraran) en el país.

9. Me sorprendió mucho que Eduardo _____ (hable, hablara) alemán con tanta facilidad.

10. Quiero que te _____ (manden, mandaran) enseguida las cosas que necesitas.

11. El padre me pidió que _____ (acompañe, acompañara) a su hija al concierto.

12. Él tendrá que seguir yendo a esa escuela aunque no le _____ (guste, gustara).

13. Me pidieron que _____ (traiga, trajera) algunos discos a la fiesta.

14. No quiero que nadie me _____ (diga, dijera) lo que debo hacer.

15. No queríamos que tú le _____ (diga, dijeras) a Juan lo que íbamos a hacer.

16. Tienes miedo que él _____ (acepte, aceptara) la oferta de la otra compañía.

17. Tenían miedo que él _____ (deje, dejara) su trabajo con ellos para trabajar en otra compañía.

18. Tus padres no quieren que tú _____ (viajes, viajaras) durante el invierno.

19. También quieren que tú _____ (esperes, esperaras) otro año para casarte.

20. Fuimos allí para que los niños _____ (vean, vieran) la exposición.

21. Prefieres que él _____ (aprenda, aprendiera) un oficio.

22. Insistían en que nos _____ (quedemos, quedáramos) todo el fin de semana.

Worksheet 12.8 Corresponding verb and noun forms

➤ Supply the corresponding noun form of each verb.

VERB FORM	NOUN FORM	VERB FORM	NOUN FORM
1. admirar		26. eliminar	
2. arreglar		27. gritar	
3. considerar		28. golpear	
4. ajustar		29. practicar	
5. pesar		30. producir	
6. tratar		31. perder	
7. aconsejar		32. fracasar	
8. probar		33. avisar	
9. acordar		34. entrar	
10. divertir		35. salir	
11. heredar		36. invertir	
12. creer		37. construir	
13. respirar		38. educar	
14. inspeccionar		39. enseñar	
15. obedecer		40. anunciar	
16. quejar		41. pintar	
17. mudar		42. comprar	
18. mirar		43. llover	
19. pensar		44. nevar	
20. criticar		45. aumentar	
21. existir		46. proceder	
22. crecer		47. ayudar	
23. enterrar		48. visitar	
24. admitir		49. cuidar	
25. coleccionar		50. planear	

Worksheet 12.9 Corresponding adjective and noun forms

➤ Supply the corresponding noun form of each adjective.

ADJECTIVE FORM	NOUN FORM	ADJECTIVE FORM	NOUN FORM
1. rápido		26. cortés	
2. loco		27. sorprendido	
3. limpio		28. curioso	
4. independiente		29. inocente	
5. maravilloso		30. orgulloso	
6. cansado		31. enfermo	
7. oscuro		32. simple	
8. excitado		33. triste	
9. joven		34. importante	
10. viejo		35. difícil	
11. popular		36. nervioso	
12. necesario		37. bello	
13. afectuoso		38. conveniente	
14. cariñoso		39. posible	
15. ambicioso		40. sarcástico	
16. famoso		41. débil	
17. regular		42. peligroso	
18. pobre		43. ausente	
19. rico		44. presente	
20. lujoso		45. religioso	
21. caliente		46. bondadoso	
22. feliz		47. silencioso	
23. diferente		48. celoso	
24. alegre		49. generoso	
25. desgraciado		50. saludable	

Name: _____ Date: _____

Vocabulary check-up—mistakes in fact

➤ Each of the following sentences has a mistake in fact, which appears in italics. Correct the mistake and write the proper form.

1. El primer mes del año es *diciembre.*_____

2. Si hoy es miércoles, anteayer fue *martes.* _____

3. Un triángulo es una figura geométrica de *cuatro* lados. _____

4. El sol se pone siempre por el *este.* _____

5. Una persona sorda no puede *ver* bien. _____

6. El tigre y el león son animales *domésticos.* _____

7. En la palabra «cafetería» el acento cae sobre la *tercera* sílaba._____

8. En una libra hay dieciséis *años.* _____

9. En el alfabeto inglés hay *veinticinco* letras. _____

10. El alfabeto español tiene *veinticuatro* letras. _____

11. En un reloj, la manecilla que indica los minutos es *más* corta que la manecilla que indica la hora.

    _____

12. El primer encuentro entre Colón y América fue en el siglo *dieciséis.* _____

13. El héroe nacional de *Venezuela* es José Martí. _____

14. El participio pasado del verbo decir es *diciendo.* _____

15. El participio pasado del verbo hacer es *haciendo.* _____

16. Por regla general, la carne se vende en una *panadería.* _____

17. Si un hombre quiere cortarse el pelo, va siempre a *un salón de belleza.* ___

18. El país más grande de Sudamérica es *el Perú.* _____

19. La capital de *Costa Rica* es San Juan. _____

20. En todos los países de Sudamérica se habla español, excepto en el Brasil, donde se habla *francés.*

    _____

21. La capital de Colombia es *Lima.* _____

22. La isla de Cuba está en el *océano Pacífico*, a la entrada del Golfo de México. ___

23. El agua de mar es *dulce.*_____

24. El joyero vende *juguetes.* _____

General review

➤ Choose the correct form and write it in the blank.

1. Janet Richards acaba de _____ (graduar, graduarse) de la escuela secundaria.

2. Esta mañana se matricula en _____ (la, el) universidad.

3. Ella habla un poco de _____ (español, el español).

4. Su padre insiste en que ella se _____ (especialice, especializara) en contabilidad.

5. Su madre prefiere que estudie _____ (por, para) enfermera.

6. Janet no quiere ser ni contadora _____ (ni, o) enfermera.

7. Ella prefiere hacer _____ (su, suya) propia decisión.

8. Lo que _____ (la, le) interesa es hacerse maestra bilingüe.

9. Ella quiere _____ (aprender, que aprenda) a hablar español perfectamente.

10. También _____ (tendrá, tuviera) que estudiar la cultura hispánica.

11. Ella ya ha _____ (comprado, comprando) muchos libros.

12. Además está _____ (leído, leyendo) unas revistas mejicanas.

13. A ella _____ (le, les) gustan sus primeros cursos.

14. A sus profesores les _____ (gusta, gustan) Janet Richards.

15. Después de cuatro años de estudios, es posible que ella _____ (pudo, pueda) enseñar en Los Ángeles.

16. Ese distrito escolar siempre necesita maestras que _____ (sean, fueran) bilingües.

17. El profesor de gramática insiste en que los estudiantes _____ (saben, sepan) bien todas las reglas.

18. Era necesario que ellos _____ (distingan, distinguieran) entre el modo indicativo y el modo subjuntivo.

19. El profesor les dijo, _____ «(Aprenden, Aprendan) bien las reglas y les servirán muy bien.»

Buscapalabras

Name: _____ Date: _____

Pirámides de palabras

➤ Lean las definiciones y escriban las palabras para formar pirámides de cuatro tamaños. Cada palabra contiene las misma letras (+ una letra nueva) que la palabra anterior.

DEFINICIONES   PIRÁMIDES

Vocal redonda   _____
Todo_____ que reluce no es oro.   _____ _____
Se parece a la lechuga.   _____ _____ _____
Enloquecido   _____ _____ _____ _____
Azul o rojo   _____ _____ _____ _____ _____

Una vocal que se pronuncia como **y**   _____
Yo creo que_____   _____ _____
Yo tengo_____ libros   _____ _____ _____
Ceremonia católica   _____ _____ _____ _____
Ves   _____ _____ _____ _____ _____
Hijas de mi tío   _____ _____ _____ _____ _____ _____

Madre _____ hija   _____
Artículo definido   _____ _____
Quiero que ella _____ este libro.   _____ _____ _____
La materia de un vestido   _____ _____ _____ _____
El tamaño de un vestido   _____ _____ _____ _____ _____
Lugar de reparaciones   _____ _____ _____ _____ _____ _____
Del lado   _____ _____ _____ _____ _____ _____ _____

Conozco _____ Orozco.   _____
Entrega   _____ _____
Un boleto de _____ y vuelta   _____ _____ _____
Hay siete _____ en una semana.   _____ _____ _____ _____
Jugo de manzana   _____ _____ _____ _____ _____
Secos   _____ _____ _____ _____ _____ _____
Esposos   _____ _____ _____ _____ _____ _____ _____
No están despiertas, están _____   _____ _____ _____ _____ _____ _____ _____ _____

Part 13

Contents

Worksheet 13.1 Future-possible conditions

Future-possible conditions are frequently expressed in inverted sentences, which consist of a dependent *if*-clause followed by the main clause. The dependent clause will be in the present indicative tense, and the main clause will be in the future tense:

EXAMPLES: **Si** Juan viene, traerá **los discos.**   *If John comes, he will bring the records.*
                    Si llueve, comeremos **en casa.**   *If it rains, we shall eat at home.*

➤ Supply the present tense form required in the *if*-clause of each sentence.

1. Si Juan _____ (venir), nos ayudará.

2. Si el tiempo _____ (ser) bueno mañana, iremos a la playa.

3. Si tú _____ (estudiar) mucho, seguramente te graduarás.

4. Si ellos _____ (poder) renovar sus visas, se quedarán otro mes.

5. Si Enrique _____ (preparar) sus lecciones, sacará buenas notas.

6. Si yo _____ (ver) a Pedro mañana, hablaremos del asunto.

7. Si él _____ (llegar) a tiempo, nos lo explicará mañana.

8. Si Guillermo _____ (estar) presente, la reunión será interesante.

9. Si _____ (llover) mañana, nos quedaremos en casa en vez de salir.

10. Si yo _____ (poder) comunicarme con él, lo invitaré a la fiesta.

11. Si no _____ (llover) mañana, haremos una excursión al campo.

12. Si María _____ (llamar) por teléfono, le daré tu mensaje.

13. Si _____ (hacer) mucho frío este invierno, necesitarás un abrigo.

14. Si usted _____ (esperar) unos minutos más, Fernando le ayudará.

15. Si el precio no _____ (ser) muy alto, compraré un automóvil.

16. Si yo _____ (tener) tiempo mañana, iré al Museo de Historia.

17. Si tú _____ (querer) aprender a manejar, te enseñaré.

18. Si Rosa _____ (preferir) quedarse con mi libro, yo compraré otro.

19. Si _____ (perder) mis llaves, llamaré al cerrajero.

20. Si Juanito _____ (portarse) mal, la maestra hablará con su padre.

21. Si nuestro equipo _____ (ganar), lo celebraremos.

22. Si yo _____ (saber) la respuesta, se la diré.

Worksheet 13.2 More on future-possible conditions

➤ Supply the future tense form required in the main clause of each sentence.

1. Si él estudia bien, seguramente _____ (pasar) sus exámenes.

2. Si mañana hace buen tiempo, nosotros _____ (ir) a la playa.

3. Si nos casamos ahora, _____ (tener) que vivir con mis padres.

4. Si usted se acuesta temprano, no _____ (estar) cansado mañana.

5. Si el mal tiempo sigue yo _____ (cambiar) mis planes.

6. Si tú esperas en esta esquina, la _____ (ver) cuando ella pase.

7. Si nosotros decidimos ir de compras mañana, lo_____ (llamar).

8. Si veo a Margarita más tarde, le _____ (dar) el mensaje de usted.

9. Si ellos salen temprano, no _____ (tener) que apurarse.

10. Si tú tomas ese curso, con tiempo _____ (aprender) a coser.

11. Si él se apura, _____ (poder) ir con nosotros.

12. Si el perro muerde a la niña, yo la_____ (llevar) al médico.

13. Si nosotros no nos apuramos,_____ (perder) el tren.

14. Si saco buenas notas, mis padres _____ (estar) muy contentos.

15. Si la compañía me da vacaciones, yo _____ (viajar) a Puerto Rico.

16. Si me invitan a la boda, les _____ (tener) que comprar un regalo.

17. Si el tren sale a las dos, ¿a qué hora _____ (llegar) allí?

18. Si invito a Raquel al baile, ¿se _____ (enojar) Dolores?

19. Si vendo mi automóvil ahora, ¿me _____ (prestar) el tuyo?

20. Si la situación económica no cambia, yo lo _____ (perder) todo.

21. Si vienen a las seis,_____ (querer) cenar con nosotros.

22. Si invertimos nuestro capital en acciones, no _____ (poder) comprar bienes raíces.

Worksheet 13.3 Present-unreal conditions

A present-unreal condition refers in general to the present and indicates a contrary-to-fact situation. The verb in the *if*-clause will be in the imperfect subjunctive, and the verb in the main clause will be in the conditional tense.

The following sentences are contrary-to-fact because John does not have a car and Mary does not know how to swim:

EXAMPLES: Si Juan **tuviera** un automóvil, **pasaría** sus vacaciones en el campo.
If John had an automobile, he would spend his vacation in the country.

Si María **supiera** nadar, **iría** a la playa todos los días.
If Mary knew how to swim, she would go to the beach every day.

➤ Supply the imperfect subjunctive form of the verb in parentheses, as required in the *if*-clause.

1. Si tú _____ (hablar) español, tendrías un buen puesto.

2. Si yo _____ (tener) dinero, compraría un automóvil nuevo.

3. Si ella _____ (hacer) sus tareas, sacaría mejores notas.

4. Si yo la _____ (conocer) bien, se la presentaría a usted.

5. Si Enrique _____ (estar) aquí, el podría ayudarles.

6. Si yo _____ (poder) ayudarles, lo haría con mucho gusto.

7. Si yo _____ (ser) usted, no hablaría más de ese asunto.

8. Si ellos me _____ (tratar) así, nunca volvería a su casa.

9. Si nosotros _____ (tener) más práctica, pintaríamos mejor.

10. Si yo me _____ (sentir) mejor, te acompañaría al teatro.

11. Si tú _____ (saber) nadar, pasaríamos el domingo en la playa.

12. Si ella _____ (estudiar) más, podría ser la mejor alumna.

13. Si él _____ (ahorrar) su dinero, podría comprar una casa.

14. Si todos _____ (caber) en el coche, iríamos juntos.

15. Si usted _____ (querer) cenar aquí, seguiríamos hablando.

16. Si tú no te _____ (haber) caído, no te habrías lastimado.

17. Si mi hijo _____ (leer) el periódico, estaría bien informado.

18. Si ella no _____ (lucir) sus joyas, no se las habrían robado.

19. Si tú _____ (probar) las espinacas, te gustarían.

20. Si nosotros _____ (comer) menos bombones, seríamos más delgados.

21. Si usted _____ (salir) con Luisa, los dos se divertirían.

22. Si tú _____ (encender) la lámpara, podrías leer mejor.

Worksheet 13.4 More on present-unreal conditions

➤ Supply the conditional tense of the verbs in parentheses, as required in the main clause.

1. Si hiciera más calor, nosotros _____ (pasar) hoy unas horas en la piscina.

2. Si él fuera un buen amigo suyo, no _____ (hablar) de usted en esa forma.

3. Si la vida aquí no fuera tan cara, _____ (venir) más turistas.

4. Si supiéramos su número telefónico,_____ (poder) llamarlo a su casa.

5. Si tú fueras millonario, _____ (viajar) por todo el mundo.

6. Si yo no estuviera tan ocupado hoy, _____ (dormir) la siesta.

7. Si los niños no hicieran tanto ruido, yo _____ (poder) concentrarme mejor en el trabajo.

8. Si supieras manejar, _____ (poder) llevarnos al aeropuerto.

9. Si ella no fuera tan joven, _____ (hacer) el viaje sola.

10. Si la situación fuera más estable, ellos _____ (mandar) a su hijo a estudiar a Europa.

11. Si yo supiera hablar español tan bien como usted, _____ (estar) muy contento.

12. Si ésta fuera una compañía más grande, yo _____ (aceptar) su oferta enseguida.

13. Si tuvieras suficiente dinero, _____ (poder) entrar en ese negocio.

14. Si este edificio no tuviera ascensor, nosotros no_____ (vivir) aquí.

15. Si ella quisiera,_____ (ir) con nosotros.

16. Si usted supiera lo que él hizo, no lo _____ (considerar) como persona de confianza.

17. Si le mandáramos un correo electrónico, él lo _____ (recibir) hoy mismo.

18. Si esos muebles no fueran tan caros, me_____ (gustar) comprarlos.

19. Si tu esposa no fuera tan gastadora, tú _____ (poder) ahorrar mucho dinero.

20. Si los Pérez no vivieran tan lejos, nosotros los _____ (visitar) con más frecuencia.

21. Si ella fuera un poco más alta, _____ (ser) una mujer muy atractiva.

22. Si escribieras el capítulo final, _____ (completar) tu primera novela.

Worksheet 13.5 More on present-unreal conditions

Supply the imperfect subjunctive of the verb in the *if*-clause, and the conditional tense of the verb in the main clause.

1. Si él _____ (manejar) con más cuidado, _____ (tener) menos accidentes.

2. Si tú _____ (estudiar) más, _____ (pasar) tus exámenes.

3. Si yo _____ (estar) en su lugar, no _____ (hablar) más de ese asunto.

4. Si Ramón _____ (estar) aquí, él _____ (poder) ayudarles en ese trabajo.

5. Si a ella le _____ (gustar) más los idiomas, le _____ (ser) más fácil aprenderlos.

6. Si ellos _____ (tener) más práctica en conversación, _____ (hablar) mejor

   español.

7. Si yo _____ (tener) más tiempo, _____ (leer) una novela española.

8. Si nosotros _____ (salir) enseguida, _____ (poder) llegar antes de la una.

9. Si tú _____ (tomar) el tren de las ocho, ¿a qué hora_____(llegar) allí?

10. Si este cuarto _____ (ser) un poco más grande, _____(ser) más fácil de

    amueblar.

11. Si usted _____ (asistir) a la clase con regularidad,_____ (adelantar) más.

12. Si él _____ (ser) una persona verdaderamente capaz, no _____ (estar) sin trabajo.

13. Si yo _____ (tener) el dinero, lo _____ (invertir) en ese negocio.

14. Si tú _____ (ser) un poco más ambicioso, _____ (poder) llegar a ser

    presidente de esa compañía.

15. Si yo _____ (vivir) en Nueva York, _____ (ir) mucho al teatro.

16. Si nosotros _____ (hablar) español bien,_____ (ir) a Sudamérica.

17. Si él me _____ (tratar) con más consideración, yo lo _____ (respetar) más.

18. Si hoy _____ (ser) sábado, yo no _____ (tener) que trabajar.

19. Si tú_____ (comprender) la astrología, no te _____ (burlar) de mí.

20. Si _____ (enriquecer) tu vocabulario, tus cartas_____ (ser) más

    interesantes.

21. Si nosotros _____ (estar) en Roma, nosotros_____ (hacer) como

    los romanos.

Worksheet 13.6 More on present-unreal conditions

➤ Change the verb in the *if*-clause to the imperfect subjunctive and the verb in the main clause to the conditional. Note the contrary-to-fact quality of the altered sentence, and write the two verbs in the blank spaces.

1. Si *tengo* tiempo, *iré* allí. _____

2. Si *estudias* mucho este semestre, *sacarás* buenas notas. _____

3. Si ella *sigue* trabajando tanto, se *enfermará*. _____

4. Si no *hace* mucho frío, *iremos* a la playa hoy. _____

5. Si *sabe* bien el español, *podrá* conseguir un buen puesto. _____

6. Si nos *gusta* el clima, *pasaremos* todo el invierno allí. _____

7. Si *veo* a Ramón, le *daré* su mensaje. _____

8. Si tú *vienes*, nos *ayudarás* con este trabajo. _____

9. Si usted *espera* unos minutos, *verá* a Elena. _____

10. Si él *trabaja* bien, le *darán* un aumento de sueldo. _____

11. Si ellos *pueden* renovar sus visas, *se quedarán* aquí otro mes. _____

12. Si me *pagan* hoy, *estaré* muy agradecido. _____

13. Si no *llueve*, *haremos* una excursión al campo. _____

14. Si tú *llegas* a tiempo, nos lo *explicarás* todo. _____

15. Si José *está* presente, la reunión *será* un éxito. _____

16. Si ella *pasa* todos sus exámenes, *se graduará* en junio. _____

17. Si yo no le *hablo* así, no me *hará* caso. _____

18. Si *llegamos* a un acuerdo, *firmaremos* el contrato hoy. _____

19. Si ella *se apura*, *podrá* ir con nosotros. _____

20. Si *se casan* ahora, *tendrán* que vivir con los padres de él. _____

21. Si *saben* la verdad, *actuarán* más rápido. _____

22. Si lo *piensas* bien, no lo *harás*. _____

Worksheet 13.7 Past-unreal conditions (past perfect subjunctive)

All subjunctives express a degree of uncertainty. In sentences with *if*-clauses, the uncertainty is total. To move the contrary-to-fact action deeper into the past, Spanish uses the past perfect (pluperfect) subjunctive in the *if*-clause and the conditional perfect in the main clause:

EXAMPLE: Si usted **hubiera hablado** con Juan, él le **habría ayudado.**
*If you **had talked** with John, he **would have helped** you.*

Note that the past perfect subjunctive employs the imperfect subjunctive of the helping verb **haber** plus the past participle:

haber			
yo	hubiera hablado	nosotros(as)	hubiéramos hablado
tú	hubieras hablado	vosotros(as)	hubierais hablado
él, ella, usted	hubiera hablado	ellos, ellas, ustedes	hubieran hablado

➤ Change the verb from the imperfect subjunctive to the past perfect subjunctive.

IMPERFECT SUBJUNCTIVE	PAST PERFECT SUBJUNCTIVE	
	Helping Verb	**Past Participle**
1. (*si*) él llegara	_____	_____
2. (*si*) yo tuviera	_____	_____
3. (*si*) ella supiera	_____	_____
4. (*si*) tú conocieras	_____	_____
5. (*si*) ellos vinieran	_____	_____
6. (*si*) nosotros pasáramos	_____	_____
7. (*si*) nosotras trabajáramos	_____	_____
8. (*si*) ella explicara	_____	_____
9. (*si*) usted estuviera	_____	_____
10. (*si*) tú fueras	_____	_____
11. (*si*) me gustara	_____	_____
12. (*si*) yo visitara	_____	_____
13. (*si*) nosotros volviéramos	_____	_____
14. (*si*) él insistiera	_____	_____
15. (*si*) yo cambiara	_____	_____
16. (*si*) ella escribiera	_____	_____
17. (*si*) él asistiera	_____	_____

Worksheet 13.8 More on past-unreal conditions (past perfect subjunctive)

The conditional perfect tense is formed with **haber** used as an auxiliary and the past participle of the main verb:

haber			
yo	habría comido	nosotros(as)	habríamos comido
tu	habrías comido	vosotros(as)	habríais comido
él, ella, usted	habría comido	ellos, ellas, ustedes	habrían comido

EXAMPLE: Si usted **hubiera cenado** en el hotel, la cena le **habría costado** más.
*If you **had dined** at the hotel, dinner **would have cost** you more.*

➤ Change the verb from present conditional to the conditional perfect, then to the past perfect subjunctive.

PRESENT CONDITIONAL	CONDITIONAL PERFECT	PAST PERFECT SUBJUNCTIVE
1. yo hablaría	habría hablado	hubiera hablado
2. él viviría		
3. ella escribiría		
4. usted vendría		
5. tú harías		
6. ellos esperarían		
7. nosotros comeríamos		
8. tú estudiarías		
9. yo tendría		
10. ellos estarían		
11. usted sería		
12. yo sabría		
13. tú pondrías		
14. usted trabajaría		
15. ella explicaría		
16. me gustaría		
17. él cabría		
18. ustedes prepararían		
19. tú dirías		

Worksheet 13.9 **More on past-unreal conditions (past perfect subjunctive)**

All the following sentences contain situations that are unreal or contrary-to-fact. Note the use of the past perfect subjunctive in the *if*-clause and the conditional perfect in the main clause:

EXAMPLE: Si Juan **hubiera tenido** un automóvil más nuevo, **habría viajado** más lejos.
*If John **had had** a newer automobile, he **would have traveled** farther.*

➤ Supply the past perfect subjunctive tense of the verbs in parentheses, as required in the *if clause*.

1. Si usted _____ (usar) su impermeable, no se habría mojado tanto.

2. Si tú _____ (ser) más razonable, habríamos llegado a un acuerdo

    fácilmente.

3. Si ustedes _____ (saber) bien las reglas, no habrían cometido tantos errores

    en sus exámenes.

4. Si sus padres _____ (dar) su permiso, él se habría alistado en la marina.

5. Si tú _____ (necesitar) dinero, se lo habrías pedido prestado a tu tío.

6. Si Ana López no _____ (estar) enferma, ella y su esposo habrían ido a Europa

    este verano.

7. Si el senador no _____ (cambiar) de opinión, la discusión no habría terminado

    nunca.

8. Si los obreros _____ (recibir) lo que merecían, habrían estado muy contentos.

9. Si el señor Iglesias no _____ (entrar) en el asunto, todo habría salido bien.

10. Si usted _____ (estudiar) más, habría pasado sus exámenes.

11. Si no _____ (hacer) tanto frío ayer, habríamos ido a la playa.

12. Susana dice que si _____ (tener) un vestido nuevo, habría ido al baile.

13. Si tú _____ (saber) algo de la historia del país, habrías entendido mejor

    las costumbres.

14. Si él _____ (venir) a tiempo, yo habría hablado con él.

15. Si yo _____ (saber) su nombre, se lo habría presentado a usted.

16. Si yo _____ (tener) su número de teléfono, lo habría llamado anoche.

17. Si tú _____ (levantarse) más temprano, no habrías llegado tarde a la

    escuela.

18. Si el muchacho _____ (saber) nadar bien, no se habría asustado.

Worksheet 13.10 More on past-unreal conditions (past perfect subjunctive)

➤ Supply the conditional perfect tense of the verbs in parentheses.

1. Si yo le hubiera puesto más azúcar, la limonada _____(ser) más dulce.

2. Si tú le hubieras echádo un poco de sal, _____(resultar) más

   sabrosa (la gallina.)

3. Si usted no hubiera roto el televisor, nosotros _____(ver) el campeonato.

4. Si hubiéramos ido con los vecinos al cine, no _____ (ver) televisión.

5. Si ella hubiera aceptado el puesto en el gobierno, _____ (avanzar)

   rápidamente.

6. Si yo no hubiera tenido que vivir en Inglaterra, me _____ (gustar) más.

7. Si los indios de Tlaxcala no hubieran ayudado a Cortés, los aztecas lo _____ (matar).

8. Si no hubiera maltratado a los indios, no _____ (morir) tantos inocentes.

9. Si no hubiéramos obtenido la tarjeta de crédito, no_____ (comprar) este

   piano.

10. Si tú hubieras practicado regularmente, lo _____ (aprender) a tocar bien.

11. Si usted hubiera llevado esa lámpara con más cuidado, no la _____ (romper).

12. Si hubiera encontrado una semejante, se la _____ (reemplazar).

13. Si tú no hubieras recorado nuestro aniversario, me _____ (enojar).

14. Si tú te hubieras enojado conmigo, me_____ (entristecer) mucho.

15. Si hubiéramos nacido en Francia, _____ (ser) franceses.

16. Si hubiéramos sido franceses,_____ (celebrar)

    el catorce de julio.

17. Si usted hubiera pescado en el otro lado del río,_____ (coger)

    más pescados.

18. Si yo hubiera ido al otro lado del río, los peces _____ (cruzar)

    a este lado.

Worksheet 13.11 More on past-unreal conditions (past perfect subjunctive)

➤ Supply the required past perfect subjunctive of the verb in the *if*-clause, and the conditional perfect tense of the verb in the main clause.

1. Si él _____ (manejar) con más cuidado, el accidente no _____
   _____ (ocurrir).

2. Si nosotros _____ (entender) español, _____
   _____ (disfrutar) más el viaje.

3. Si ella _____ (tener) más experiencia, _____
   _____ (obtener) ese trabajo.

4. Si tú _____ (estudiar) más, _____
   _____ (aprobar) los exámenes.

5. Si ellos no _____ (ser) tan pobres, _____
   _____ (mandar) a su hija a una escuela privada.

6. Si la casa _____ (ser) un poco más grande, sin duda nosotros la _____
   _____ (comprar).

7. Si usted _____ (llegar) cinco minutos antes, _____
   _____ (poder) hablar con el jefe.

8. Si yo _____ (conocer) mejor a esa muchacha, la _____
   _____ (invitar) a salir conmigo.

9. Si el jefe me _____ (tratar) así, yo _____
   _____ (buscar) trabajo en otra compañía.

10. Si tú _____ (asistir) a la clase todos los días, _____
    _____ (progresar) más.

11. Si ellos _____ (venir) en taxi, no _____
    _____ (llegar) tan tarde.

12. Si ayer _____ (ser) domingo, nosotros _____
    _____ (ir) a la iglesia como de costumbre.

13. Si ayer no _____ (llover), Juan y yo _____
    _____ (ir) al juego de pelota.

14. Si yo no _____ (estar) tan cansado anoche, _____
    _____ (ir) al juego de pelota con ustedes.

15. Si ella _____ (poner) más atención en clase, se _____
    _____ (graduar) con honores.

Worksheet 13.12 More on past-unreal conditions (past perfect subjunctive)

➤ Transform these sentences to the past-unreal pattern by changing the verb in the *if* -clause to the past perfect subjunctive and the verb in the main clause to the conditional perfect tense.

1. Si ella *pasara* sus exámenes, se *graduaría* en junio. _____
   _____

2. Si él *fuera* buen amigo suyo, no *hablaría* de usted en esa forma. _____
   _____

3. Si ella *comiera* menos, *estaría* más delgada. _____
   _____

4. Si tú *estuvieras* allí, la fiesta *sería* más agradable. _____
   _____

5. Si usted *se quedara* aquí más tiempo, *aprendería* a hablar español mejor. _____
   _____

6. Si le *dieran* un aumento de sueldo, *estaría* más contento en su trabajo. _____
   _____

7. Si *tuviéramos* su número de teléfono, lo *llamaríamos* enseguida. _____
   _____

8. Si tú *te acostaras* más temprano, no te *sentirías* tan cansado. _____
   _____

9. Si él *tuviera* más paciencia, *sería* mejor profesor. _____
   _____

10. Si no *hiciera* tanto calor, *tendríamos* más ganas de trabajar. _____
    _____

11. Si él *supiera* manejar, *buscaría* trabajo como chofer. _____
    _____

12. Si yo *tomara* el avión de las ocho, ¿a qué hora *llegaría* a Bogotá? _____
    _____

13. Si él *fuera* más ambicioso, no *estaría* contento con un puesto insignificante. _____
    _____

Worksheet 13.13 *Quisiera*

To express *want* in Spanish, we use the verb **querer.** To soften this expression, we often substitute the past subjunctive for the present indicative:

EXAMPLES: WANT TO   WOULD LIKE TO…
     Yo **quiero bailar** con Rosa.   Yo **quisiera bailar** con Rosa.
     Ellos **quieren bailar** con Rosa.   Ellos **quisieran bailar** con Rosa.

The verb **querer** never takes a preposition. Remember that only the infinitive of a verb may directly follow another verb.

If there is a change in subject after **quisiera,** a dependent clause with a past subjunctive verb must be introduced:

EXAMPLE: Él **quiere** que usted lo **acompañe.**   He **wants** you to **accompany** him.
     Él **quisiera** que usted lo **acompañara.**   He **would like** you to **accompany** him.

➤ Introduce a subordinate clause beginning with **que usted** and change the verb to the imperfect subjunctive.

1. Él quisiera *volver* más tarde. …que usted _____
2. Yo quisiera *hacerlo* en seguida. …que usted _____
3. Yo quisiera *llegar* temprano. …que usted _____
4. El médico quisiera *ir* al hospital ahora. …que usted _____
5. Yo quisiera *tener* más tiempo para estudiar. …que usted _____
6. Yo quisiera *comprarle* un buen regalo. …que usted _____
7. Mi madre quisiera *acompañarnos* al baile. …que usted _____
8. Yo quisiera *ser* menos gastador. …que usted _____
9. Yo quisiera *poder* viajar a la Argentina. …que usted _____
10. El profesor quisiera *esperar* un día más. …que usted _____
11. Yo quisiera *estar* de vuelta a la una. …que usted _____
12. Yo quisiera *hablar* español perfectamente. …que usted _____
13. Yo quisiera *conocer* la mejor. …que usted _____
14. Él quisiera *ir* directamente al pueblo. …que usted _____
15. Ellos quisieran *ver* la exposición. …que usted _____
16. Él quisiera *ponerse* la chaqueta nueva. …que usted _____
17. Nosotros quisiéramos *estudiar* con ellos. …que usted _____
18. Yo quisiera *sacar* mejores notas este semestre. …que usted _____
19. Él quisiera *conocer* las costumbres aztecas. …que usted _____
20. Nosotros quisiéramos *tocarle* una canción. …que usted _____

Worksheet 13.14 Subjunctives after compound relative pronouns

Compound relative pronouns, such as **quienquiera** (*whoever*), **cualquiera** (*whatever, whichever*), **dondequiera** (*wherever*), and **como quiera** (*however*), are always followed by **que** and the subjunctive if a future action is implied:

EXAMPLES: **Quienquiera** que lo vea, lo admira mucho.
Dondequiera que vayamos, podremos oír español.

The subjunctive is also used after **ojalá (que)**, to express wish or hope. This interjection is a remnant of the 781-year Moorish occupation of Spain. Its literal Arabic meaning, *Allah willing*, does not apply in Spanish.

EXAMPLE: **Ojalá** (*I hope*) que ella venga al concierto conmigo.
Ojalá (*I wish*) que yo la conociera mejor.

➤ Supply the required subjunctive form for the verbs in parentheses.

1. Quienquiera que _____ (leer) este libro, le gustará.

2. Como quiera que _____ (ser), ella es mi hermana.

3. Ojalá que no _____ (llover) mañana.

4. Quienquiera que lo _____ (conocer) bien, no lo olvidaré.

5. Dondequiera que tú _____ (ir), verás las mismas condiciones.

6. Ojalá que ellos _____ (llegar) a tiempo al aeropuerto.

7. Ojalá que yo _____ (aprobar) todos mis exámenes este año.

8. Ojalá que yo _____ (saber) la respuesta.

9. Ojalá que tú _____ (hablar) hoy con ellos sobre el asunto.

10. Ojalá que yo _____ (tener) esta información para la semana próxima.

11. Ojalá que el tiempo mañana _____ (ser) mejor que ayer.

12. Ojalá que no _____ (hacer) mucho frío en la playa.

13. Cualquiera que _____ (ser) la causa, el resultado es el mismo.

14. Dondequiera que él _____ (estar), lo encontraremos.

15. Dondequiera que ustedes _____ (ir), oirán esta canción.

16. Quienquiera que _____ (recibir) la noticia, se alarmará.

17. Ojalá que Roberto _____ (recibir) el trofeo permanente.

18. Ojalá que tú _____ (aliviarse) muy pronto de la gripe.

19. Este libro será útil para quienquiera que lo _____ (estudiar).

20. Usted podrá hacerse entender dondequiera que _____ (ir).

Worksheet 13.15 Corresponding noun and verb forms

➤ Supply the corresponding verb form for each of the following nouns.

NOUN	VERB	NOUN	VERB
1. decisión	_____	26. explicación	_____
2. viaje	_____	27. golpe	_____
3. deseo	_____	28. grito	_____
4. empleo	_____	29. prueba	_____
5. pelea	_____	30. aumento	_____
6. susto	_____	31. cuidado	_____
7. sorpresa	_____	32. nieve	_____
8. limpieza	_____	33. lluvia	_____
9. confianza	_____	34. descripción	_____
10. promesa	_____	35. traducción	_____
11. pregunta	_____	36. arreglo	_____
12. fracaso	_____	37. ayuda	_____
13. entierro	_____	38. cambio	_____
14. protección	_____	39. producción	_____
15. ganancia	_____	40. abrazo	_____
16. pérdida	_____	41. beso	_____
17. repaso	_____	42. mirada	_____
18. remedio	_____	43. reservación	_____
19. robo	_____	44. satisfacción	_____
20. invitación	_____	45. aprendizaje	_____
21. queja	_____	46. nacimiento	_____
22. examen	_____	47. paseo	_____
23. paquete	_____	48. pago	_____
24. mentira	_____	49. aburrimiento	_____
25. llegada	_____	50. castigo	_____

Worksheet 13.16 Reflexive verbs—special meanings

You already know that **hacer** means *to do* or *to make*, but you may not know that **hacerse**, the same verb used reflexively, means *to become*. Here are some other verbs that have special meanings in their reflexive forms:

acostarse	*to go to bed*	**irse**	*to go away*	**ponerse**	*to put on*
caerse	*to fall down*	**levantarse**	*to get up*	**ponerse a**	*to begin to*
perderse	*to get lost*	**llamarse**	*to be named*	**quitarse**	*to take off*
despertarse	*to wake up*	**morirse**	*to die*	**reírse de**	*to ridicule*
dormirse	*to fall asleep*	**parecerse**	*to resemble*	**romperse**	*to break*
enamorarse	*to fall in love*	**pintarse**	*to (apply) make up*	**sentarse**	*to sit down*

➤ Choose either the reflexive or the nonreflexive form of the verbs in parentheses, as required by the meaning of the sentence.

1. Nuestro profesor _____ (llama, se llama) Alberto López.

2. _____ (Llamé, Me llamé) a la puerta, pero nadie contestó.

3. _____ (Quita, Quítate) el sombrero en el ascensor.

4. ¿Cómo _____ (quitamos, nos quitamos) esas manchas en el mantel?

5. Los niños _____ (pusieron, se pusieron) a llorar.

6. Cuando habla con muchachas, Luis _____ (pone, se pone) colorado.

7. El pobre viejo _____ (cayó, se cayó) en las escaleras.

8. Las jóvenes _____ (pintaron, se pintaron) los labios.

9. La señora _____ (sentó, se sentó) cerca de sus hijos.

10. Tu madre _____ (parece, se parece) más delgada que nunca.

11. Tú _____ (pareces, te pareces) mucho a tu padre.

12. Ellas _____ (levantan, se levantan) a las siete y media.

13. Si no me entiendes, _____ (levanta, levántate) la mano.

14. Con tanto ruido _____ (vuelvo, me vuelvo) loco.

15. Mi padre _____ (hizo, se hizo) rico en los negocios.

16. Por fin _____ (acostamos, nos acostamos) a los niños.

17. Ellos _____ (acostaron, se acostaron) muy tarde anoche.

18. Mañana _____ (vamos, nos vamos) a comer en un restaurante.

19. El concierto es muy aburrido. Yo ya _____ (voy, me voy).

20. El chico _____ (perdió, se perdió) en la gran ciudad.

21. El presidente del club _____ (apellida, se apellida) Romero.

22. Siento mucho _____ (haber dormido, haberme dormido) en clase.

Worksheet 13.17 **Reciprocal action verbs**

If two or more subjects of a verb perform the action of the verb upon each other, the action is reciprocal. The verb will be identical in form to a reflexive verb and must, of course, be plural.

EXAMPLES: Los recién casados **se besaron.**   *The newlyweds **kissed each other.***
Nos ayudamos con los quehaceres.   ***We helped one another** with the chores.*

➤ Using the preterite or imperfect tense, change the verb in parentheses to the reciprocal form.

1. Los boxeadores _____ (pegar) mucho.

2. Mi padre y yo _____ (abrazar).

3. Cuando llega el tren, ellos _____ (despedir).

4. Los coches _____ (chocar) el uno con el otro.

5. Carlos y Marta _____ (conocer) en la biblioteca.

6. Los dos campeones _____ (felicitar).

7. Tú y yo _____ (saludar) en la plaza.

8. Mi esposa y yo _____ (regalar) relojes.

9. El perro y el gato _____ (mirar) con curiosidad.

10. Hace diez años las gemelas _____ (parecer) más.

11. Los dos soldados _____ (sorprender) con su valor.

12. Los tres primos _____ (prometer) viajar juntos.

13. Las dos actrices _____ (admirar) en secreto la una a la otra.

14. Los familiares _____ (saludar) en el jardín.

15. Las hermanas _____ (prestar) vestidos con frecuencia.

16. Nosotros nunca _____ (pelear).

17. Los dos hombres _____ (reconocer) en seguida.

18. Los muchachos _____ (lastimar) en la lucha.

19. Los payasos _____ (reír) los unos de los otros.

20. El otro candidato y yo _____ (desear) buena suerte.

21. Ella y su hermana nunca _____ (hablar) de sus novios.

22. El plomero y el carpintero _____ (ayudar) anteayer.

Worksheet 13.18 Relative pronouns *que, quien*

As a relative pronoun, **que** may introduce an adjectival clause or a noun clause.

EXAMPLES:	ADJECTIVE CLAUSE TO MODIFY A PERSON	Este es el sombrero **que** compré en México.
	ADJECTIVE CLAUSE TO MODIFY A THING	Este es el médico **que** conocí en México.
	NOUN CLAUSE AS DIRECT OBJECT	Yo sé **que** hoy es tu cumpleaños.

After a preposition, **quien (quienes)** usually replaces **que. Quien** may also replace **que** to clarify that it refers to a person rather than a thing.

EXAMPLES:	INTRODUCTION (OF A CLAUSE)	Dáselo a **quien** llegue primero.
	INTRODUCTION/CLARIFICATION	Él es el hombre a **quien** vi en la iglesia.
		Hablé con las muchachas con **quienes** fui a la escuela.

➤ Supply **que, quien, or quienes** as required.

1. Por fin llegaron los libros _____ yo pedí hace tiempo.

2. Las muchachas a _____ invitamos a la fiesta no pueden venir.

3. Washington es el héroe de _____ estamos hablando.

4. ¿Cuál es la casa en _____ viven los Pérez?

5. Vi a la señora a _____ le hablé ayer.

6. Él es el médico _____ curó a mi mamá.

7. Tú eres una persona en _____ se puede confiar.

8. Ellos son los dos hermanos con _____ Pablo va a estudiar.

9. Ésta es la jaula en _____ trajimos el pájaro.

10. Era un general _____ siempre inspiraba a sus soldados.

11. ¿Dónde está la carta _____ acabo de recibir?

12. Ese es el colegio en _____ estudiaba Cristina.

13. Ella es la persona en _____ cayeron las sospechas.

14. Los soldados a _____ condecoraron eran todos héroes.

15. ¿Has visto el automóvil _____ Eduardo acaba de comprar?

16. Ésta es la silla en _____ mi abuelo se sentaba siempre.

17. Ellos son los amigos de _____ les he hablado tanto.

18. Todas las cosas _____ compramos en Venezuela son originales.

19. Ésta es la pluma con _____ firmaron las Leyes de la Reforma.

20. Pienso mucho en Anita, de _____ les he hablado muchas veces.

Worksheet 13.19 *El cual, la cual, los cuales, las cuales*

In cases of ambiguity, where there is more than one possible antecedent for a relative pronoun, **el cual, la cual, los cuales, las cuales** may often be found instead of **que, quien, quienes.** All of these forms agree in number and gender with the antecedent, thus avoiding any chance of error. These are often used after the preposition *por* and after adverbial phrases such as **después de, además de, . . .**

EXAMPLES: Vi la película en el Teatro Nacional, **el cual** me gustó mucho.
    (*Clearly,* **el cual** *refers to* **el Teatro Nacional.***)
    Un chico trajo los paquetes **por los cuales** han venido las muchachas.
    (***Por los cuales*** *refers to* **los paquetes,** *not to* **un chico***)

➤ Supply **el cual, la cual, los cuales, las cuales,** as required.

1. Esa mesa, encima de _____ usted puso las flores, es un mueble de mucho valor.

2. Cervantes peleó en la batalla de Lepanto, en _____ fue herido.

3. El hierro es un metal con _____ se hacen cosas útiles.

4. Anoche vimos una película de vaqueros, _____ nos gustó.

5. La sociedad de _____ él es miembro es muy exclusiva.

6. ¿Es éste el automóvil por _____ pagaste más de dos mil dólares?

7. El petróleo es un producto, la falta de _____ podría afectar mucho nuestra economía.

8. Ésta es la mesa detrás de _____ él siempre se sentaba.

9. Éste es el cuadro con _____ el pintor ganó el premio.

10. Éstas son las telas entre _____ usted puede seleccionar.

11. José me prestó un libro, _____ leeré este fin de semana.

12. Ayer recibí mis notas, _____ son mejores que antes.

13. El edificio de la esquina, en _____ ya hay inquilinos, todavía no está terminado.

14. La sala tiene dos ventanas, una de _____ da al parque.

15. Ellos tienen cuatro hijos, dos de _____ están en Brasil.

16. Los perros son animales a _____ yo enseño a obedecer.

17. El cartero trajo una carta, en _____ recibí un cheque.

18. En mi clase hay seis muchachas, de _____ la más bonita es Rosa Salinas.

Worksheet 13.20 *Cuyo, cuya, cuyos, cuyas*

The relative pronouns **cuya, cuya, cuyos, cuyas** are translated as *whose,* which should not be confused with the interrogative pronoun *whose?* (**¿de quién?, ¿de quiénes?**).

EXAMPLES: Él es el muchacho de **cuyo** padre te hablé ayer.
*He is the boy about **whose** father I spoke to you yesterday.*

Él es el profesor **cuyas** hijas estudian en Europa.
*He is the professor **whose** daughters study in Europe.*

➤ Supply either **cuyo, cuya, cuyos,** or **cuyas,** as required.

1. Él es un hombre _____ fama nunca morirá.

2. Un hombre de _____ nombre no me acuerdo, me dio este libro.

3. María, _____ padres están en Asia, me explicó esa costumbre.

4. Ricardo, _____ tío es autor, ya empezó a escribir una novela.

5. El capitán, _____ conducta es conocida, fue condecorado.

6. Los pájaros, _____ nidos fueron destruidos, se han ido.

7. Mi padre era un hombre _____ generosidad no tenía límite.

8. El médico, _____ dirección me pediste, salió para París.

9. El filósofo, _____ ideas odiamos, fue muy debatido.

10. El galán, _____ actuación nos impresionó, fue premiado.

11. El niño, _____ padres murieron, fue adoptado por sus tíos.

12. Los Pérez, en _____ casa nos conocimos, regresaron a Francia.

13. La profesora, _____ clase es muy aburrida, ha pedido un traslado.

14. Alicia, _____ paciencia es increíble, empezó a estudiar ruso.

15. Él es un hombre _____ honradez es conocida en todas partes.

16. Jorge es un amigo por _____ lealtad yo respondo.

17. Isabel es una joven _____ belleza llama la atención.

18. Pepe es un chiquillo _____ majaderías lo hacen insufrible.

19. Luis, _____ vacaciones terminan hoy, vendrá a trabajar mañana.

20. Mi primo, _____ padres viven en Miami, nos visitó anteayer.

21. El payaso, _____ actuación es muy graciosa, es la atracción principal.

22. Ana, _____ padres son ricos, va a heredar un dineral.

Worksheet 13.21 *Deber de haber*

Haber hablado, haber salido (*to have spoken, to have gone out*), etc. are perfect infinitives. **Haber,** in this case, must be preceded by another helping verb to convey the meaning of *must have,* and needs to be preceded by **deber de.***

EXAMPLES: Juan no está aquí. Él **debe de haber salido** con María.
*John is not here. He **must have gone out** with Mary.*
Debe de haber llovido mientras estábamos en el cine.
*It **must have rained** while we were at the movies.*

***Deber de** (with the preposition) indicates probability or conjecture.
Deber (without the preposition) indicates duty or obligation.

➤ Substitute the correct form of **deber de haber** for the words in italics, keeping in mind that the meaning remains the same.

1. Pablo *probablemente fue* al cine. _____

2. *Probablemente esperaron* allí mucho tiempo. _____

3. Su tía *probablemente salió* de la ciudad. _____

4. Usted *probablemente esperó* en otro lugar. _____

5. Él *probablemente nos escribió* el lunes. _____

6. Tú *probablemente dejaste* el libro en casa. _____

7. Él *probablemente vino* en taxi. _____

8. Ellos *probablemente estuvieron* cansados. _____

9. Ella *probablemente tradujo* este artículo. _____

10. Rafael *probablemente trajo* el dinero. _____

11. Ella *probablemente compró* ese traje aquí. _____

12. Él *probablemente nació* en España. _____

13. Tú *probablemente descubriste* la verdad. _____

14. *Probablemente* Elena *estaba* enferma ayer. _____

15. Tú *probablemente gastaste* un dineral allí. _____

16. Él *probablemente estaba* enojado contigo. _____

17. Ella *probablemente estudió* italiano. _____

18. Pedro *probablemente sabía* nuestros planes. _____

19. Mi abuela *probablemente murió* de pulmonía. _____

20. Anita *probablemente perdió* sus llaves. _____

Worksheet 13.22 *Deber haber*

As previously noted, the **de** of **deber de haber** is dropped in order to express duty or obligation. The past tense of *should* combines the conditional tense of **deber (debería)** and the perfect infinitive (**haber hablado):**

EXAMPLES: El **debería haber estudiado** más.
*He **should have** studied more.*
Usted **debería haberme llamado** por teléfono anoche.
*You **should have called me** by telephone last night.*

➤ Replace the verb in parentheses with the correct form of **debería haber** plus the infinitive.

1. Tú _____ deberías haber hablado _____ (hablar) con él.

2. Ella no _____ (gastar) tanto dinero en la lotería.

3. Ustedes _____ (mandarle) un mensaje hoy mismo.

4. Él _____ (poner) más atención en la clase.

5. Ellos no _____ (hacer) eso sin consultarme.

6. Usted _____ (decirle) eso inmediatamente.

7. Ella no _____ (pasar) tanto tiempo en casa.

8. Ustedes _____ (llevar) al niño a un buen médico.

9. Alguien _____ (llamar) una ambulancia.

10. Nosotros _____ (darle) al profesor un regalo.

11. Él no _____ (leer) tanto anoche.

12. Ellos _____ (esperar) unos minutos más.

13. Nosotros _____ (levantarnos) más temprano.

14. Ella _____ (pasar) todo el día en la playa.

15. Ellos _____ (hacer) menos ruido en la clase.

16. Usted _____ (poner) más cuidado en la tarea.

17. Nosotros _____ (ir) allí en taxi.

18. Tú _____ (escoger) otra carrera.

19. Ella _____ (dar) un paseo todas las tardes.

20. La criada no _____ (chismear) tanto.

Worksheet 13.23 *Pero/sino, y/e, o/u, o/ó*

If the conjunction **pero** (*but*) joins a negative predicate to an affirmative predicate that corrects (or contradicts) the information in the first predicate, **pero** is replaced by **sino.**

EXAMPLE: La pluma no es mía, **sino** de ella.   *The pen is not mine, **but** hers.*
           Ella no va a la Argentina, **sino** a Chile.   *She is not going to Argentina, **but** to Chile.*

The conjunction **y** before an [i] sound will be written **e**; the conjunction **o** before an [o] sound will be written **u.** This is necessary to keep these words from being absorbed by the following word in speech (**y hierba, o hora**). The conjunction **o** will be written **ó** between two Arabic numerals.

EXAMPLES: Hablan francés **e** italiano.   Había siete **u** ocho personas allí.
            Son padre **e** hijo.   Había 5 **ó** 6 gatos en el patio.

➤ Choose the correct conjunction and write it in the blank at the right

1. No quieren vivir en Madrid _____ (pero, sino) Barcelona.

2. Él no quería tomar agua, _____ (pero, sino) un refresco.

3. Pedro _____ (y, e) Elena se van a casar pronto.

4. Eduardo _____ (y, e) Isabel vinieron juntos a la fiesta.

5. Chabela no es rica, _____ (pero, sino) tiene mucho talento.

6. Isabel no es rica, _____ (pero, sino) pobre.

7. Para coser se necesita aguja _____ (y, e) hilo.

8. La aguja _____ (y, e) el hilo que tengo no sirven.

9. Tengo ocho _____ (o, ó) nueve dolares en mi cartera.

10. Tengo 8 _____ (o, ó) 9 dolares en mi cartera.

11. No hablaste con la directora, _____ (pero, sino) con la secretaria.

12. No se si trabaja en Tokío _____ (o, u) Osaka.

13. ¿Es usted de Ohio _____ (o, u) Michigan?

14. El no solamente es guapo, _____ (pero, sino) inteligente.

15. Ellos van a salir, _____ (pero, sino) nosotros vamos a quedarnos.

16. No importa que el empleado sea mujer _____ (o, u) hombre.

17. El viejo habrá tenido setenta _____ (o, u) ochenta años.

18. Su dirección es 332 _____ (o, ó) 233 de la calle Séptima.

19. La fiesta escolar es para madres _____ (y, e) hijas.

20. El automóvil no es grande _____ (pero, sino) tampoco es muy pequeño.

Worksheet 13.24 Diminutives

You may hear someone use a word like **requetechiquitito** and never realize that it is simply **chico** with two diminutive prefixes and two diminutive suffixes. Diminutives are much more common in Spanish than in English, especially in the speech of some women. The commonest, by far, are **-ito,-cito, -ecito, -illo,** and **-ico,** each with corresponding plural and feminine forms.

1. For words of two or more syllables ending in a vowel, remove the vowel and add **-ito** (**-illo**).
2. For one syllable words ending in a consonant, add **-ecito** (**-ecillo**).
3. For most words ending in an **-e,** remove the **-e** and add **-cito** (**-cillo**).
4. For longer words ending in a consonant, add **-cito** (**-cillo**).

EXAMPLES:	coche	**cochecito**	pan	**panecillo**
	libro	**librito**	ventana	**ventanilla**
	mujer	**mujercita**	voz	**vocecita**

➤ Supply a diminutive for each of the words in italics.

1. Voy a llevar a mi *hermano* al parque. _____

2. Le gusta hablar con la *mujer* que siempre está allí _____

3. Yo prefiero oír los *pájaros* que cantan en los árboles. _____

4. Me gusta andar con mi *perro* por la tarde. _____

5. Hay muchos *chicos* jugando en la calle. _____

6. Siempre le doy limosnas al *viejo* de la esquina. _____

7. Mis tíos tienen un *rancho* no muy lejos de aquí. _____

8. Vamos allí para ver los nuevos *pollos*. _____

9. Nos encantan también los *conejos*. _____

10. Ya compramos nuestro *árbol* de Navidad. _____

11. Espero que mis padres me regalen un *gato* blanco. _____

12. Yo tengo que comprar unas *cosas* para dar a mis primos. _____

13. Me gusta mirar el campo desde la *ventana* del tren. _____

14. Veo las charcas llenas de *patos*. _____

15. Me encantan especialmente los pintorescos *cerros*. _____

16. *La hija* de mi amigo tiene una colección de muñecas. _____

17. Ella tiene una *cama* para cada una de sus muñecas. _____

18. También tiene una mesita y cuatro *sillas*. _____

19. Me gusta la *voz* de esa cantante ranchera. _____

20. Ella me recuerda a una *joven* que conocí en México. _____

Worksheet 13.25 Absolute superlatives

The absolute superlative of many adjectives (occasionally of adverbs) is formed by adding the suffix **-ísimo** (**-ísima, -ísimos, -ísimas**). This is the same as adding *very, most,* or *extremely* before the adjective in English.

EXAMPLES:
facilísimo	*very easy*
dulcísimo	(drop *e* from **dulce**), *very sweet*
malísimo	(drop *o* from **malo**), *very bad*
riquísimo	(observe *c* to *qu* spelling change), *very rich*
larguísimo	(observe *g* to *gu* spelling change), *very long*

In the case of adverbs, simply use the suffix **-ísimamente.**

➤ Supply the absolute superlative equivalent of the italicized words.

1. La casa que acabamos de comprar es *muy grande*. _____

2. Desgraciadamente pagamos *mucho* por ella. _____

3. Ustedes tienen un jardín *muy bello*. _____

4. Esas rosas tienen una fragancia *muy dulce*. _____

5. Los rascacielos de Nueva York son *muy altos*. _____

6. Los dueños de esos edificios son *muy ricos*. _____

7. Después de la lluvia esta carretera es *muy peligrosa*. _____

8. No obstante, la vista desde el mirador es *muy bella*. _____

9. Esa familia muy pobre me da *mucha* tristeza. _____

10. Para alguna gente la vida es *muy dura*. _____

11. El viaje a San Diego es *muy largo*. _____

12. Pero mis hijos se ponen *muy contentos* allí. _____

13. El tráfico en este sector de la ciudad es *muy malo*. _____

14. Hay que manejar con *mucho* cuidado a cada momento. _____

15. El zoológico de San Diego es *muy famoso*. _____

16. Los chimpancés juegan *muy contentos*. _____

17. Los tigres son *muy feroces*. _____

18. Uno de los pájaros tropicales es *muy hermoso*. _____

19. Con tanto que ver, el día pasa *muy rápido*. _____

20. Si no fuera *tan lejos*, regresaríamos con frecuencia. _____

Worksheet 13.26 Exclamations

Most exclamations are expressed with **¡Qué…!** When a verb, and adjective or adverb are included, the verb will normally be placed last, or not used at all.

EXAMPLES: **¡Qué** pálida está! **¡Qué** bien canta! **¡Qué** lindo día!

When no verb is included, the exclamation usually contains **tan** or **más.**

EXAMPLES: **¡Qué** corbata tan bonita! **¡Qué** vestido más elegante!

When only a verb is **used, cómo** replaces **qué.**

EXAMPLES: **¡Cómo** hablas! **¡Cómo** comieron!

➤ Change the following sentences to exclamations.

1. Es un día muy hermoso. _____

2. Eres muy inteligente. _____

3. Son unas blusas muy lindas. _____

4. Hace mucho calor. _____

5. Tú bailas muy mal. _____

6. Bailas muy bien. _____

7. Fue un regalo muy extraño. _____

8. Es un hombre muy guapo. _____

9. Se ponen muy tristes. _____

10. Fue una película aburrida. _____

11. Tienes ojos muy lindos. _____

12. Tus ojos son muy verdes. _____

13. Son montañas muy altas. _____

14. Es un paisaje muy hermoso. _____

15. Tiene manos muy fuertes. _____

16. Tocas bien el piano. _____

17. Tocas el piano. _____

18. Tocas. _____

19. Raúl aprende rápidamente. _____

20. Son flores muy exóticas. _____

21. Es un administrador eficiente. _____

22. Está contento con su automóvil. _____

Worksheet 13.27 **Prepositions**

➤ Supply the preposition required to complete the meaning of each sentence. Use contractions (**al**, **del**).

1. Mi familia y yo acabamos _____ llegar a Guadalajara.

2. Ésta es una de las ciudades más bonitas _____ México.

3. Alquilamos un coche _____ ir a la ciudad.

4. Empezó _____ llover cuando salimos del aeropuerto.

5. El camino _____ el aeropuerto a la ciudad es muy largo.

6. Cuando dejó _____ llover, el viaje se hizo más agradable.

7. Bajamos del coche _____ frente a un mercado.

8. Antes _____ seguir el camino, tomamos un refresco.

9. Yo escogí un refresco popular que sabe _____ toronja.

10. En la ciudad traté _____ encontrar un hotel económico.

11. Pasamos la primera noche _____ el Hotel del Parque.

12. Nos acostamos a las diez _____ la noche.

13. Después del desayuno, mandé unas postales _____ correo aéreo.

14. Entonces llevamos _____ los niños al Parque Agua Azul.

15. Es el parque más conocido _____ Guadalajara.

16. De vez _____ cuando hay conciertos en ese parque.

17. La catedral de Guadalajara es una joya _____ la arquitectura.

18. El teatro Juárez es otro edificio que da _____ la plaza.

19. Fuimos _____ ese teatro la segunda noche.

20. Vimos un drama que tiene lugar alrededor _____ el año 1910.

21. La distancia _____ el hotel al teatro es corta.

22. Los turistas vienen _____ todas partes del mundo.

23. Algunos norteamericanos no regresan _____ los Estados Unidos.

24. Ellos piensan mucho _____ las ventajas de vivir en Guadalajara.

25. Ellos creen que es un lugar ideal _____ jubilarse.

26. Yo no voy _____ ser residente permanente de Guadalajara.

27. _____ cambio, voy a regresar año tras año.

28. Es difícil visitar aquí _____ divertirse mucho.

Vocabulary check-up

➤ Choose the correct form and write it in the blank at the right.

1. Un sinónimo de perezoso es _____ (tarde, amable, delgado haragán).

2. Lo opuesto de frecuentemente es _____ (a menudo, rápidamente, rara vez, siempre).

3. Una persona muda no puede _____ (ver, oír, hablar, caminar).

4. Lo opuesto de levantarse es _____ (acostarse, cansarse, aburrirse).

5. ¿Cuál de estos objetos se encuentra siempre en una aula? _____

   (pizarra, maleta, cubiertos, espejos).

6. ¿Cuál de estas palabras es femenina? _____ (libro, mano, teléfono, año).

7. ¿Cuál de estas palabras es masculina? _____ (mesa, problema, escuela, revista).

8. Actualmente quiere decir _____ (después, realmente, ahora, lentamente).

9. ¿Cuál de estos animales se encuentra principalmente en el desierto? _____

   (león, camello, lobo, pantera).

10. La frase dar cuerda se usa cuando se habla de _____

   (computadoras, relojes, sortijas, zapatos).

11. ¿Cuál es el sustantivo que corresponde a construir? _____

   (construido, construcción, construye, construyó).

12. Para barrer se necesita _____ (una pistola, una escoba, un borrador, una

   computadora).

13. Para borrar se necesita _____ (un lápiz, una barrera, una regla, un

   borrador, una máquina de coser).

14. El padre de mi esposa es mi _____ (cuñado, suegra, suegro, hijastro).

15. Lo opuesto de agrio es _____ (fino, largo, amargo, dulce).

16. Un sinónimo de estrecho es _____ (hermoso, largo, angosto, alto).

17. Un deporte de origen vasco que se juega con una cesta es _____

   (fútbol, tenis, jai alai, baloncesto).

18. En una corrida de toros, el hombre que va montado a caballo es el _____

   (matador, picador, banderillero).

19. Un sinónimo de asombrado es _____ (cansado, educado, sorprendido,

   prohibido).

20. Para coser se necesita aguja _____ (y un clavo, e hilo, y un martillo).

General review

➤ Choose the correct form and write it in the blank.

1. Cuando Doroteo Arango _____ (tuvo, tenía) dieciséis años tuvo que huir de su rancho en Durango.

2. Para proteger _____ (su, a su) hermana, había fusilado al hijo del hacendado.

3. Doroteo _____ (escondió, se escondió) en la Sierra de de Chihuahua.

4. _____ (Para, Por) ganarse la vida, aprendió a ser bandido.

5. Como bandido dejó de _____ (llamándose, llamarse) Doroteo Arango y adoptó el nombre Pancho Villa.

6. Dondequiera que usted _____ (va, vaya) en México, oirá el nombre de Pancho Villa.

7. No sólo fue bandido _____ (pero, sino) jefe de bandidos.

8. Francisco I. Madero le ofreció el puesto de general de _____ (su, suyo) ejército.

9. Más _____ (que, de) nada, Madero quería derribar el gobierno del dictador Porfirio Díaz.

10. Villa le dijo a Madero que _____ (aceptara, aceptaría) el título de general.

11. Villa quería que Madero se _____ (hiciera, haría) presidente de México.

12. El sabía que Madero _____ (ayudara, ayudaría) a los indios y a los pobres de México.

13. El general Villa luchó_____ (valiente, valientemente) contra las tropas del gobierno.

14. En poco más _____ (que, de) un año, Villa entró victoriosamente en la capital.

15. Emiliano Zapata, otro general que llegó del sur, se reunió con _____ (General, el general) Villa.

16. Estos dos héroes _____ (del, de la) revolución ocasionaron el deseado cambio de gobierno.

17. Porfirio Díaz huyó a Francia, donde permaneció sin _____ (regresando, regresar) nunca a México.

18. Francisco Villa _____ (se, les) despidió de sus oficiales y sus tropas.

19. Les dijo que _____ (regresaron, regresaran) a sus ranchos para gozar de la libertad que habían ganado.

20. Pancho Villa es el héroe_____ (cuyo, cuya) vida sigue fascinando a muchos en Méjico.

21. La casa de Villa, Quinta Luz, _____ (todavía, tampoco) está en la ciudad de Chihuahua.

22. Una de las páginas _____ (más, la más, las más) tristes de la historia de México fue el asesinato de Villa en 1923.

Buscapalabras

Nombres difíciles

The 46 nouns in this puzzle do not end in **-o** or **-a**. As you find them, circle them and write them together with their definite articles in the spaces provided after the English equivalents in the accompanying list

EXAMPLE: *la parte*

accident _____

actress _____

afternoon _____

angel _____

balcony _____

baseball _____

chess _____

corn _____

cough _____

crime _____

dance _____

diamond _____

elephant _____

emperor _____

eraser _____

father _____

flavor _____

generosity _____

glove _____

honesty _____

interest _____

judge _____

light _____

report _____

rice _____

salt _____

scar _____

meat _____

menu _____

D	E	T	A	T	E	L	E	V	I	S	I	O	N	C
I	R	A	C	L	O	T	E	T	S	A	P	Z	E	A
A	B	R	T	E	N	T	I	G	R	E	S	E	M	N
M	A	D	O	T	J	U	V	E	N	T	U	D	I	S
A	L	E	N	R	A	C	Z	N	I	A	V	A	R	I
M	C	E	L	O	B	S	I	E	B	E	T	R	C	O
T	O	T	A	P	M	I	A	R	R	O	Z	N	E	N
E	N	N	I	E	D	O	M	O	S	D	U	O	T	C
J	O	A	N	R	E	P	D	S	A	L	E	H	A	I
A	I	U	P	I	R	A	M	I	D	E	T	J	R	C
R	N	G	B	O	R	R	A	D	O	R	I	Z	A	A
T	T	R	I	E	L	E	F	A	N	T	E	N	P	T
R	E	I	P	O	V	D	A	D	A	L	C	O	S	R
O	R	M	A	D	R	E	X	E	L	I	A	B	I	I
P	E	R	D	A	P	O	I	R	O	B	A	S	D	Z
A	S	A	C	C	I	D	E	N	T	E	Z	E	U	J
V	E	R	D	A	D	Z	I	R	T	C	A	L	L	E

interest _____

judge _____

light _____

report _____

rice _____

salt _____

scar _____

meat _____

menu _____

mother _____

net _____

nonsense _____

oil _____

pie _____

pyramid _____

rail _____

song _____

steamship _____

street _____

suit _____

television _____

tiger _____

truth _____

wall _____

youth _____

Vocabulary

Vocabulary

This master vocabulary list contains all the words from the exercises in *Workbook in Everyday Spanish*.

a, to, at
  a alguna parte, somewhere
  a causa de, because of
  a lo largo de, along
  a menudo, often
  a pesar de, in spite of
  a plenitud, fully
abandonar, to leave
abdicar, to abdicate
abierto, -a, open
abogado, -a, lawyer
abrazar, to embrace
abrazo, embrace, hug
abrigo, shelter; coat
abrir, to open
abuela, abuelita, grandmother, granny
abuelo, abuelito, grandfather, gramps
abuelos, grandparents
aburrido, -a, boring
aburrimiento, boredom
aburrir, to bore
aburrirse, to be bored
acabar, to finish
  acabar de…, to have just…
Acapulco, Mexican resort city
acción (f), action
accidente (m), accident
aceite (m), oil
  aceite de oliva, olive oil
aceituna, olive
acento, accent
aceptar, to accept
acera, sidewalk
acerca de, about, concerning
acero, steel
acompañar, to accompany
acordarse, to remember
acordeón (m), accordion
acostar [ue], to put to bed
acostarse [ue], to go to bed
acostumbrarse, to become accustomed
acta, certificate, statement
actitud (f), attitude
actor (m), actor
actriz (f), actress

actuación (f), performance
actualidad (f), present time
actualmente, at present
actuar, to act, perform
acuarela, watercolor
acuático, -a, aquatic
acueducto, aqueduct
acuerdo, accord
  de acuerdo con, in agreement with; according to
acusado, -a, accused
adecuado, -a, adequate
adelantar, to advance
adelante, forward
además, besides
adivinar, to guess
admirar, to admire
admitir, to admit
adoptado, -a, adopted
adornar, to adorn, to decorate
adquirir, to acquire
aeropuerto, airport
afán (m), zeal, eagerness
afectar, to affect
afectuoso, -a, affectionate
afeitar(se), to shave
aficionado, -a, fan (sports)
afilado, -a, sharp, sharpened
afilar, to sharpen
afinar, to tune (instrument)
afortunado, -a, lucky, fortunate
afuera, outside
agosto, August
agradable, pleasant
agradecer [zc], to thank
agradecido, -a, thankful, grateful
agradar, to please
agrado, pleasure
agravio, offense, grievance
agregar, to add
agrícola, agricultural, farming
agricultor, -a, agriculturist, farmer
agrio, -a, sour
agua (f), water
  agua filtrada, filtered water
aguja, needle
ahogar(se), to drown

ahorrar, to save (money, time, etc.)
ahorros, savings (as in a bank)
aire (m), aire
  aire libre, open air
ajedrez (m), chess
ajeno, -a, belonging to someone else; distant, detached
ajo, garlic
ajustar, to adjust
al, (a + el), to the, at the; upon
  al mediodía, at noon
  al revés, inside out
alabanza, praise
alarmar, to alarm
Albéniz (Isaac) (1860–1909), Spanish composer
alcachofa, artichoke
alcanzar, to reach (a place or point)
alcohol (m), alcohol
aldea, village
alegrar(se), to please
alegre, pleased, merry
alegría, joy, merriment, gaiety
alemán, -ana, German
alfabeto, alphabet
alfiler (m), (straight) pin
alfombra, carpet
algazara, noise
álgebra (m), algebra
algodón (m), cotton
alguien, someone, somebody
algún, -una, algunos, -as, some
Alhambra (la), Moorish palace in Granada, Spain
alistarse, to enlist
aliviar, to alleviate
allá, there, over there
allí, there
alma, soul
almacén, store
almanaque (m), calendar
almeja, clam
almirante (m), admiral
almorzar [ue], to eat lunch
almuerzo, lunch
alquilar, to rent
alrededor (de), around

alrededores, environs, surrounding area
altiplano, plateau
alto, -a, high; tall; stop, halt (sign)
altura, height
alumno, -a, pupil, student
Alvarado (Pedro de) (1485–1541),
 Spanish explorer
ama: ama de casa, housewife
amable, nice, friendly
amargo, -a, bitter
amarillo, -a, yellow
ambición (f), ambition
ambicioso, -a, ambitious
ambos, -as, both
ambulancia, ambulance
ameno, -a, pleasant, agreeable, nice
americano, -a, American
amigo, -a, friend
amistad (f), friendship
amplio, -a, wide; full, roomy
amueblar, to furnish
ancho, -a, wide
anciano, -a, elderly person
andar, to walk; to ride; to go
andino, -a, of the Andes (mountains)
anécdota, anecdote, story
ángel (m) angel
 ángel de la guarda, guardian angel
angosto, -a, narrow
ángulo, angle
anillo, ring
 anillo de compromiso, engagement ring
aniversario, anniversary
anoche, last night
anónimo, -a, anonymous
anteayer, the day before yesterday
anterior, previous
antes, before
antigüedad (f), antiquity; antique
antiguo, -a, antique, old
Antillas Mayores, Greater Antilles
antiséptico, antiseptic
año, year
 año pasado, last year
anteojos (m, pl), (eye)glasses
antepasados, ancestors
anual, annual
anunciar, announce
apagado, -a, turned off
apagar, to turn off
aparato, appliance; device; fixture
aparecer [zc], to appear
apariencia, appearance
apartamento, apartment (*departamento*
 in México)

apellidarse…, to have…as a last name
apellido, surname, last name
apenado, -a, embarrassed, grieved
apetito, appetite
aplaudir, to applaud
aplauso, applause
aplicado, -a, studious; industrious
aplicar, to apply
apoderarse, to overpower
apogeo, peak, height (of fame, power)
apoyar, to support
apreciar, to appreciate, to value
aprender, to learn
aprendizaje (m), apprenticeship
apretado, -a, tight, close
aprobación (f), approval
aprobar [ue], to approve; to pass (a test)
apropiado, -a, appropriate
apurarse, to be in a hurry
aquel, that (over there)
aquél, that one (over there)
aquí, here
Arango, Doroteo (Pancho Villa),
 (1878–1923) Mexican general
árbol (m), tree
 árbol navideño, Christmas tree
arboleda, grove of trees
arco, arch
 arco iris, rainbow
aretes (m), earrings
argentino, -a, Argentine, Argentinian
armario, closet
armar, to assemble
armonia, harmony
arpa (f), harp
arqueólogo, -a, archeologist
arquitecto, architect
arquitectónico, -a, architectural
arquitectura, architecture
arreglar, to arrange, to regulate
arreglo, arrangement
arriesgar, to risk
arrodillarse, to kneel
arroyo, brook; gutter, stream
arroz (m), rice
 arroz con pollo, chicken with rice
arrugar (se), to wrinkle
artículo, article
artista, (m/f), artist
artritis, arthritis
arzobispo, archbishop
ascenso, ascent; rise
ascensor (m) elevator
asegurar, to assure, to insure
así, so

asiento, seat
asignatura, school course, subject
asistir a…, to attend…
asombrar, to astonish, astound
aspiradora, vacuum cleaner, sweeper
asunto (m), affair
asustar, to frighten, startle
atacar, to attack
Atahualpa (1710–1756), Peruvian Indian
 chief
ataque cardíaco, heart attack
atención (f), attention
atentado, aggression
atentamente, sincerely
Atlántico, Atlantic (Ocean)
atlas (m), atlas
atractivo, -a, attractive
atraso, delay, slowness; under
 development
atravesar [ie], to cross
atribuir [y], to attribute
audiencia, audience; hearing
auditorio, auditorium
aula, classroom
aumentar, to augment, increase
aumento, increase
aunque, although
ausencia, absence
ausente, absent
autobús (m), bus
autogiro, autogyro
automóvil (m), automobile
autopista, freeway
autor, -a, author
auxilio, help, assistance
 primeros auxilios, first aid
avanzar, to advance
avenida, avenue
aventurero, -a, adventurer
averiguar, to find out
avisar, to notify, advise
aviso, notice; warning
ayer, yesterday
ayuda, help, aid
ayudar, to help, to aid
azteca (m/f), Aztec
azúcar (m), sugar
azufre (m), sulphur
azul, blue

bailar, to dance
bailarín, -ina, dancer
baile (m), dance

bajar, to lower

  bajar de peso, to lose weight, reduce

bajo, short; beneath

balar, to bleat

Balboa, Vasco Núñez de (1475–1517),
  Spanish explorer

balcón (m), balcony

baloncesto, basketball

ballet folklórico, folkloric ballet

banco, bank; bench

bandeja, tray (*charola* in México)

banderillero, bullfighter on foot with
  darts

bando, faction, party

bandoneón (m), large
  Argentinian concertina

bañar (se), to bathe (oneself)

bañista (m/f), bather, swimmer

barato, -a, cheap, inexpensive

bárbaro, -a, barbarous, barbaric

barbero, barber

barco, boat, ship

barraca, hut, cabin

barrer, to sweep

barrio, neighborhood, district

bastante, enough, sufficient

basura, trash, garbage

Batalla de Lepanto (1571), Battle on the
  Gulf of Corinth

bebé (m), baby

beber, to drink

beca, scholarship

béisbol (m), baseball

belicoso, -a, belligerent

belleza, beauty

bello, -a, beautiful

  bellas artes, fine arts

Benalcázar, Sebastián de (1480–1551), a
  Spanish conqueror of Peru

beneficio, benefit, profit

Biblia, Bible

biblioteca, library

bibliotecario, -a, librarian

bicicleta, bicycle

bien, well

  bienes raíces, real estate

bilingüe, bilingual

billete (m), ticket; bill (currency) (*boleto* in
  México)

biología, biology

blanco, -a, white

Blasco Ibáñez, Vicente (1867–1928),
  Spanish novelist

blusa, blouse

boca, mouth

boda, wedding

bodega, cellar, warehouse; grocery store

Bogotá, capital of Colombia

boleto, ticket (México)

bolígrafo, ball-point pen

boliviano, -a, Bolivian

bolsillo, pocket

bomba, bomb; pump

bombero, firefighter

bombones, chocolates, candy

bondadoso, -a, good, kind

bonito, -a, pretty

borrador (m), eraser; first draft

borrar, to erase

bota, boot

botella, bottle

bostezar, to yawn

botón (m), button

botiquín (m) **de emergencia,** first aid kit

boxeador, boxer

boxeo, boxing

Brasil, Brazil

brasileño, -a, Brazilian

breve, brief, short

  en breve, in short; soon

brillante, brilliant

brincar, to jump, skip

brindis (m), toast (as with wine)

broma, joke

bromear, to joke

bruja, witch

brujo, sorcerer

buen(o), -a, good

Buenos Aires, capital of Argentina

bufanda, scarf

búho (m), owl

bujías, spark plugs

bulevar (m), boulevard

burlón, -ona, fond of pranks

buscapalabras (m), word-search puzzle

buscar, to look for, to search (for)

buzón (m), mail box

  echar al buzón, to mail

C

cabalgar, to ride (a horse)

caballo, horse

cabecera, head (table or bed)

caber, to fit

cabeza, head

Cabeza de Vaca, Álvar Núñez
  (1500–1560), Spanish explorer

cable (m) cable; rope, line

cacahuate/cacahuete (m), peanut

cacique (m), Indian chief

cada, each

  cada vez, each (every) time

caer, to fall

  dejar caer, to drop, let drop

caerse, to fall down

café (m) coffee; coffee shop

cajetilla, small box, pack (of cigarettes)

calculadora, calculator

cálculo, calculus; calculation

Calderón de la Barca, Pedro (1600–1681),
  Spanish dramatist

calendario, calendar

calentar [ie], to heat, warm up

cálido, -a, warm; hot

caliente, hot

calificar, to qualify

  calificar papeles, to grade papers

caló (m), Gypsy dialect; jargon

calor (m) heat; warmth

  tener calor, to be hot

calle (f), street

cama, bed

cámara, camera: chamber

camarero, -era, waiter/waitress

cambiar, to change, to exchange

  cambiar un cheque, to cash a check

cambio, change (money)

  en cambio, on the other hand

camelia, camellia

camello, camel

caminar, to travel, to walk

camino, road

camión (m), truck

camioneta, station wagon

camisa, shirt

campana, bell

campeón, -ona, champion

campeonato, championship

campo, field, country; camp

Canadá (m), Canada

canasta, basket

cancelar, to cancel

canción, song

cancionero, -a, collection of songs

candidato, -a, candidate

canela, cinnamon

canoa, canoe

cansado, -a, tired

cansarse, to grow tired

cantante (m/f), singer

cantar, to sing

cántaro, pitcher, vessel, jug

  llover a cántaros, to rain cats and dogs

cantidad (f), quantity

Cantinflas (Mario Moreno) (1911–1993), Mexican comic actor

cantor (m), singer

cañón (m), cannon; canyon

capaz, capable

capital, capital (city); funds

capitán, (m) captain

capítulo, chapter

captura, capture, seizure

carabela, caravela, old sailing ship

características, characteristics

Caracas, capital of Venezuela

carcajadas, loud laughs
  echarse a carcajadas, to burst out laughing

cárcel, jail, prison

carecer [zc], to lack

carga, cargo

cari (m), curry

caribe, of or from the Caribbean

caricatura, cartoon, caricature

cariñoso, -a, affectionate

carne (f), meat, flesh

carnicero, butcher

caro, -a, dear; expensive

carpintería, carpentry

carpintero, carpenter

carta, letter

cartera, wallet, billfold; briefcase; handbag

cartero, letter-carrier

carrera, career; race

carretera, highway

carro, cart, car

casa, house

casarse, to get married

casi, almost

caso, case; event, occurrence
  hacer caso (de), to pay attention (to)

castellano, -a, Castilian

castigar, to punish

castigo, punishment

catalán, -ana, from Cataluña, Spain; also language of the region

catarro, head cold

catástrofe, catastrophe

catedral (f), cathedral

católico, -a, Catholic

catorce, fourteen

cautela, caution

cazador (m), hunter

cazar, to hunt

cebada, barley

celebración, celebration

celebrar, to celebrate

célebre, famous, noted

celos, jealousy
  tener celos, to be jealous

celoso, -a, jealous

cenar, to eat dinner, dine

centeno, rye

centroamericano, -a, Central-American

cepillar(se), to brush

cerca, fence, hedge
  cerca (de), near, close by

cercano, -a, near

cereza, cherry

Cervantes: Miguel de Cervantes Saavedra (1547–1616), Spanish author

cerrajero, locksmith

cerrar [ie], to close, shut
  cerrar con llave, to lock

césped (m), grass, lawn, (*zacate* [m] in México)

cesta, basket

ceviche, appetizer of raw fish marinated (in lemon juice)

chachachá (m), chachacha (dance)

chaqueta, jacket

charca, pond, pool

charreada, Mexican display of horsemanship

charro, Mexican horseman; dancer of *jarabe tapatío*

cheque (m), check
  cheque de viajero, traveler's check

chica, girl

chico, boy

chico, -a, small,

chícharos, dried peas (México)

chileno, -a, Chilean

chimpancé (m), chimpanzee

china poblana, Mexican national costume; female dancer of the *jarabe tapatío*

chino, -a, Chinese

chiquillo, rowdy child

chismear, to gossip

chiste (m), joke

chistoso, -a, funny, amusing

chocar (con), to crash (into)

chocolate (m), chocolate

chofer (m), driver

chuleta de cerdo, pork chop

churrigueresco, -a, Churrigueresque (ornate architectural style)

cicatriz (f), scar

cicatrizar, to heal

cielo, sky

cien, (one) hundred

ciencia, science

científico, -a, scientific; scientist

cierto, -a, certain; true

cigarrillos, cigarettes, (*cigarros* in México)

cilantro, coriander

cilindro, cylinder

cima, summit, top

cinc (m), zinc

cinco, five

cincuenta, fifty

cine (m), movie (theater), motion picture

cinematografía, cinematography

cinturón (m), belt

circo, circus

círculo, circle; club

circunstancia, circumstance

cirquero, circus performer

ciruela, plum

cirujano, surgeon

cita, date, appointment

ciudad, city

ciudadano, -a, citizen

civilización, civilization

claro, -a, clear, light; of course!

clase (f), class

clásico, -a, classical

clavado, dive (in swimming)

clavel (m), carnation

clavo, nail (carpentry); clove (spice)

claxon (m), automobile horn

clérigo, clergyman

clima (m), climate

clínica, clinic, hospital

club (m), club

cobrar, to charge (money) to collect (a bill)

cobre (m), copper

cocer [ue], to cook, boil

cocina, kitchen, cuisine

cocinero, -a, cook

coche (m), automobile, car; baby carriage

cochecito, small car; baby carriage

coger, to take, to grasp

cohete (m), skyrocket; firecracker

col (m), cabbage

cola, tail; glue

colección (f), collection

coleccionar, to collect

colegio, school

colesterol (m), cholesterol

colina, hill

colombiano, -a, Colombian

colorado, -a, red; red-faced, blushing

combate (m), combat

comedia, comedy; stage play (Spain)
comentario, commentary
comenzar, to begin
comer, to eat
cometer, to commit
cómico, -a, comic(al), funny; comedian
comida, meal; dinner, banquet
comienzo, beginning
como, as, since, because
como, cómo, how
cómodo, -a, comfortable
compañero, -a, companion, pal; associate, colleague
compañía, company
compasión, compassion, pity
competencia, competition
competir [i], to compete
complacer [y], to please; to accommodate
completar, to complete
complicado, -a, complicated
cómplice (m/f), accomplice
componer, to compose
componerse (de), to be made of
composición (f), composition
compositor (m), composer
comprador (m), buyer, shopper
comprar, to buy, to purchase
comprender, to understand; to comprise
computador, -a, computer
comunicar, to communicate
comunidad, community
con, with
  con ganas, willingly, eagerly
concentrar (se), to concentrate
concierto, concert
concluir (y), to conclude
concurso, contest; race, competition
condecorar, to decorate, award (medal, honor, etc.)
condición (f), condition
condimentos, seasonings
conducir [zc], to conduct, to drive
conducta, conduct, behavior
conejo, rabbit
confianza, confidence, trust; informality
confiar, to trust
conjunto, group; rock group
conmigo, with me
conocer [zc], to be acquainted with
conocido, -a, well-known, distinguished
conquistador (m), conqueror
conseguir [i], to get, obtain
consejo, advice, counsel
considerar, to consider
consideración (f), consideration

consiguiente, consequent
  por consiguiente, consequently
constar (de), to consist (of)
construcción (f), construction
construir [y], to construct
consulado, consulate
consulta, consultation
  libros de consulta, reference books
consultar, to consult
contabilidad (f), accounting
contar [ue], to count; to tell
contador, -ora, accountant; meter (gas, water)
contagio, contagion, infection
contener [ie], to contain
contento, -a, gay, joyful; satisfied
contestar, to answer
contienda, struggle, contest
contigo, with you (informal)
contraer matrimonio, to marry, get married
contratar, to contract, to hire
contrato, contract
contribuir, to contribute
conveniente, convenient
conversación (f), conversation
conversar, to converse, chat
convertir (se) [ie], to change, convert
cooperar, to cooperate
cooperativo, -a, cooperative
copiar, to copy
copista (m/f), copyist, copier
copla, verse; popular ballad
corbata, necktie
corcho, cork
cordial, friendly, pleasant
cordillera, mountain range
coro, chorus, choir
coronel (m), colonel
correcto, -a, correct
corregir [i], to correct
correo, mail
  correo electrónico, e-mail
  (por) correo aéreo, (by) air mail
correr, to run
corrida de toros, bullfight
corriente, current; common
cortar, to cut; to sever
cortarse el pelo, to get a haircut
corte (f), court
Cortés, Hernán (1485–1547), Spanish explorer/conqueror of México
cortés, courteous, polite
cortina, curtain
corto, -a, short

coser, to sew
costar, to cost
costarricense (m/f), Costa Rican
costo (de la vida), cost (of living)
costumbre (f), custom, habit
cotidiano, -a, daily
crear, to create
crecer [zc], to grow; to increase
creciente, increasing, growing
creer, to believe
criada, maid, servant
crímen (m), crime
criollo, -a, Creole
cristal (m), (pane of) glass
Cristóbal Colón, Christopher Columbus
criticar, to criticize
crucigrama (m), crossword puzzle
crudeza, rawness; roughness
cruzar, to cross
Cruz Roja, the Red Cross
cuaderno, notebook
cuadro, picture, painting
cual, which (one)
cualquiera, whichever
cuando, when
  de vez en cuando, from time to time
cuantioso, abundant, substantial
cuanto, -a, how much
cuarto, room; (one) fourth
  cuarto de baño, bathroom
cuates, twins; pals (México only)
cuatro, four
cubano, -a, Cuban
cubeta, pail, bucket
cubierta, covering; bedspread; ship deck; book jacket
cubierto, place setting; past participle of **cubrir**
cubito de hielo, ice cube
cubrir, to cover
cuchara, spoon
cuchillo, knife
cuenta, account, bill
cuerpo, body
cueva, cave
¡Cuidado!, (Be) careful!
cuidadoso, -a, careful
cuidar, to take care
culpable, guilty
cultivar, to cultivate, grow
cultivo, cultivation, crop
cultura hispánica, Hispanic culture
cumbre (f), top, summit
cumpleaños, birthday

cumplir, to fulfill; to comply

   cumplir años, to have a birthday

cuñada, sister-in-law

cuñado, brother-in-law

curar, to cure

curiosidad (f), curiosity

curioso, -a, curious

curso, course

cuyo, -a, whose

 D

daltonismo, color-blindness

damas, ladies

   damas chinas, Chinese checkers

danza, dance

daño, harm, damage, injury

dar, to give

   dar cuerda, to wind (as a watch)

   dar gracias, to thank, express
   gratitude

   dar risa, to be laughable

dátil, (m) date (fruit)

dato, fact

de, of, from

   de una u otra, from (of) one or the
   other

debajo (de), under

deber, to owe; should

debido, -a, owing to, due to

débil, weak

decaer, decline, depress

decidir, to decide

decir, to say

decisión (f), decision

declamar, to declaim, to recite poetry

decorar, to decorate, trim, adorn

dedicar, to dedicate

dedo, finger

   dedo pulgar, thumb

deducir [zc], to deduce; to deduct

defender(se) [ie], to defend (oneself)

definición (f), definition

definido (artículo definido), definite article

dejar, to leave, to let

   dejar de, to stop (doing)

del, of the *[de + el]*

delantal (m), apron

delante, before, in front

deleitar, to delight; to amuse

deletreo, spelling

delito, crime, offense

demás: los demás, the rest, the others

demasiado, -a, too much (pl), too many

demostrar [ue], to demonstrate

dentadura, set of teeth

   dentadura postiza, false teeth

dentista (m/f), dentist

dentro (de), inside

depender (de), to depend (on)

dependiente (m/f), store clerk

deporte (m), sport

   deporte acuático, water sport

derecha, right (hand, direction)

   a la derecha, to the right

derecho, law

   escuela de derecho, law school

derribar, to knock down, overthrow

desafortunado, -a, unfortunate, unlucky

desagradar, to displease

desaguar, to drain, empty

desarrollar, to develop

desaparecer [zc], to disappear

desastre (m), disaster

desayunar (se), to eat breakfast

descalzo, -a, barefoot

descansar, to rest

descanso, rest

desconocer (zc), to not know, be
   ignorant of

describir, to describe

descripción (f), description

descubridor, discoverer

descubrimiento, discovery

descubrir, to discover

desde, since, from

   desde hace… años, … years ago

desdichado, -a, unhappy

desear, to want, to desire

desembarcar, to disembark, to land

desembocar, to flow into

deseo, wish

desesperado, -a, desperate

desfilar, to parade, to march

desfile (m), parade

desgraciadamente, unfortunately

desgraciado, -a, unfortunate

desierto, desert

desnudo, -a, naked

desnudarse, to get undressed

despachar, to send, dispatch

despedida, farewell

   despedida de soltera, bridal shower

despedirse [i] (de), to say goodbye (to)

despegar, to take off (aircraft)

despensa, pantry, larder

despertador (m), alarm clock

despertar (se) [ie], to wake up

despierto, -a, awake

después, after(wards)

destino, destiny, destination

destacar, to stand out; emphasize

destreza, skill

destruir [y], to destroy

detalle (m), detail

detenidamente, carefully

detrás, behind

deuda, debt

devolver [ue], to return (something)

devuelto, returned, sent back (from
   devolver)

día (m), day

   de día, by day, in the daytime

   Día de los Inocentes, April Fool's Day
   (held December 28)

   Día de los Muertos, Halloween (México
   only)

diamante (m), diamond

diariamente, daily

diapositiva, slide

Diario, daily; Daily, popular name for
   newspapers

dibujante (m/f), draftsman, designer,
   cartoonist

dibujar, to draw

diccionario, dictionary

diciembre, December

dicho, saying; **-a,** a forementioned (from
   verb *decir*)

dichoso, -a, happy; fortunate

dictador (m), dictator

dictar, to dictate

dieciséis, sixteen

diez, ten

diferente (m/f), different

difícil, difficult

dificultad (f), difficult

digno, -a, worthy; dignified

diligente, diligent; industrious

dineral (m), fortune, a lot of money
   (colloq.)

dinero, money

dinosaurio, dinosaur

director, -a, director, principal

disco, (phonograph) record, disc

   disco compacto, compact disc

disculpa, excuse

disculpar, to excuse

discurso, discourse, speech

discusión (f), argument, discussion

discutir, to discuss; to argue

disfraz (m), costume, disguise

disfrutar, to enjoy

disgustar, to displease, to be
   displeasing

dislocar, to dislocate, sprain
Disneylandia, Disneyland
disparate (m), nonsense, big mistake
disponible, available
dispuesto, -a, ready
distinguir, to distinguish
distraído, -a, distracted
distribuir [y], to distribute
distrito, district
divertido, -a, fun
divertir [ie], to amuse
divertirse [ie], to have a good time
dividir, to divide
doblar, to double; to fold
doce, twelve
doctor, -ora, doctor
dólar (m), dollar
doler [ue], to hurt, ache, feel pain
dolor (m), pain
doméstico, -a, tame; domestic
domingo, Sunday
domingo de Pascua, Easter Sunday
don, mister (with first name)
donde, dónde, where,
dondequiera, wherever
Don Juan Tenorio, a popular Spanish
  drama
dormir [ue], to sleep
dormitorio, bedroom
dos, two
dos veces, twice
dosis, dose
drama (m), drama
dramático, -a, dramatic
dramaturgo, dramatist
duda, doubt
  sin duda, without a doubt
dudar, to doubt
dudoso, -a, doubtful, dubious
dueño, -a, owner, boss
duo, duet,
dulce, sweet; dessert
duplicar, to duplicate, double
durante, during
duro, -a, hard, difficult

e, and (before [i] sound)
economía, economy
económico, -a, economical
echar, to throw, to toss, put out
  echar de menos, to miss (someone or
  something)
  echarse a reír, to burst out laughing

edad, age: **¡Qué edad tienes?** How old
  are you?
  Edad Media, Middle Ages
edificio, building
Edison, Thomas Alva (1847–1931),
  American inventor
editor(a), editor, publisher
educado, -a, educated, refined
educar, to educate
egipcio, -a, Egyptian
Egipto, Egypt
ejercicio, exercise
el, the (masculine)
él, he
elección (f), election,
electricidad (f), electricity
eléctrico, -a, electric
elefante (m), elephant
elegante, elegant
eliminar, to eliminate
elogiado, -a, praised
ella, she
ellas, they (feminine)
ellos, they
embarcación, boat, vessel
embarcarse, to board (as a ship)
emergencia, emergency
emocionado, -a, moved; thrilled
empaquetar, to pack(age)
empeño, determination, tenacity
  casa de empeño, pawnshop
empeorar, to make worse, worsen
emperador (m), emperor
empezar [ie], to begin, start
empleado, -a, employee
empleo, job
empresa, company
en, in, on
  en aquel entonces, at that time, in
  those days
  en cambio, on the other hand
  en cuanto a…, as for…
  en ninguna parte, nowhere
  en punto, on the dot (time),
  en voz alta, aloud, in a loud voice
enamorarse (de), to fall in love (with)
encantado, -a, charmed, enchanted,
  delighted
encantar, to enchant, to charm
encanto, charm, enchantment
encargarse de, to take charge of
encender, to light
encima, on top of
encogerse de hombros, to shrug one's
  shoulders

encontrar [ue], to meet, to encounter; to
  find
encuentro, meeting
enemigo, -a, enemy
enero, January
enfadarse, to become angry
enfermedad (f), illness, disease
enfermera, -o, nurse
enfermo, -a, sick, ill; sick person
enfriar, to chill, make cold
engordar, to grow fat, to gain weight
enloquecer [zc], to drive crazy
enloquecerse [zc], to go crazy
enojado, -a, angry
enojar, to anger
enojarse, to become angry
enorme, enormous
enriquecer(zc), to enrich
ensalada, salad
  ensalada de papas, potato salad
ensayista (m/f), essayist
ensayo, essay; rehearsal
enseguida, right away
enseñar, to teach; to show
ensuciarse, to soil, to get dirty
entender(ie), to understand
entero, -a, entire
enterrar(ie), to bury
entierro, burial
entrada, entrance
entrar, to enter
entre, between
entregar, to deliver; to surrender
entrenador, -ora, coach, trainer
entrenamiento, training, coaching
entrenar, to train, to coach
entrevista, interview
entristecer(zc), to sadden
entusiasmo, enthusiasm
envidiar, to envy, to be envious
epistolar, in the form of letters or epistles
época, period (of time), epoch
equipaje (m), luggage
equipo, team (sports); equipment
equivocación (f), error, mistake
equivocado, -a, wrong
equivocarse, to be wrong
error (m), error, mistake
escala, port of call, stopover
  hacer escala, to make a stop, lay over
  (in travel)
escaleras, stairs
escena, scene
esclavo, -a, slave
escocés, -esa, Scottish, Scotch

escoger, to choose
escolar, pertaining to school
esconder, to hide, conceal
escopeta, shotgun
escribir, to write
  escribir a máquina, to type(write)
escrito, -a, written; past participle of
  escribir
escritorio, desk
escuchar, to listen
escuela, school
esculpir, to sculpt
espacio, space
España, Spain
español, -ola, Spanish
espantar, to frighten
espanto, fear, fright
espantoso,-a, frightening
especialidad (f), specialty
especializarse, to specialize
espejo, mirror
esperar, to wait (for)
espía, spy
espinacas, spinach
esposa, wife
esposo, husband
esposos, husband and wife
esquiar, to ski
estable, stable, steadfast, firm
establecer [zc], to establish
estación (f), season (of year); station
estacionar, to park
estadio, stadium
estado, state
Estados Unidos, United States
estallar, to burst, explode, erupt
estante (m), (book)shelf
estaño, tin
estar, to be
  estar de acuerdo, to agree
  estar de vuelta, to be back
  estar enfermo, -a, to be sick
estatal, pertaining to the state
estatua, statue
este (m), East
este, esta, esto, this
éste, ésta, this one
estilo, style
estómago, stomach
estornudar, to sneeze
estrecho, -a, narrow; strait (geography)
estrella, star
estudiante (m/f), student, pupil
estudiar, to study
estudioso, -a, studious; (m/f) scholar

estufa, stove
Europa, Europe
europeo, -a, European
evitar, to avoid, to evade
exacto, -a, exact
examen (m), exam, examination, test
excelente, excellent
excitar, to excite
excluir [y], to exclude
exclusivo, -a, exclusive
excursión, excursion, hike, trip
exhibición, exhibit
exigente, demanding
exigir, to demand
existir, to exist
éxito, success
  tener éxito, to be successful
experiencia, experience
experto, -a, expert, capable
explicación (f), explanation
explicar, to explain
explorador, -a, explorer
explorar, to explore
exportación (f), export
exposición, exhibition
extenso, -a, large, extensive
exterior, el exterior, abroad
expulsar, to expel
extranjero, -a, foreigner
extrañar, to seem strange; to miss,
  pine for
extraño, -a, strange
extraviado, -a, lost, missing

 F

fábrica, factory
fachada, façade
fácil, easy
facilidad (f), ease
facultad (f) **de medicina,** college of
  medicine, "med school"
faja, strip, band, sash
falda, skirt; foothill
falta, lack (of); fault; error
faltar, to lack; to be missing
  faltar a clase, to be absent from class,
  "cut class"
fama, fame, reputation
familia, family
familiar, close relative; familiar
famoso,-a, famous
fantasma (m), ghost, phantom
fascinar, to fascinate
favorito,-a, favorite

fecha, date
fecundo,-a, fertile
felicitar, to congratulate
feliz, happy
femenino,-a, feminine
fenicio,-a, Phoenician
feo,-a, ugly
feria, fair, bazaar
feroz, ferocious, wild
ferroviario,-a, pertaining to railroads,
  railway
ferviente, fervent, ardent
fiebre (f), fever
fiel, faithful
fiesta, party, festival
figura, figure
fila, row, line
filósofo,-a, philosopher
filtrado,-a, filtered
fin (m), end;
  a fines de, at the end of (date)
finca, country estate, farm
fingir, to feign, pretend
Finlandia, Finland
fino, -a, fine, good
firmar, to sign
físico,-a, physical
flaco,-a, thin
flamenco, pertaining to Spanish gypsies
  (music, dance)
flecha, arrow
flor (f), flower
florecer [zc], to flower, bloom, flourish
florero, vase
flota, fleet
fluir [y], to flow
folklórico,-a, folkloric
fomentar, to encourage, promote
fonógrafo, phonograph,
  record player
fondos, funds
forma, form; shape
formal, formal; reliable
formar, to form; to shape
forzado, -a, forced; strained
foto (f), photo
fotografia, photograph
fracasar, to fail, be unsuccessful
fracaso, failure
fragancia, fragrance
fragua, forge
frambuesa, raspberry
francés,-esa, French
Francia, France
frase (f), sentence, phrase

frecuencia, frequency
  con frecuencia, frequently
frecuente, frequent
fregar [ie], to scrub, wash (dishes)
frenos, brakes
frente (f), forehead
frente (m), front
  en frente de, in front of
fresco, -a, fresh, cool; cheeky, brazen
frío, -a, cold
  tener frío, to feel cold
frito, -a, fried
fruta, fruit
fuego, fire; light (flame)
  fuegos artificiales, fireworks
fuente (m), fountain; source; platter
  pluma de fuente, fountain pen
fuerte (m), fort, strong
fumador, -a, smoker
fumar, to smoke
fundador, -a, founder
fundar, to found
fútbol (m), football
futbolista (m/f), football player
futuro, future
fusilar, to shoot, execute

gabinete (m), cabinet; office
galardón (m), reward, prize
gallego, -a, Galician
galleta, cracker, cookie
gallina, hen
ganancia, earning, profit, gain
ganar, to gain, to earn; to win
ganarse la vida, to earn a living
ganas: tener ganas de …, to feel like …
gancho, hook; hairpin; lure
garaje (m), garage
garantizar, to guarantee
garganta, throat; gorge, ravine
gastador, -a, spender, spendthrift
gastar, to spend
gastos, expenditures, outlay
gato, -a, cat; (m) jack (lifting tool)
gaveta, drawer
gaviota, (sea)gull
gelatina, gelatin
gemelos, -as, twins; (m), binoculars; cuff links
general (m), general
género, kind, class
generosidad (f), generosity
generoso, -a, generous
gente (f), people

geografía, geography
geométrico, -a, geometric(al)
gerente, manager, director
gimnasia, gymnastics
ginebra, gin; **Ginebra**, Geneva, city in Switzerland
gitano, -a, gypsy
glándula, gland
gobernador, -ora, governor
gobierno, government
golfo, gulf
golondrina, swallow
golpear, to strike, to hit
gordo, -a, fat; (m/f), fat person
grabado, -a, recorded (as on tape)
grabar, to engrave; to record (as on tape)
gracioso, -a, funny; graceful
graduado, -a, graduate, graduated
graduarse, to graduate
gramática, grammar
gran, great, large (before a noun)
grande, large, great
grato, -a, pleasant, pleasing
gratis, free (no charge)
griego, -a, Greek
grifo, faucet
gripe (f), flu, influenza
gris, gray
gritar, to shout
grito, shout, cry
grúa, derrick; tow truck
grueso, -a, thick; fat
grupo, group
guantes (m), gloves
guapo, -a, handsome; bold, brave
guardar, to save, to keep, to guard
  guardar cama, to stay in bed
  gubernativo, -a, pertaining to the government
guerra, war
  Guerra Civil, Civil War
guerrillero, -a, guerrilla
guía (m/f), guide
guisantes (m), peas
guitarra, guitar
gusano, worm
gustar, to be pleasing, to please, delight
gusto, taste

habitación (f), room, bedroom
habitante (m/f), inhabitant
hábito, habit, custom
hablador, -a, talkative
hablar, to speak

hacendado, landowner; rancher
hacer, to make, to do
  hacer frío/calor, it's cold/hot
  hacer caso, to pay attention
  hacer escala, to have a stop-over or lay-over (in travel)
hacia, toward
hacienda, (country) estate, ranch
hacha, hatchet
hada, fairy
halagar, to please, flatter
hallar (se), to find; to be located
hamaca, hammock
hambre (m), hunger
hambriento, -a, hungry
haragán, -ana, idler, loafer
hasta, until
hay, there is, there are
hazaña, feat, exploit, deed
hecho, fact; past participle of *hacer*
hegemonía, leadership, national dominance
helado, ice cream
helicóptero, helicopter
heredar, to inherit
heredero, -era, heir(ess)
herido, -a, wounded
hermana, sister
hermano, brother
hermoso, -a, beautiful
héroe (m), hero
heroína (f), heroine
hiedra/yedra, ivy
hielo, ice
hierba, grass
hierro, iron
higiene (f), hygiene
hija, daughter; dear girl
hijastro, step-son
hijo, son; dear boy
hilo, thread
hipnotizar, to hypnotize
hipódromo, race track
hispano, -a, Hispanic
hispanoamericano, -a, relative to a part of America where Spanish is spoken
hispanoparlante (m/f), Spanish speaker
historia, history, story
historiador, -a, historian
histórico, -a, historic, historical
hogar (m), home
hogareño, -a, homey, pertaining to the home
hoja, leaf; sheet (of paper)
hojalata, tin(plate)
holandés, -esa, Dutch

holgazán, -ana, lazy (person)
hombre (m), man
hombro, shoulder
  encogerse de hombros, to shrug one's
  shoulders
honesto, -a, honest, upright
honor (m), honor
honradez (f), honesty
honrado, -a, honest, trustworthy
hora, hour
hormigón (m), concrete
horno, oven
horrible (m/f), horrible
hospital (m), hospital
hotel (m), hotel
hoy, today
  hoy día, nowadays, these days
hubo, there was, there were
huelga, labor strike
huerta/huerto, garden, orchard
hueso, bone
huevo, egg
  huevos rancheros, fried eggs with
  tortilla and chile sauce
huir [y], to flee
humorístico, -a, humorous, funny
hundirse, to sink

ibérico, -a, Iberian
iberoamericano, -a, related to the Iberian
  Peninsula and Latin America
idéntico, -a, identical
identificar, to identify
idioma (m), language
iglesia, church
imaginar, to imagine
imitar, to imitate
impermeable (m), raincoat
imponente, imposing, impressive, stately
imponer, to impose
importancia, importance
importante, important
importar, to be important; to import
  (from abroad)
impresor, -ora, printer
impresionar, to impress
impresión (f), impression
imprimir, to print
inaugurar, to inaugurate
incendio, fire
incluir [y], to include
incorrecto, -a, incorrect
increíble, incredible

independiente (m/f), independent
indeseable, undesirable
indicar, to indicate
indio, -a, Indian
indispensable (m/f), indispensable
industrializar, to industrialize
inesperado, -a, unexpected
infancia, infancy
influenza, influenza, flu
influir [y], to influence
informado, -a, informed
informática, computer technology
informe (m), report
ingeniero, -a, engineer
Inglaterra, England
inglés, -esa, English
ingrediente (m), ingredient
inmediate (m/f), immediate
inmigración (f), immigration
inocencia, innocence
inocente, innocent
inolvidable, unforgettable
inquilino, -a, tenant, lessee
insignificante (m/f), insignificant
insistir, to insist
inspeccionar, to inspect
inspirar, to inspire
instrucción, instruction
instruir [y], to instruct
insuficiente, insufficient
insufrible, unbearable
inteligente, intelligent
intentar, to attempt, try
interés (m), interest
interesante, interesting
interesar, to interest
intérprete (m/f), interpreter
interrogar, to interrogate
interrumpido, -a, interrupted
interrumpir, to interrupt
invención (f), invention
inventar, to invent
invento, invention
inventor (m), inventor
invierno, winter
inversión (f), investment
invertir [i], to invest; to invert
investigar, to investigate
invitación (f), invitation
ir, to go
irse, to leave
Irlanda, Ireland
Isabel, Elizabeth
isla, island
istmo, isthmus

Italia, Italy
italiano, -a, Italian
izquierda, left

jai alai (m), Basque ball game
jaleo, spree, racket, fuss
jamás, never
Japón, Japan
japonés, -esa, Japanese
jarabe tapatío, Mexican Hat Dance
jardín (m), garden
jardinero, gardener
jaula, cage
jefatura, leadership; headquarters
jefe, boss, chief
jinete (m/f), rider, horseman
jirafa, giraffe
jota, Spanish dance; letter [j]
joven (m/f), young, young person
joya, jewel
joyería, jewelry
joyero, jeweler
jubilarse, to retire (from working)
juego, game
juez (m), judge
jugada, play (sports)
jugador (m), player; gambler
jugar, to play
juglar (m), minstrel
jugo, juice
juguete (m), toy
juguetón, -ona, playful
julio, July
junio, June
junto a, next to
juntos, together
justo, -a, just, fair
juventud (f), youth

kilo, kilogram
kilómetro (cuadrado), (square) kilometer

la, the (fem. article); you, her, it (pronoun)
La Habana, Havana (Cuba)
labio, lip
laboratorio, laboratory
labrado, -a, carved; wrought
labriego, -a, farmhand, peasant
lado, side
ladrar, to bark

ladrón,-ona, thief
lago, lake
lamentar, to lament
lámpara, lamp
lana, wool
lanzador (m), pitcher (baseball)
lanzar, to throw, fling, pitch, hurl
La Paz, seat of government of Bolivia
lapicero, pencil holder, mechanical pencil
lápiz (m), pencil
largo,-a, long
las, the (fem. article); you, them (pronoun)
lástima, pity
lastimado, -a, injured, hurt
lastimar, to injure, hurt
lastimarse, to get hurt
latino, -a, Latin; (person) who speaks a
    Romance language
lavado,-a, washed
lavadora, washing machine (clothes or
    dishes)
lavandera, laundress
lavar, to wash
lazar, to lasso, rope
Lazarillo de Tormes, anonymous Spanish
    picaresque novel
lealtad, loyalty
lección (f), lesson
lectura, reading
leche (f), milk
leer, to read
legumbres (f), vegetables
lejos (de), far (from)
lengua, tongue; language
    lengua extranjera, foreign language
    lenguas romances, Romance languages
lentes (m), lenses, eyeglasses
lentitud (f), slowness
lento, -a, slow
león, -ona, lion
Lepanto, Corinthian Gulf battle site
    where Cervantes was wounded (1571)
letra, letter (of alphabet); lyrics (of a song)
levantarse, to get up, to rise
ley (f), law
libertad (f), liberty
libra, pound (measurement)
libre, free
librería, bookstore
librero, bookshelf
libro, book
licencia, license
liderato, leadership
lienzo de charreadas, field where charros
    perform

ligero, -a, light (in weight); swift
límite (m), limit
limón (m), lemon, lime (in Latin America
    and Spain)
limonada, lemonade
limpiar, to clean
limpieza, cleaning
limpio,-a, clean
lindo,-a, pretty
línea, line; stripe; queue
lío, mess, snarl
Lisboa, Lisbon (Portugal)
lista, list; menu
listo,-a, ready; clever
llamar, to call
llamarse, to be named
llano, plain
llano, -a, level, smooth, even
llanta, tire (vehicle)
llave (f), key (for locking); faucet
llegada, arrival
llegar, to arrive
llenar, to fill
lleno,-a, full
llevar, to carry
llorar, to cry
llover [ue], to rain
    llover a cántaros, to rain cats and dogs
lluvia, -as, rain
lluvioso, -a, rainy
lo, it
    lo opuesto, the opposite
lobo, wolf
loco, -a, crazy
localizar, to locate
Londres, London, capital of England
loción, lotion
locutor, -ora, TV or radio announcer
lograr, to manage (to)
Lope de Vega, Félix (1562–1635), Spanish
    dramatist
loro, parrot
los, the (masc. article plural); you, them
    (pronouns)
lote (m), lot (plot of land)
    lote de estacionamiento, parking lot
lotería, lottery
loza, china, crockery
lucir [zc], to shine; to show off
lucha, struggle
luchar, to struggle, to fight, to wrestle
lugar (m), place
    tener lugar, to take place
lujoso, -a, luxurious
luna, moon

lunes (m), Monday
luto, mourning
    estar de luto, to be in mourning
luz, light
    luz eléctrica, electric light

macizo, -a, solid, pure (metals)
madera, wood, lumber
madre (f), mother
Madrid, capital of Spain
madrileño, -a, of or from Madrid
madrugada, dawn, daybreak
madrugar, to get up early
maestría, mastery; teacher's degree
maestro,-a, teacher
maíz, (m), corn
majadería, silliness
majestad (f), majesty
malagueño, -a, of or from Málaga (Spain)
maleta, suitcase
malgastar, to waste
(La) Malinche or Doña Marina, Aztec
    woman interpreter and companion
    of Cortés
maltratar, to mistreat
mamá, mother
mancha, stain, spot
mandar, to send
manecilla, hand (clock or watch)
manejar, to drive; to handle
manera, manner, means; method, mode
manganeso, manganese
manifestación, demonstration, rally
mano (f), hand
mantel (m), tablecloth
mantequilla, butter
manzana, apple
mañana, tomorrow
mapa (m), map
máquina, machine
    máquina de coser, sewing machine
    máquina de escribir, typewriter
maquinaria, machinery
mar (m), sea
maravilloso, -a, marvelous
margarina, margarine
mariachi (m), mariachi, Mexican musical
    group
marinero, sailor
mariscos, shellfish
martes (m), Tuesday
Martí, José, (1853–1895), Cuban poet and
    liberator

martillo, hammer
marzo, March
Marruecos, Morocco
más, more
masa, dough
masculino, -a, masculine
masticar, to chew
matador (m), matador; killer
matar, to kill
matemáticas, mathematics
materia, (school) subject; material, stuff
matricularse, to register
matrimonio, marriage; married couple
maullar, meow (cat)
máximo, -a, maximum
mayo, May
mayor, older; larger; greater
mayoría, majority
me, directly or indirectly involving me
mecánico, mechanic
mecánico, -a, mechanical
medalla, medal
mediados: a mediados de, in the middle of (period of time)
medianoche (f), midnight
mediante, by means of
medicamento, medication
medicina, medicine
médico, physician, doctor
medio, -a, half
mediodía (m), noon
medir [i], to measure
mejor, better, best
mellizo, -a, twin
memorizar, to memorize
mencionar, to mention
menor, younger; smaller
   el menor, la menor, the youngest
menos, minus, less, least
mensaje (m), message
mentira, lie, falsehood
menudo, -a, tiny, very slim
   a menudo, often
menú (m), menu
mercado, market
merecer, to deserve
mermelada, marmalade
mes (m), month
mesa, table
meseta, plateau
mestizo, -a, half-breed
meta, goal
meter, to introduce, to put inside
mexicano, -a, Mexican
mezcla, mixture, blend

mezclar, to mix
mezquita, mosque
mi, my
mí, me (as object of prepositon)
microbio, microbe
miedo, fear
   tener miedo, to be afraid
miembro (m/f), member
mientras, while
miércoles (m), Wednesday
militar, military
millonario, -a, millionaire
mío, -a, mine
mirada, (a) look
mirador (m), vantage-point, lookout
minuto, minute
mirar, to look (at)
Misisipi (m), Mississippi
mismo, -a, same
misterioso, -a, mysterious
mitad, half
Moctezuma, Aztec emperor
moda, style, fashion
modelo (m/f), model
modo, mood
   modo sujuntivo, (subjunctive mood)
mojarse, to get wet
mojado, -a, wet
molestar, to disturb
moneda, coin
mono, -a, monkey; cute; pretty
monosilábico, -a, monosyllabic
montaña, mountain
Montañas Rocosas, Rocky Mountains
montar, to mount; to ride
   montar a caballo, to ride a horse
morder [ue], to bite
Morelos: José María Morelos y Pavón (1765–1815), Mexican general
moreno, -a, dark, brunet(te)
morir(se) [ue], to die
morisco, -a, Moorish
moro, -a, Moor; Moorish
mosca, housefly
mostrar, to show, demonstrate
motocicleta, motorcycle
motor (m), motor
muchacha, girl
muchacho, boy
mucho, -a, much
mudar, to change
mudéjar, Moorish style of architecture
mudo, -a, unable to speak
mueble (m), furniture
mujer (f) woman

muelle (m), wharf, quay; spring (as in a watch)
muerto, -a, dead; past participle of morir
multa, fine
multar, to fine
mundial, worldwide
mundo, world
muñeca, doll; wrist
museo, museum
música, music
músico, musician
mulsulmán, -ana, Moslem
muy, very

nacer [zc], to be born
nacimiento, birth
nación (f), nation
nacional (m/f), national
Naciones Unidas, United Nations
nada, nothing
nadador, -a, swimmer
nadar, to swim
nadie, nobody
naranja, orange
naranjada, orangeade
nariz (f), nose
natación (f), swimming
naufragio, shipwreck
navaja de afeitar, shaving razor
nave (f), ship
navegar, to navigate, to sail
Navidad (f), Christmas
navideño, -a, pertaining to Christmas
neblina, mist
necesario, -a, necessary
necesidad (f), necessity
necesitar, to need
negar [ie], deny
negarse a [ie], to refuse to
negro, -a, black
nervioso, -a, nervous
netamente, purely, clearly
nevar [ie], to snow
ni, nor
   ni la mitad, not even half
nicaragüense, of or from Nicaragua
nido, nest
nieta, granddaughter
nieto, grandson
nietos, grandchildren
nieve (f), snow
ningún, -una, no, not one
ninguno, -a, none

niña, girl

niño, boy

nobleza, nobility; goodness

noche (f), evening, night
  de noche, in the evening, at night
  esta noche, tonight

Nochebuena, Christmas Eve

nombre (m), name, noun

noreste, northeast

nos, directly or indirectly involving us;
  ourselves

nosotros, we, us

nosotras (f), we, us

nota, note; grade (school)

noticia, news item; notice

novela, novel

noventa, ninety

novio, -a, sweetheart; bridegroom; bride

nublado, -a, cloudy

núcleo, nucleus

nuestro,-a, our(s)

Nueva Jersey, New Jersey

Nueva York, New York

nueve, nine

nuevecito, -a, brand new

nuevo, -a, new

nuez (f), nut, walnut; Adam's apple

número, number

numeroso, -a, numerous

nunca, never

nutrición (f), nutrition

nutritivo,-a, nutritious

o, or

ó, or (between Arabic numerals, as in 2 ó 3)

obedecer (zc), to obey

obligado, -a, obliged, forced to

obra, work, work of art

obrero, -a, worker

observar, to observe

obtener, to obtain

ocasionar, to cause, produce

océano Pacífico, Pacific Ocean

ochenta, eighty

ocho, eight

octava, octave

octavo, -a, eighth

octubre, October

ocupado, -a, busy, occupied

ocurrir, to occur

odiar, to hate

oferta, offer; sale, bargain

oficio, trade, occupation

ofrecer, to offer

oído, (inner) ear; heard (from *oír*)

ojalá, used to express hope or wish;
  God willing

oír, to hear

ojo, eye

ola, wave

oler (ue), to smell

olimpiadas, olympics

olímpico, -a, olympic

olmeca, Olmec (Mexican Indian
  civilization)

olla, pot

olvidar, to forget

olvidar (se), to forget

once, eleven

onza, ounce

ópera, opera

opinión, opinion

oportunidad, opportunity

optómetra (m/f), optometrist

oración, sentence, phrase; prayer

orden (f), order

ordenar, to order

oreja, (outer) ear

orgullo, pride

orgulloso, -a, proud

oriente (m), Orient, east

origen (m), origin, source

original (m/f), original

orilla, shore, bank; edge

oro, gold

orquesta, orchestra

ortografía, spelling

os, to you, for you

oscuro, -a, dark

oso, bear

otoño, autumn

otro,-a, other, another
  otra vez, again, another time

paciencia, patience

paciente, patient

Pacífico, Pacific (Ocean)

padre (m), father

Padre Hidalgo, "Father of Mexican
  Independence" (1753–1811)

padres, parents (both mother and father)

paella, Spanish national dish (shellfish,
  chicken and rice)

pagar, to pay

página, page

pago, payment

país (m), country, nation

paisaje (m), landscape, countryside, scenery

pájaro, bird

pala, shovel

palabra, word

palacio, palace

Palacio de Bellas Artes, Palace of Fine Arts

paloma, dove

pampa, Argentine plain

pan (m), bread

panadería, bakery

panadero, baker

panameño,-a, Panamanian

panecillo, dinner roll, small loaf of bread

pantalla, movie screen

papa, potato (original Indian name)

papá, (m), papa, dad

papel (m), paper

paquete (m), package

par (m), pair

para, for; in order to

paraguas, umbrella

pararrayos (m), lightning rod

parecer [zc], to seem

parecerse [zc] **(a),** to resemble

pared (f), wall

pariente (m/f), relative (family)

parque (m), park

parte (f), part
  en ninguna parte, nowhere

participar, to participate

particular, private; personal

parrafo, paragraph

pasado mañana, the day after tomorrow

pasajero,-a, passenger

pasaporte (m), passport

pasar, to pass, spend (time), to go

pasear, to walk, stroll

paseo, walk, stroll
  dar un paseo, to take a walk
  de paseo, strolling, out for a walk
  Paseo de la Reforma, major Mexico City
  boulevard

pastel (m), pie, pastry; cake

pasteurizar, to pasteurize

patata, potato (Spain)

patín (m), skate

patinar, to skate

pato, -a, duck

patrimonio, inheritance, heritage

patriótico, -a, patriotic

patrón, -ona, boss, employer; (m) pattern

pavo, -a, turkey (*guajolote/guajalote*
  in México)

payaso, clown

paz (f), peace
peatón (m), pedestrian
pedazo, piece, fragment
pedir [i], to ask (for)
pegar, to hit, strike; to glue, stick
peinar (se), to comb (oneself)
pelear (se), to fight, to quarrel
película, film
peligro, danger
peligroso,-a, dangerous
pelota, ball; jai alai
pelotero, ball player
peluquería, beauty salon,
   hairdresser's shop
pensar [ie] (en), to think (about)
peor, worse, worst
pequeño, -a, small, little
pera, pear (fruit)
perder [ie], to lose; to misplace
perderse [ie], to get lost
perdón, pardon
perecer [zc], to perish
peregrino, -a, pilgrim
perezoso, -a, lazy
perfeccionar, to improve
perfecto, -a, perfect
perfume (m), perfume
período, period
periódico, newspaper
periodista (m/f), reporter, journalist
permiso, permission
permitir, to permit
permanecer [zc], to remain, to stay
pero, but, yet
persa (m/f), Persian
perseguir [i], to persecute
persiana, louver door or window,
   Venetian blind
persona (f), person
pertenecer [zc], to belong
perteneciente a, belonging to,
   pertaining to
peruano, -a, Peruvian
perro, -a, dog
pesado,-a heavy
pesar, to weigh, to regret
pesca, fishing; catch
pescado, fish (out of water)
pescador (m), fisherman
pescar, to fish
pesebre (m), manger, crib
peseta, former monetary unit of Spain
peso, weight
peso, monetary unit of México, Bolivia,
   Colombia, Cuba, and Dominican Republic

petróleo, petroleum, oil
pez (m), fish (alive)
pianista (m/f), pianist
piano, piano
   piano de cola, grand piano
picador (m), mounted lancer in
   bullfight
Picasso, Pablo Ruiz (1881–1973), Spanish
   painter
pie (m), foot
   a pie, on foot
   de pie, standing
piedra, stone
pieza, piece, one of several parts
pillete (m), young rascal
pingüino, penguin
pintar, to paint
pintarse, to apply makeup
pintor, -a, painter
pintoresco, -a, picturesque
pintura, painting; paint
pionero, -a, pioneer
pirámide, pyramid
pirata (m), pirate
Pirineos, Pyrenees Mountains
piscina, swimming pool
piso, floor
pista, track; runway
   pista de hielo, ice rink
pizarra, chalk board
Pizarro, Francisco (1475–1541), Spanish
   explorer of Perú
placer (m), pleasure
plan (m), plan
planchar, to iron, press
planear, to plan
plano, map, street map; plan of a building
planta, plant
   planta baja, ground floor
plantar, to plant
plata, silver
plátano, banana
plática, informal talk, chat
plato, plate, dish
playa, beach
plaza, square
   plaza de toros, bullring
plenitud (f), fullness, abundance
plomero, plumber
plomo, lead (metal)
pluma, feather; pen
población, population; town
poblado, town, village
pobre, poor
pobreza, poverty

poco, little (in amount)
   poco a poco, little by little
   poco, -a, little (in amount)
poder (ue), to be able to
podio, podium
poesía, poetry
poeta (m/f), poet
policía (m), police officer; (f), police force
político, -a, politician; political
pollito, chick
pollo, chicken
Ponce de León, Juan (1460–1521),
   Spanish explorer
ponche (m), punch (beverage)
poner, to put, place
   poner atención, to pay attention
ponerse, to put on (as clothing);
   to become
   ponerse a, to begin to
por, by, for, through
   por consiguiente, consequently
   por lo visto, apparently
   por primera vez, for the first time
   por todas partes, everywhere
   por qué, why
porque, because
portafolio, portfolio
portarse, to behave
portugués, -esa, Portuguese
poseer, to possess
posguerra, postwar
posible (m/f), possible
posición (f), position
postre (m), dessert
práctica, practice
practicar, to practice
práctico, -a, practical
pradera, meadow, prairie
precaución (f), caution, precaution
precio, price
precioso, -a, precious; beautiful
preciso, -a, precise
preferir (ie), to prefer
pregunta, question
preguntar, to ask (a question)
premiado, -a, awarded
premio, award
prender, to light, to turn on
preocuparse, to be concerned, worried
preparar, to prepare
prepararse, to get ready
presentar, to present; to introduce
presente (m/f), present
presentir, to have a foreboding, suspect
presidente (m), president

préstamo, loan
prestar, to lend
prevención (f), prevention
primavera, spring
primo, -a, cousin
primer(o), -a, first
  primeros auxilios, first aid
primordial, basic, essential
princesa (f), princess
principal (m/f), main
principiar, to begin
príncipe (m), prince
principios: a principios de, at the
  beginning of
privado, -a, private
probable (m/f), probable
probar (ue), to prove
problema (m), problem
proceder, to proceed
producción (f), production
producir [zc], to produce
producto, product
profesión (f), profession
profesor, -a, professor
profundo, -a, deep, profound
programa (m), program
prohibir, to prohibit
promesa, promise
prometer, to promise
pronombre (m), pronoun
prontitud (f), promptness
pronto, soon; quickly
pronunciación, pronunciation
pronunciar, to pronounce
propina, tip (gratuity)
propio, -a, own, one's own
próspero, -a, prosperous
protección, protection
protector, -a, protective
proteger, to protect
provenzal, Provençal, language
proverbio, proverb
próximo, -a, next, near
prueba, proof, test
psicólogo, -a, psychologist
publicar, to publish, publicize
pudín (m), pudding
pueblo, town; people
puente, bridge
puerta, door
puertorriqueño, -a, Puerto Rican
puesto, post, position
puño, fist; cuff
puntual, punctual, on time
pupitre (m), desk (of a student)
purificar, to purify

que, that, which, than
qué, what
quedarse, to remain, to be left
quehacer (m), chore
quejarse, to complain
quejas, complaints
quemar(se), to burn, burn down,
  get burned
querer [ie], to want, to wish; to love
queso, cheese
quien, quién, who
quienquiera, whoever
quince, fifteen
quitar, to take away or off
quitarse, to remove, take off
Quito, capital of Ecuador
quizá, quizás, perhaps, maybe

rabo (m), tail
radicar (en), to live (in) (a town or city)
radio (m), radium, radius; (f) radio
rama, branch (of a tree)
ramo, bunch, bouquet; branch, field
  (of endeavor)
ranchero, -a, rancher, farmer; from the
  ranch
rápidamente, rapidly
rapidez (f), speed, rapidity
rápido, -a, rapid, fast
rascacielos (m), skyscraper
rasurador (m) razor
raza, race (of people)
razón (f), reason
  tener razón, to be right
realizar, to realize, make happen
rebelde (m/f), rebel
rebuznar, to bray
recado, message
receta, recipe
recibir, to receive
recibo, receipt
recién casados, newlyweds
recién llegado, newcomer
recién pintado, -a, just painted,
  "fresh paint"
recio, -a, strong, stout
recipiente (m), vessel
recoger, to gather
recomendar [ie], to recommend
reconocer, to recognize
recordar [ue], to recall, to remember
recreo, recreation, recess

recuerdo, memory; souvenir
red (f), net
redactor, -a, editor
redondez (f), roundness
redondo, -a, round, spherical
reducir [zc], to reduce
reemplazar [zc], to replace
referencia, reference
reformar, to reform; to renovate
refresco, refreshment
refrigerador (m), refrigerator
refugio, refuge, shelter
regadío, irrigation, irrigated land
regalo, gift, present
regalar, to make a gift
regañar, to scold
regar [ie], to water, irrigate
regatear, to haggle, to bargain
región (f), region, area
regla, rule; ruler
regresar, to go back
regular, to regulate, medium, fairly good
reina, queen
reinado, reign
reino, kingdom
reír(se), to laugh
  reírse de, to make fun of, laugh at
relámpago, lightning
religioso, -a, religious
relinchar, to neigh, whinny
reloj (m), clock, watch
relucir [zc], to shimmer, to sparkle
remar, to row
remediar, to remedy, repair
remedio, remedy, cure
remendar [ie], to mend
remolcar [ue], to tow
renacimiento, Renaissance; rebirth
renovar, to renew
reparación (f), repair
reparar, to repair
repartir, to distribute, divide, share
repasar, to review
repaso, review
repetido, -a, repeated
repetir, to repeat
reportar, to report
reporte (m) report
República Dominicana, Dominican
  Republic
resbalar, to skid
reservación (f), reservation
reservar, to reserve
resfriado, resfrío, cold, chill
residente (m/f), resident
resolver [ue], to resolve, solve

respaldar, to back, support
respeto, respect
respirar, to breathe
responder, to respond
responsabilidad (f), responsibility
respuesta, answer
restaurante (m), restaurant
resultar, to result
retirarse, to retire, withdraw
retraso, delay
reunión (f), meeting, gathering
revista, magazine
revolución (f), revolution
rezar, to pray
rico, -a, rich
riel (m), rail
riesgo, risk
rima, rhyme
rincón (m), corner, nook
río, river
risa, laughter
ritmo, rhythm
rizar, to curl
robar, to steal; to rob
robo, robbery, theft
rodeado, -a, surrounded
rodilla, knee
rojo, -a, red
Roma, Rome, capital of Italy
romance, coming from Latin (language)
romántico, -a, romantic
romper, to break
roncar, to snore
ropa, clothes, clothing
ropero, closet
roquero, -a, rock artist or musician
roto, -a, broken, torn
rubio, -a, blond(e)
ruido, noise
ruidoso, -a, noisy
rumbo a, in the direction of, headed toward
ruso, -a, Russian
ruta, route

 S

sábado, Saturday
sábana, sheet (bedding)
sabana, savanna, treeless plain
saber, to know
sabio, -a, wise
sabor (m), flavor
sabroso, -a, flavorful, tasty
sacar, to take (out of)
   sacar fotos, to take photographs

sacerdote (m), priest
sacudir, to shake, to dust
sal, salt
sala, living room
salir, to leave, go out
salón (m), large room
salsa (f), sauce, (m) kind of dance
salto, leap
salud (f), health
saludable, healthy (good for you)
saludar, to greet
salvavidas (m/f), life-preserver, lifeguard
samba, popular dance in Brazil
San Juan, capital of Puerto Rico
sanar, to cure, recover
Sancho Panza, servant to Don Quixote
sano, -a, healthy
saquear, to ransack, sack
sarampión (m), measles
sarcástico, -a, sarcastic
satisfacción (f), satisfaction
sastre (m) tailor
sátira, satire
satisfacer, to satisfy
satisfecho, -a, satisfied
secadora, dryer (clothes, hair)
secar, to dry
sección (f), section
seco, -a, dry
secretaria, secretary
secreto, -a, secret
secundario, -a, secondary
sed (f), thirst
seda, silk
seguir, to continue
según, according to
segundo, -a, second
seguridad (f), security
seguro, -a, secure, certain, safe
seguro, insurance
seis, six
selección (f), selection
seleccionar, to select
selva, jungle
selvático, pertaining to wilderness or jungle
sembrar [ie], to sow, to plant
semejante, similar
semestre (m), semester
semilla, seed
senador, -a, senator
sendero, path
sentado, -a, seated, sitting
sentar(se), to sit
señalar, to signal, point out
señor, (m), mister, sir; man
señora, Mrs.; woman; lady

señorita, miss; young woman; young lady
sentir(se) [ie], to feel
separar, to separate
septiembre (m), September
sequedad (f), dryness
sequía, dry spell, drought
serio, -a, serious
serrucho, saw; kingfish
servir, to serve, to be useful
servicial, attentive
servilleta, napkin
sesenta, sixty
setenta, seventy
seudónimo, pseudonym
si, if, whether
sí, yes
sicólogo, -a, psychologist
sidra, sparkling cider
siempre, always
siesta, nap, afternoon snooze
   dormir una siesta, to take a nap
siete, seven
siglo, century
   Siglo de Oro, Golden Age [of Spanish literature]
significar, to mean, to signify
sílaba, syllable
silencioso, -a, silent, quiet
silla, chair, seat
sillón (m), easy chair, armchair
simpático, -a, nice, likable
simple (m/f), simple
sin, without
   sin duda, undoubtedly, without a doubt
sincero, -a, sincere
sinfónico, -a, symphonic
sino, but (used for contradicting)
sinónimo, synonym; -a, synonymous
síntoma (m), symptom
situación (f), situation
soberanía, sovereignty
sobre, over, above; (m) envelope
sobrepasar, to surpass
sobre todo, above all
sobretodo, overcoat
sobrio, -a, moderate, temperate, sober
sofá (m), sofa
sol (m), sun
solamente, only
soldado, soldier
soler (ue), to be in the habit of, to be accustomed to
solicitar, to solicit, to request
solo, -a, alone
sólo, only (shortened form of *solamente*)
soltero, -a, unmarried

sombrero, hat
sombrilla, parasol, umbrella
sonrisa, smile
soñar [ue] (con), to dream (about)
sopa, soup
sordo, -a, deaf
sorprendente, surprising
sorprender, to surprise
sorprendido, -a, surprised
sorpresa, surprise
sortija, ring; ringlet of hair, curl
sospecha, suspicion
sospechar, to suspect
sospechoso, -a, suspicious; suspect
sótano, cellar
Soto, Hernando de (1500–1542), Spanish
  explorer
su, his, her, your, their
suave (m/f), soft
subdirector, vice principal, assistant
  director
subir, to go up, ascend
suceder, to happen, occur; to succeed
  (a king)
suceso, event, happening
sucio, -a, dirty
Sudamérica, South America
sueco, -a, Swedish
suegra, mother-in-law
suegro, father-in-law
sueldo, salary
suelo, floor; soil
sueño, dream; sleep
  tener sueño, to be sleepy
suerte, luck
suéter (m), sweater
suficiente, sufficient, enough
sufrir, to suffer
Suiza, Switzerland
sumar, to add
suntuoso, -a, sumptuous, lavish
superficie (f), surface
supermercado, supermarket
suplir, to supplement; provide
sur (m), south
surgir, to arise, emerge, appear
sustantivo, substantive, noun or pronoun
susto, fright, scare
suyo, -a, his, hers, yours, theirs

T

tabaco, tobacco; cigar
tabla, board, plank
tamaño, size

también, also, too
tambor (m), drum
tampoco, neither
tan, so, as
tanto, -a, so much, as much
tantos, -as, so many, as many
tardar, to delay, be late
tarde, late; (f) afternoon
tarea, task, assignment
tarjeta, card
tarjeta de crédito, credit card
taxi (m), taxi
taxista (m/f), taxi driver
taza, cup
te, to you
té (m), tea
teatro, theater
tecla, key
teclado, keyboard
técnico, -a, technical; (m/f), technician
tela, cloth, fabric
telefonear, to telephone
telefónico, pertaining to telephones
teléfono, telephone
telegrama (m), telegram
teleguía, TV program guide
televisión (f), television
televisor (m), televison set
tema (m), theme, subject
temblor (m), earthquake; quiver, tremor
temer, to fear
tempestad (f), storm, tempest
templado, -a, moderate, temperate;
  lukewarm
temporada, season
  temporada de pesca (caza), fishing
  (hunting) season
  temporada de lluvias, rainy season
temprano, early (in the day)
tener, to have; to hold
  tener calor, to be hot
  tener éxito, to be successful
  tener frío, to be cold
  tener hambre, to be hungry
  tener lugar, to take place
  tener miedo, to be afraid
  tener razón, to be right
  tener sed, to be thirsty
  tener sueño, to be sleepy
tenis (m), tennis
tenista (m/f), tennis player
teoría, theory
Tenochtitlán, capital of the Aztec Empire
Teotihuacán, cultural and religious center
  of the Aztec Empire

tercer(o), -a, third
terminado, -a, finished
terminar, to finish
término, term, word
termo, thermos
ternura, tenderness
terremoto, earthquake
terreno, plot of land
tesorero, -a, treasurer
testificar, to testify
testigo (m/f), witness
  testigo ocular, eyewitness
tía, aunt
tiempo, time; weather
  hace buen tiempo, it's good weather
  tiempo libre, free time
tienda, store; tent
tigre (m), tiger
tijeras, scissors
timbre (m), electric bell; stamp
timidez, shyness
tímido, -a, timid, shy
tinta, ink
tintorería, dry cleaners
tío, uncle
típico, -a, typical
tirantes (m), suspenders
título, title; diploma
tiza, chalk
toalla, towel
tocar, to touch; to play (instrument)
  tocar a la puerta, to knock on the door
todo, -a, all
tolteca (m/f), Toltec, Toltec Indian
tomar, to take; to drink
tomate (m), tomato [*jitomate* in
  México]
tonto, -a, foolish
torero, bullfighter
tormenta, storm
torneo, tournament
toro, bull
  corrida de toros, bullfight
toronja, grapefruit
torre, tower
tortilla, tortilla (Mexico); omelet
tos (f), cough, coughing
toser, to cough
trabajar, to work
trabajo, work
tradición (f), tradition
traducción (f), translation
traducir (zc), to translate
traer, to bring
tráfico, traffic, commerce

tragedia, tragedy
traidor, -a, traitor
traje (m), suit (of clothes)
  traje de baño, bathing suit
tranquilo, -a, tranquil, calm
transistor (m), transistor
tránsito, traffic
tranvía (m), streetcar
tras, behind, after
traslado, transfer, move
tratar, to treat
  tratar de, to try to
travesía, crossing, voyage
travieso, -a, mischievous
treinta, thirty
  treinta y uno, thirty-one
tren (m), train
trenza, braid (hair)
tres, three
triángulo, triangle
trigo, wheat
trío, trio
tripulación (f), crew (of a ship)
triste, sad
tristeza, sadness
triunfo, triumph
trofeo, trophy
trono, throne
tropa, troop
truco, trick
trueno, thunder
tu, your
tú, you (familiar)
turco -a, Turk; Turkish
turista (m/f), tourist
turquesa, turquoise (gem)
tuyo, -a, yours

u, or (before [u] sound)
últimamente, lastly, finally; lately
último, -a, last (in line or number)
ultramarino, -a, overseas
un, -a, a, an, one
Unamuno, Miguel de (1864–1936),
  Spanish novelist and poet
unidad (f), unity, unit
  unidad monetaria, monetary unit
unificar, to unify
uniforme (m), uniform
universidad (f), university
uno, one
uña, fingernail
usar, to use
uso, use; usage; wear and tear

usted, -es, you (formal)
útil, useful
utilizar, to use, utilize
uva, grape

vacación (f), vacation
vacío, -a, empty; (m), void, vacuum
vacunar, to vaccinate
valentía, courage, valor
valer, to be worth
  valer la pena, to be worth the trouble
  or effort
valiente, brave
valioso, -a, valuable, useful, worthwhile
valor (m), value; courage
vals (m), waltz
vaquero, cowboy
varios, -as, various
vasco/vascongado, -a, Basque
vascuence (m), Basque (language)
vaso, glass (for drinking)
vecino, -a, neighbor
vehículo, vehicle
veinte, twenty
veinticinco, twenty-five
veintinueve, twenty-nine
velocidad (f), speed, velocity
venado, deer, stag; venison
venda, bandage
vendedor, -a, salesperson, vendor
vender, to sell
venezolano, -a, Venezuelan
vengar, to avenge
venir [ie], to come
venta, sale; selling
ventana, window
ver, to see, to look
verano, summer
verbo, verb
verdad (f), truth
verdadero, -a, true
verde, green
verduras, greens, vegetables
vergüenza, shame; shyness
  tener vergüenza, to be embarrassed,
  to be shy
vértigo, vertigo, dizziness
vestido, dress
vestir(se), to dress
vez (f), time, instance
  de vez en cuando, from time to time
  diez veces, ten times
  en vez de, instead of

  otra vez, again
  por primera vez, for the first time
  una vez, once
viajar, to travel
viaje (m), trip, journey
viajero, -a, traveler
víctima (m/f), victim
vida, life
viejo, -a, old
viento, wind
viernes, Friday
villancicos, Christmas songs
violín (m), violin
violinista (m/f), violinist
virreinato, viceroyalty
visa (f), visa
visitante (m/f), visitor
visitar, to visit
vitaminas, vitamins
vivir, to live
vocal (f), vowel, vocal
volar [ue], to fly
volver [ue], to return (from somewhere)
vosotras (f), you (plural familiar)
vosotros, you (plural familiar)
voto, vote
voz (f), voice
  en voz baja, in a soft voice
  voz pasiva, passive voice
vuelo, flight
vuelta, return
  boleto de vuelta, return trip ticket
  boleto de ida y vuelta, round-trip ticket
  estar de vuelta, to be back
vuelto, change (money); past participle
  of *volver*

y, and
ya, already, now
yeso, plaster; chalk
yo, I
yodo, iodine
yuca, cassava
yucateco, -a, of or from Yucatán, México

zapatería, shoe store
zapatero, maker or seller of shoes,
  cobbler
zapato, shoe
zarzuela, Spanish operetta
zoológico, zoo